D1603786

ALTRUISM, SOCIALIZATION, AND SOCIETY

J. Philippe Rushton

The University of Western Ontario

Prentice-Hall, Inc.
Englewood Cliffs, New Jersey 07632

Library of Congress Cataloging in Publication Data

Rushton, J   Philippe.
      Altruism, socialization, and society.

      (Prentice-Hall series in social learning theory)
      Bibliography: p.
      Includes indexes.
          1. Altruism.   2. Human behavior.
      3. Socialization.   4. Social institutions.
      i. Title.
      HM291.R77   303.3'2   80-11344
      ISBN 0-13-023408-7

35, 6 26

PRENTICE-HALL SERIES IN SOCIAL LEARNING THEORY
Albert Banudra, *series editor*

Editorial/production supervision and interior design by Natalie Krivanek
Manufacturing buyer: Edmund W. Leone

Printed in the United States of America

10   9   8   7   6   5   4   3   2   1

Prentice-Hall International, Inc., *London*
Prentice-Hall of Australia Pty. Limited, *Sydney*
Prentice-Hall of Canada, Ltd., *Toronto*
Prentice-Hall of India Private Limited, *New Delhi*
Prentice-Hall of Japan, Inc., *Tokyo*
Prentice-Hall of Southeast Asia Pte. Ltd., *Singapore*
Whitehall Books Limited, Wellington, *New Zealand*

This book is dedicated to my mother,
Andrea Marie Elizabeth Rushton

to my father,
John Rushton

and to my son,
Stephen Philippe Rushton.

"Greater love hath no man than this,
that a man lay down his life for his
friend."
John 15:13.

CONTENTS

PREFACE

Altruism is essential for the existence of society. The question of how it is that a human being, brought into the world with apparently no other thought than its own gratification, eventually becomes capable of living its life with concern for others, is of central importance. Why do people live with prosocial consideration for others by being honest, generous, helpful, and compassionate, and desist from engaging in such antisocial behavior as lying, cheating, stealing, and aggression? Why is it some people do learn to behave in a socially responsible manner while others do not? The answer appears to lie in social learning. Without adequate socialization, complex and diverse societies such as those we have today are impossible.

This book, then, is about altruism, socialization, and society. It is only during the last fifteen years or so that the study of human altruism has grown to be of major importance. Reviews of the earlier literature by Berkowitz (1972), Bryan and London (1970), Krebs (1970), Latané and Darley (1970), Macaulay and Berkowitz (1970) and Wispé (1972), clearly established altruism as a major topic in the behavioral sciences. Today many introductory textbooks in, for example, developmental and social psychology devote a complete chapter to the topic. More recently there has been another spate of reviews, now constituting full books in their own right (Bar-Tal, 1976; Hornstein, 1976; Mussen & Eisenberg-Berg, 1977; Staub, 1978, 1979; Wispé, 1978). In addition the study of altruism has been immeasurably broadened by analyses from anthropological, biological, and sociological perspectives (Wilson, 1975, 1978).

To date there has not been a fully integrated conceptual analysis of this now vast literature. This book attempts to do this through the framework of social learning theory. Social learning theory bids to become the first generally accepted integrative paradigm in the behavioral sciences. It has substantially advanced our understanding of human behavior in a variety of areas including: aggression (Bandura, 1973), cognition (Rosenthal & Zimmerman, 1978), personality (Mischel, 1976), and psychopathology (Wilson & O'Leary, 1980), to name but a few. Several years ago Albert Bandura, now, the leading exponent of social learning theory, wrote perhaps

> The worth of a psychological theory must be judged not only by how well it explains laboratory findings, but also by the efficacy of the behavioral modification procedures that it produces.   (Bandura, 1969, Preface)

Even its critics seem to agree that, of all the paradigms in the behavioral sciences, at the very least, social learning is of practical utility. This befits a valid conceptual model of human behavior.

A large portion of this book is devoted to demonstrating how social learning occurs, sometimes inadvertently, at both the individual and the social systems levels, to produce either positive forms of altruistic behavior or a lack thereof.

The book is arranged as follows. Chapter 1 provides a discussion, description, and definition of the phenomenon of altruism. Chapter 2 reviews the evidence for altruism in other animals and suggests that humans have the capacity for altruism because of their evolutionary history. Chapter 3 considers the motivations for altruistic behavior and suggests that empathy and personal norms are the primary psychological mechanisms by which human altruism is mediated. This leads, in Chapter 4, to the question of whether there are individual differences in altruism, and the conclusion that, indeed, some people are consistently more altruistic than others. Chapter 5 discusses the vitally important principles of social learning with specific reference to ways individuals internalize the personal norms and empathy that are proposed in Chapter 3 to underlie human altruism. In Chatper 6, 7, and 8 the societal level of the family, mass media, and educational systems are discussed in terms of their roles in socializing altruism. It is concluded that, because of recent changes in the economic system, the family is increasingly an ineffective anti-social direction, and the educational system isn't socializing them at all. It is even suggested that we are in danger of producing a society of undersocialized personalities. The final thesis of the book, presented in Chapter 9, is that behavioral science has much to offer in bringing about a better social environment and that this will be accomplished in large part through the influence of the forces of socialization of our disposal.

ACKNOWLEDGMENTS

Many people have discussed, criticized, extolled the virtues of, and generally commented on the ideas presented in this book. The five years required for completion have resulted in considerable debts. First, very special thanks are due to Professor Albert Bandura, who served as the Prentice-Hall series editor for this book and whose extensive comments on the manuscript proved exceptionally valuable, and saved me from my worst excesses. His scholarship is indeed exemplary. Major thanks are also due to Professor Joan E. Grusec and Dennis L. Krebs, whose insightful on an earlier draft of the manuscript provided a great deal of useful feedback. Many persons read individual chapters. I would especially like to thank Professor Mel Goodale for his comments on Chapter 2, The Sociobiology of Altruism. Otherwise I must thank people collectively: to the colleagues who collaborated in research, to the friends and colleagues who read chapter drafts out of interest, and to the students who read them in course, I extend gratitude for discussions. I would particularly like to thank those at the

London School of Economics and Political Science (1970-73), the University of Oxford (1973-74), York University (1974-76), the University of Toronto (1976-77), and the University of Western Ontario (1977-80). Though many of those thanked herein may disagree with particular aspects of the book, it is clearly better as a result of the time and consideration that they provided.

I would like to thank Lynne Mitchell, my secretary, for working so diligently on the many "final" versions that the manuscript went through, and also John Isley, Natalie Krivanek, and the staff at Prentice-Hall for their graciousness while bringing it into print. Beyond this, it behooves me to thank all of those who conduct research and who publish their work, for it is they who make progress in knowledge possible.

Now, at the very end, I would like to express my deep appreciation to several particularly close friends. Forever associated in my mind with the writing of this book will be: Jeanne Grant, Yvette Uddin, Jean Graham, Robin Russell, Anne Campbell, Florinda Xavier and, most especially, Cheryl Lawrence.

J. Philippe Rushton
London, Ontario

chapter 1

ALTRUISM AS
A UNIVERSAL VALUE

Our view of ourselves as a species focuses more on the aggressive and destructive sides of our nature than on the more positive ones. This is probably a legacy from (a) Freud, (b) the popular ethologists such as Konrad Lorenz and Desmond Morris, and (c) the result of the antisocial behaviors that we *do* see or hear about. I suggest that the resulting perception of ourselves is wrong. Rather than being a selfish and aggressive species, as is so often depicted, we might better be characterized as helpful, cooperative, empathic, loving, kind, and considerate. Is it not for this reason that acts of violence and destruction result so readily in moral outrage and behavior?

This book is about altruism and some of the factors—biological, individual, and societal—that influence it. Behavioral scientists usually study the more negative sides of human behavior: aggression; violence; outgroup prejudice;

anxiety; fear; and, of course, mental illness. These are very important problems that scientists need to study in order to help alleviate suffering and to improve the human condition. There is, however, another side to human nature —a pervasive, positive side which also must be studied if we are to strengthen its prominence. One of the major themes of this book is how society can increase the socialization of altruism. Humans can be a very prosocial species, who engage in numerous helping, kind, considerate, and loving behaviors. This is exemplified in both values and behavior.

EXAMPLES OF HUMAN ALTRUISM

"Regard for others" is a virtually universal value of all human societies and forms the basic tenet for most of the world's great religious, social reformist, and revolutionist movements. From Christianity we have "Do unto others as you would have them do unto you" and "Greater love hath no man than this, that a man lay down his life for his friend." From Article 73 of the United Nations Charter (1945) we have: "Members of the United Nations which have or assume responsibility for . . . territories whose people have not yet attained a full measure of self-government . . . accept as a sacred trust the obligation to promote to the utmost . . . the well being of the inhabitants of the territories." Thus it is recognized that even a state can be under a moral obligation to help not only other states but also communities that are hardly nation-states at all.

Behaving with regard for others is almost universally hailed as a virtue, despite exceptions. For example, Machiavelli's (1532) counsel for political leaders in his book, *The Prince*, consisted of such advice as "To maintain the state a prince is often obliged to act against charity, humanity and religion. . . ." In more modern times the American novelist Ayn Rand (1964) in a book entitled *The Virtue of Selfishness* asserted that ethical altruism is bad because it tends to develop dependent, unenterprising, and sentimentalistic personalities. Overwhelmingly, however, altruism has been viewed through the ages as a valuable, if not indispensable, necessity for the existence and good functioning of society. Before attempting to define the term altruism formally, let us consider several examples of what we might wish to include under the general rubric of "altruistic behavior." Included in this category are highly noteworthy acts of rescue behavior:

In 1904 the Carnegie Hero Fund Commission was established to award medals for "outstanding acts of selfless heroism performed in the United States and Canada." The requirements for receiving a Carnegie Medal are that (1) the act is voluntary, (2) the actor has to risk his or her own life to an extraordinary degree, (3) the actor must not be directly related to the victim, and (4) the actor must not be in an occupational role in which duty would have required the act to have been performed (such as the police or lifeguards). In 1977 the commission awarded fifty-six medals for acts of outstanding heroism. Eight of the medals were awarded to individuals who died in their rescue attempts. The fifty-six emergencies included twenty instances of drowning, sixteen of burning in automobiles or buildings, six suffocations from smoke or fumes, four rock falls, three cases of electric shock, two oncoming trains, two attacking animals, one shooting, one falling sheet of metal, and one possible fall from a tree. A quotation from the Carnegie Hero Fund Commission's 1977 annual report will illustrate:

Bronze Medal awarded to Billie Joe McCullough, who helped to save Bradley T. VanDamme from burning, Fulton, Ill., October 10, 1975. In a one-car accident at night, VanDamme, aged 18, unconscious from injuries received, was in the right front seat of a station wagon on which flames burned across the rear and along the passenger side. McCullough, aged 22, laborer, and another man ran to the vehicle, where the driver's door had been torn off. Flames had spread into the front seat area. Kneeling on the seat, McCullough and the other man with some difficulty freed VanDamme, who was afire, and removed him from the vehicle, which soon afterward was engulfed in flames. VanDamme was hospitalized for injuries and extensive burns. He recovered.

Wartime, too, often provides occasions for altruistic behavior. The most extreme kind is giving one's own life in order to save others. There is considerable evidence that this occurs. The highest award in the United States Army is the Congressional Medal of Honor. This has been awarded posthumously on several occasions for such actions as throwing one's body on a live hand grenade and muffling the explosion, thus saving the lives of comrades who otherwise would have been hit by the blast. Similarly, the Victoria Cross of Great Britain has been awarded for crawling out of relatively safe trenches into no-man's-land to rescue wounded comrades and, even when wounded, to go back repeatedly to complete additional rescues, eventually dying of wounds in the process.

The human propensity to die for beliefs and values might be illuminating here. The Japanese *kamikaze* pilot who flew his plane, loaded with bombs, into American vessels during World War II believed that by sacrificing his own life, his emperor, his fellow Japanese, and the greater glory of Japan might live. Most other nations, too, have produced, with little difficulty, soldiers and individuals willing to die for an idea or for a greater group loyalty. Thus the one thousand Greek Spartan soldiers who in 480 B.C. stood firm against the thousands of Persians attempting to go through the narrow pass at Thermopylae, buying with their lives sufficient time for the Greek cities to prepare a defense against the invaders. History is full of such examples.

Organ transplants are a form of altruism likely to increase in frequency with advances in medical science. For example, hundreds of people live with only one kidney, having donated the other one to someone who would have died without the transplant. A number of such kidney donors were studied by Fellner and Marshall (1968) who noted, among other things, that often the decision to give was made almost instantaneously. The donor did not have to ponder over the merits and costs, nor the worthiness of the potential recipient. It was a clear and obvious choice for them to give, they "couldn't refuse," they felt good about their decision, and they continued to feel good about their decision nine years later (Marshall & Fellner 1977). A less extreme form of medical donation is the thousands of individuals who habitually donate their blood at some cost and inconvenience to themselves so that others may benefit. Altruistic motives "to help others" are obvious in such behavior (Titmuss 1970). It is possible to arrange for altruistic organ transplant even after death. Today people have the choice of carrying permission cards around with them (in some places as part of their driver's license) so that, should they die suddenly, as in an automobile accident, there are instructions for their kidneys or eyes to be donated to others, or their entire bodies to science—the final act of a human being.

Much altruistic behavior also goes on in quite everyday circumstances, most of which is taken for granted. A number of published studies allow us to assess the amount of this kind of altruism. Latané and Darley (1970) sent a team of investigators to the streets of New York City to make a variety of requests for help. Passersby were asked for the time, for directions, for change for a quarter, and for the person's name. Apart from the last request, people almost always responded with help. Eighty-five percent of New Yorkers gave the time of day and directions to an inquirer, and 73 percent gave change for a quarter. Only 29 percent, however, gave their name. Passersby also were asked for ten cents. 34 percent gave when asked directly; 50 percent gave when the asker gave his name first; and 64 percent gave when the asker claimed that he needed to make a telephone call. This figure went up to 72 percent if the requester reported that his wallet had been stolen. In a similar study it was found that over 50 percent of women shoppers in a midwestern American city would give a male university student forty cents for bus fare when the student explained that his wallet had "disappeared" (Berkowitz 1972).

Responses to such requests vary as a function of many situational variables, one of which is urban density. It generally has been found that people in big cities are less altruistic than people in small towns. Milgram (1970), for example, provided evidence that city dwellers were less trusting (allowing a stranger into their house) and less helpful (telephoning a number for a caller who had run out of money and had dialed the subject's number in error) than were town dwellers. Merrens (1973) found that city dwellers were less likely to respond to requests for help from passersby than were town dwellers. Korte and Kerr (1975) found on three different measures (request to make an important phone call; deliberate overpayment of money to a clerk; and losing a stamped, addressed postcard) that city people were less helpful than town dwellers. Finally, Takooshian, Haber, and Lucido (1977) had six-to-ten-year-old children stand on a busy street and say to passersby "I'm lost. Can you call my house?" Only 46 percent of people in big cities helped, whereas 72 percent of people in smaller towns did so.

All of these studies directly compared a large city with a small town. A study carried out subsequently examined whether the above findings could be (a) replicated in a Canadian context and (b) generalized to a suburban setting as a midpoint between a "small town" and a "large city" (Rushton 1978). A variety of requests were made of passersby at three different locations: downtown in the Canadian city of Toronto (pop. 2,125,000), in the suburbs of the same city, and in a small town just outside the same city. The four requests were similar to those used previously by Latané and Darley (1970). They were: "Excuse me, I wonder if you could . . ." (a) "tell me what time it is?" (b) "tell me how to get to the nearest post office?" (c) "give me change for a quarter?" and (d) "tell me what your name is?" The percentage of people helping is shown in Table 1.1 as a function of locale and question asked. The New York data of Latané and Darley (1970) also are shown in this table.

TABLE 1-1

Percentage of People Helping in Response to Type of Request
in Areas Differing in Urban Density

Type of Request	Amount of Density							
	Low		Medium		High		High	
	Small Town		City Suburbs		Inner City		New York City*	
	% Helping	Sample N	% Helping	Sample N	% Helping	Sample N	% Helping	Sample N
Time	97[a]	92	95[a]	150	91[ab]	272	85[b]	92
Directions	97[a]	85	90[ab]	150	88[b]	276	85[b]	90
Change	84[a]	100	73[ab]	150	70[b]	279	73[ab]	90
Name	51[a]	65	39[a]	150	26[b]	246	29[b]	277

Note.—Within each type of request those having different superscripts are significantly different by chi square ($p < .05$).
*Based on data from Latané & Darley 1970.

Reprinted with permission of author and publisher from Rushton, J. P., Urban density: helping strangers in a Canadian city, suburb, and small town. PSYCHOLOGICAL REPORTS, 1978, 43, Table 1, page 989.

From Table 1.1 we see that in Toronto for every request there is a drop off in giving as urban density increases. The probability of getting this rank ordering by chance alone for one request is 1/3 or $p = .17$. To get it four times in a row has an associated probability of $p < .001$. The data collected by Latané and Darley (1970) in New York City are in the main compatible with the hypothesis. There seems to be very little difference between downtown Toronto and downtown New York, however. Middle scores in altruism were noted in the suburbs. Further research into the causes of these disturbing findings is definitely needed. The principal interpretation to be made from Table 1.1 at this time, however, is that regardless of density, the average person is in fact very helpful to strangers.

Researchers using more ingenious ways of measuring altruism in natural situations also found it abundant. On the streets of New York, for example, 50 percent of people will mail back an apparently lost wallet to its owner (Hornstein, Fisch, & Holmes 1968). Even on the New York subway people are altruistic; in one study, the investigator fell to the ground pretending to have a knee injury. When this happened, 83 percent of the people in the subway car offered their help (Latané & Darley 1970). In another study, the investigator would repeatedly fall down, pretending to be either physically infirm or drunk. On the occasions he pretended to be physically infirm, he was assisted by a bystander on 100 percent of the occasions. Even when he fell to the ground pretending to be drunk, he was given offers of help on 70 percent of the episodes (Piliavin, Rodin, & Piliavin 1969).

Three- to five-year-old children also engage in altruistic behavior toward both peers and teachers. Strayer, Wareing, and Rushton (1979) videotaped twenty-six children ranging from three to five years of age, for thirty hours during free play at a university preschool. The children's play then was coded into one of sixteen possible categories of prosocial behavior. Approximately twelve hundred altruistic acts, that is, one and one-half per child per hour, were observed. This actually is a very conservative figure, for each child was not always in the room to be videotaped. When a "real-time" correction was introduced, the number of altruistic acts engaged in was fifteen and one-half per hour. Nearly 60 percent of these behaviors were directed toward peers and 40 percent toward teachers. The kinds of altruistic behaviors noted were of four main kinds, the frequency and rate of which can be seen in Table 1.2.

TABLE 1-2

Observed Altruistic Activity among 26 Children during 30 Hours of Free Play at a University Preschool

Behavioral Category	Observed Frequency	Percent of Total Activity	Mean Individual Rate per Hour
Object-related Activity	362	30%	7.60
Cooperative Activity	581	49%	6.66
Helping Activity	197	16%	0.94
Empathic Activity	55	5%	0.46
Total	1195	100%	15.56

Source: Based on data from Strayer, Wareing, & Rushton, *Ethology and Sociology,* 1979.

The first type, called *object-related activity* was donating and sharing such objects as toys, for instance, if a child walked across the room and offered another child a toy with which to play. The second type of altruism was *cooperative activities*. This included task cooperation, defined as working together to achieve a common goal, and such activities as unpacking a box of toys and moving furniture around the room. *Helping activities* comprised the third general class of behavior. An example would be assisting another child to accomplish a goal such as putting on a smock or doing up buttons. The final class of altruistic behavior was *empathic activity*. Comforting an upset peer is an example of this. In Table 1.2 we see that on average each child cooperated at a rate of more than six and one half times per hour, shared an object over six and one half times every hour, and engaged in helping nearly once every hour. Of course, these behaviors occurred within the generally benign atmosphere of a university preschool. Were the social ecology of the preschool to be altered drastically, this pattern of behavior might change as well. Nonetheless, it is clear from these data that even very young children often engage in altruistic behavior. Other evidence suggests that forms of both sharing and comforting are present as early as the second year of life (Rheingold, Hay, & West 1976; Waxler, Yarrow, & King, 1979). Altruistic behavior is very human activity; it occurs at a very high rate and is ubiquitous in many different situations.

So far we have described a series of behaviors that would necessarily be included in any category of altruism that we define. These included the documented cases of Carnegie Heroes who attempt to rescue other people from dangerous situations, the anecdotal examples from wartime, the examples of people donating body organs before or after they die, and examples from the experimental and observational studies of the everyday altruism of ordinary adults and children.

DEFINITION OF ALTRUISM

What do all these acts of rescue, sacrifice, donation, and helping have in common to warrant their inclusion in the superordinate category of altruism? One common characteristic is that they are all behaviors apparently *carried out in order to benefit another*. This is essential to the definition of altruism. If, however, the behavior results in helping the self as well, we might hesitate to call the behavior altruistic, depending on how we define the person's intentions. This is made clear in such formal definitions of altruism as Macaulay's and Berkowitz's: "behavior carried out to benefit another without anticipation of rewards from external sources" (1970, p. 3). This definition is all encompassing. It defines altruism as both intention and behavior, and has received general acceptance among psychologists.

The conceptualization offered in this book differs slightly. Here altruism will be defined primarily in behavioral terms. Altruism is defined as *social behavior carried out to achieve positive outcomes for another rather than for the self.* Egoism, the opposite of altruism, is defined as *social behavior carried out to achieve positive outcomes for the self rather than for another.* These definitions emphasize more clearly than others the behavioral continuum on which altruism lies. At the extreme altruistic end of the continuum are those behaviors in which the outcome is maximized for another, even at the expense of the self. At the extreme egoistic end are those behaviors in which the outcome is maximized for the self, even at the expense of others.

One advantage of the continuum idea of altruistic behavior is that it explicitly suggests that there are degrees of altruism (just as there are degrees of egoism). When thinking of degrees of altruism (e.g., "extremely altruistic" as opposed to "very altruistic") the involvement of a process of social judgment or attribution becomes clear. We cannot look directly into the minds of people to see their intentions. The conceptual advantage of focusing on behavior becomes evident when we consider altruism among animals. As will be examined in the next chapter, most social species engage in altruistic behavior. The most altruistic of all species, for example, are the social insects who readily sacrifice their lives in defense of their nest-mates. Obviously, it would be problematic to infer that insects have altruistic intentions, but there is no doubt of their behavior. Altruistic intentions are inferred from behavior and the social context in which the behavior takes place.

In fact, it is often problematic to infer altruistic intentions even among humans. It is quite possible that the person does not know the degree to which his or her intentions are altruistic. As Nisbett and Wilson (1977) point out, much decision making occurs rapidly and at a preconscious level. Often only the *consequences* or *results* of processed information enter the consciousness, not the processing itself. This helps explain why, when people are asked to specify the reasons for their actions, they often report a series of conflicting motivations. People are not always aware of why they act the way they do. If we refer to the kidney donors studied by Fellner and Marshall (1968), we will note that the donors reported that their decisions were made almost instantaneously. The donor did not weigh the pros and cons involved. He or she just "couldn't refuse." Similarly, in emergency situations, people do not spend time to deliberate consciously whether or not to act. They act or they do not act. Verbal, conscious reasons often come later.

If it is true that on many occasions people cannot be sure of the reasons for their behavior, how do researchers determine whether or not an intention is altruistic? Researchers often escape this problem by deliberately creating well-controlled situations in which it would be reasonable to infer altruistic motivations for behavior because other possible motivators have been controlled for. This use of *operational defintions* within well-controlled situations allows a variety of variables to be manipulated and their effects on the amount of subsequent altruistic behavior observed. These methods are being used extensively by behavioral scientists interested in the study of altruism. We shall discuss some of their studies later. However, using operational definitions within well defined specific contexts does not solve all definitional problems. The choice of behaviors to be called altruistic is not arbitrary. In the final analysis it would have to be one which would be judged altruistic by most people. Researchers measure *behavior* in well-controlled situations and infer altruistic motivations when other possible motivations have been controlled. Thus, the researcher, like other individuals, infers altruistic rather than selfish motivations from the overall social context. One advantage to the behavioral continuum concept proposed in this book, therefore, is that it brings definitions into accord with research practice.

Defining altruism behaviorally does not preclude looking for the psychological and other mechanisms by which this behavior is activated. In chapter 3 a number of psychological motivations are considered. These include personal standards of behavior, rules of reciprocity, and empathic responsivity. By focusing attention on behavior, these motivations are seen for what they are—hypothetical constructs invented in order to explain the regularities in observed behavior. It is the behavior that must remain of primary importance for our research attention.

A second advantage to the idea that altruism lies on a behavioral continuum is that it places the concept in opposition to the notion of egoism. By considering altruism as opposed to egoism, we bring the usage into accord with that of Auguste Comte (1798-1857) who originated the term. Comte (1851-1854) 1966) wrote much about the development of the "sympathetic instincts" in opposition to egoistic ones. He believed that the purpose of an advanced society was to foster the love, even the worship of, humanity, and that positivistic science, especially the discipline of sociology (a term he also coined), would produce this new set of values. Curiously enough, Comte also believed that he had located the anatomical site of the altruistic motives:

> As to the locality of these three instincts (attachment, veneration, benevolence) Gall's solution, except for the first of them, may be left untouched . . . the great founder of cerebral physiology had been induced to place Attachment in close relation to the egoistic organs and away from the two other sympathetic instincts. But with the organ of Benevolence he was more successful. . . . Allotting (it to) the highest median portion of the frontal division. . . . Veneration should be placed immediately behind it. . . . Attachment I would place laterally to Veneration. Its organ sloping from before backwards connects itself below with that of the Love of Approbation.
>
> (*System of Positive Polity,* Vol. 1, p. 569)

Finally the behavioral definition also solves the endless, and fruitless, debate as to whether such a thing as *true* altruism exists. For example, it may be true that there will never be a total absence of *all* possible rewards, including such *internal* ones as the relief of guilt, pleasure for having lived up to an internal standard, reduction in a sense of injustice, or termination of a sympathetic feeling of pain for another. We shall discuss the nature of motivations to behave altruistically in chapter 3. For the present however, let us note that there is a class of behaviors which are carried out that benefit others. Furthermore, these behaviors often are carried out in the absence of immediate reward and sometimes at some cost. Most people consider such behavior by their peers a virtue. It is useful to have a word for such behavior, and "altruism" is the one designated. It seems unreasonable to rule this class of behavior out of existence by using stringent criteria—playing definitional games can rule virtually any phenomenon into or out of existence. To the behavioral scientist as well as to the social engineer, altruistic behaviors are of great interest. The thesis of this book is that complex societies cannot exist without a large degree of concern for others on the part of the populace, and this book will specify some of the means by which society influences the degrees of altruism in existence.

SUMMARY

Rather than being the selfish and aggressive species so often depicted, human beings might better be characterized as helpful, compassionate, loving, kind, and considerate. Examples of this are numerous, and include the documented cases of Carnegie Heroes who attempt to rescue other people from dangerous situations, the examples of people donating body organs before or after they die, and the everyday altruistic behavior of ordinary adults and children who provide help to others on a routine basis. Altruism is a pervasive part of human society, and constitutes a universal value.

Altruism may be defined as social behavior carried out to achieve positive outcomes for another rather than for the self. It refers to a class of behaviors without which complex societies, such as our own, cannot survive. Indeed an increase in altruism may be a necessity if we are to ensure the survival of the human race. This book will consider some of the factors—biological, individual, and societal—that influence altruism.

chapter 2

THE SOCIOBIOLOGY
OF ALTRUISM

To what extent is human nature basically helpful, loving, and considerate of others? To what extent, on the other hand, is it basically selfish and egoistic? Or do we really have no "basic" nature; that is, are we a "blank slate" waiting to be filled in by environmental experiences? These are important questions, the answers to which will determine how we come to view ourselves as a species. Luckily we are approaching the day when such questions will be answered.

By "basic nature" we mean the genetic endowment that determines or predisposes people to behave in particular ways. How is a person's reaction to different situations influenced by genetic endowment, how is it influenced by life experiences, and how do these two interact to produce behavior? Cross-fertilization among the sciences of zoology, genetics, and experimental psychology has led to the point at which answers to these sorts of questions are beginning to be possible.

All species of life on this planet, including human beings, share a common origin. Over millions of years many different species with quite different traits and characteristics have evolved. Darwin's (1859) theory of evolution specifying *natural selection* and *survival of the fittest* attempted to explain how this worked.

DARWIN'S THEORY
OF NATURAL SELECTON

The first stage in Darwin's theory of natural selection requires that individual members of a group show some genetic differences from each other that are capable of being passed on to their offspring. Such differences may have arisen previously from the natural mutations and recombinations that occur with genetic material. The second stage requires that some individual members of the group be more successful than others in producing offspring that grow to successful reproductive maturity. This differential success in reproduction results in certain genetic characteristics increasing in frequency in the next generation and others decreasing in frequency. This change in the frequency of characteristics over generations *is* evolution. Natural selection is the *mechanism* by which evolution occurs.

The term "survival of the fittest" needs to be clarified. By fitness, Darwin meant reproductive success. Thus "fit" individuals are those individuals of the species that, for whatever reasons, successfully reproduce themselves in the next generation, and "unfit" individuals are those that, for whatever reasons, do not reproduce. The term has no meaning outside this definition, and the definition is entirely in terms of reproductive consequences. Darwin's theory of natural selection necessarily requires, however, that the presence of certain traits increases some individuals' "fitness," whereas the absence of these same traits decreases it in others.

Natural selection is perhaps easiest to understand in terms of such readily observable physical dimensions as coloring. An example might be taken from the time of the industrial revolution in England when a great deal of soot had been deposited on trees and background areas. At this time, a local moth previously of a quite light color, became considerably darker in the industrial regions (although not in the nonindustrial areas). This occurred because the light moths stood out against the dark, sooty backgrounds and became easier prey for birds. They thus were less likely to reproduce themselves. They were less "fit" to survive. The few dark moths that existed, however, proliferated as their color gave them camouflage against the dark background. The genetic mutations that had resulted in their being a darker color had increased their genetic "fitness," and thus dark moths came to predominate (Kettlewell 1956).

The difference in human beings' skin coloring also is due to natural selection.

In hotter climates, individuals are more likely to survive when there is more pigment in their skin. This is because pigment absorbs the excessive ultraviolet radiation that occurs in these latitudes before it can reach and harm the sensitive layers of the skin beneath. Similarly, in regions of high latitude and seasonal cloudiness, a white skin is advantageous, at least in winter, for it permits a maximum of vitamin-D irradiation, which would be greatly impeded by more pigment granules. Thus, it is no surprise to find that the peoples indigenous to hot climates are darker skinned, and peoples indigenous to cold and cloudy climates are lighter skinned.

Behavior capacities and dispositions are like skin color. Examples of the inheritance of behaviors with which we all are familiar would include horses that run fast, dogs that point or round up sheep, and cats that like the company of human beings. Such animal traits have been selectively bred by humans for centuries, and experimental studies in laboratories have extended these to include such exotic traits as alcohol preference in mice (Lindzey, Loehlin, Manosevitz, & Thiessen 1971), courtship and mating speed in fruit flies (Manning 1965), and aggressiveness in domestic fowl (Siegel 1972). Many behaviors thus far studied in selective breeding experiments have demonstrated genetic links to the behavior in question. Let us consider an example of how this may happen. The behavior of herding occurs in a number of species. Many herd animals show signs of great discomfort when taken away from the herd. This could be naturally selected for by having predators such as lions killing off and eating those animals that did not stay with the herd. Thus, any genes that disposed the animal to depart from the herd would be selected out, but genes that disposed the animal to stay with the herd would be selected in.

A particularly good example is the development of language among humans. Those individuals within a group who were genetically more disposed to use or to comprehend language would have a greater chance of survival than those who did not because they would be more likely to utilize a greater amount of information for survival. For example, they would be more likely to learn in advance of certain dangers of a particular hunt. Those who paid no heed to such warnings would be more likely to fall into danger and be killed. Thus, the genes that determined their poor language capabilities would not be passed on to future generations, but those best suited to language development would prosper and multiply. They would be able to communicate about food sources and cooperate to hunt and gather it. Those who were least able to cooperate would lose out in the natural competition for food and thus leave fewer progeny.

In summary, the basic notion of natural selection is that those genetic endowments that occur completely by chance and that increase the "fitness" of the individuals having them are more likely to be handed down in the genes to offspring than are genetic characteristics that occur, also by chance, but that decrease the fitness of the individuals having them. Furthermore, the characteristics in question need not be only morphological in nature, they also can be behavioral.

ALTRUISM AMONG ANIMALS

The question then arises: Could a social behavior such as *altruism* possibly have been selected for and hence genetically determined? Are human beings genetically predisposed to be altruistic toward each other? Certainly Charles Darwin thought this was a distinct possibility. He devoted chapters 4 and 5 of his *Descent of Man* (1871) to the moral faculties, speculating that although it was the human being's moral sense that most distinguished people from other animals, it arose from two interacting aspects, both part of natural selection. The first is a person's intellectual powers, the second is his or her sociability.

Darwin (1871) detected such morality in other animal species as well and provided a series of examples of how sociable, cooperative, and helpful animals are to each other. He described how horses nibble and cows lick each other at any spots that itch; how chimps groom each other and remove external parasites, thorns, and burrs; how leaders of monkey troops act as sentinels and utter cries of danger or safety to their fellows; how rabbits warn each other of potential predators by stamping loudly with their hindfeet, and how sheep apparently do the same by stamping with their forefeet, uttering a whistle at the same time; and how bull bisons in North America, when there is danger, drive the cows and calves into the middle of the herd, while they defend the outside.

Since Darwin's observations, much additional data have been gathered to support the idea of animal altruism. E. O. Wilson (1975) brought together a great deal of evidence for altruism in animals in his book *Sociobiology: The New Synthesis*. Sociobiology, a new science, he defined as "the systematic study of the biological basis of all social behavior" (p. 4). Ultimately, Wilson suggested the same underlying principles of social behavior will apply to termite colonies, troops of rhesus macaques, and even *Homo sapiens*. Accounting for altruism he sees as the central theoretical problem of sociobiology: "How can altruism, which by definition reduces personal fitness, possibly evolve by natural selection?" (p. 3). We shall return to this very important question after we review some of the evidence demonstrating the presence of altruism among animal species other than our own. I shall attempt to organize this review under five not entirely separate categories: parental behavior, cooperative defense, rescue behavior, cooperative hunting, and food sharing.

Parental Behavior.

Parental behavior has evolved just as surely as physical characteristics have. Different species have very different kinds of parental care. The lowest level of parental care is that of producing eggs and sperm and discharging them into the water as frogs do. A higher level is laying an egg in the ground with provision of pollen or honey for the future needs of the progeny as wasps do. A step beyond this includes continuing to bring food to the hatched larvae, thus ministering to the continuing needs of the offspring. With mammals, there is a great deal of altruistic self-sacrifice in parental care of the young. In females there is the physiological burden of gestation, the ordeal of delivery, the production of milk, and then the activities of caring for and protecting the young. Interestingly, with developed parental care among mammals come the first indicators of affection, which most of the higher mammals appear capable of demonstrating toward one another. Affectional ties are possibly a mechanism by which nature ensured that altruistic caring for the young would occur, with its attendant sacrifice.

Much care for the young is given also by species other than mammals. Birds, for example, will work very hard for their offspring or potential offspring, not only in building the nest and later feeding the young, but also in protecting them once they are born (actually even before they are born). Examples of such altruism are the distraction displays used to attract the attention of potential enemies and to lure them away from the bird's eggs or newly hatched young. Typically, the distraction display involves feigning injury by flying slowly close to the ground, perhaps using only one wing to do so, and even landing close to the intruder. In this way the predator's attention is diverted from the nest, and the young are saved. There is very little doubt that the adults engaged in these distraction displays are placing their own lives in danger.

Parental care for the young is often aided by "helpers." Among the Florida scrub jays, Woolfenden (1973) reported that approximately half of the breeding pairs are assisted by helpers. Although the helpers are not active in nest construction or incubation, they participate in every other activity, including defense of the territory and nest from other jays, attacks on predators, and feeding the young. In almost every case it is close kin that are helped in this manner. Alloparents (helpers) occur in most advanced animal societies. This form of altruism is displayed par excellence by the sterile worker castes in the higher social insects (Wilson 1971). These animals pose a unique problem for evolutionary theory, since their workers forego reproduction themselves but labor for the reproductive success of their mother, the queen. This is a particularly good example of altruism. Among mammals the phenomenon of alloparents has been reported in porpoises and in both the African and Asiatic elephants. Alloparental care, however, is perhaps best expressed in primates whose adult females are attracted to the newborn infants of others and, depending on the particular species of primate, attempt to care for them. Among rhesus monkeys, mothers come to trust these other females and use them as baby sitters while on foraging trips.

In many primate species, males also care for offspring—again the kind of care given varies with the species under consideration. In species characterized by the presence of a single male in the troop, the males tend to show an almost maternal solicitude toward infants. At one extreme, the male marmoset *(Calli-*

thrix) carries his twin offspring until their combined weight equals his own, turning them over to his mate only for feeding.

Before leaving parental care, we must briefly mention perhaps the most altruistic type of all, that is, adoption. Jane Goodall (1968, 1971) described several cases of orphaned chimpanzees who were adopted by adult siblings. Estes and Goddard (1967) described how adult males in a pack of wild dogs continued to feed and care for nine pups after their mother died. This continued until such time as the pups were able to join the pack on hunting trips.

Mutual Defense.

Cooperation is a prototype of altruistic behavior. Altruistic, cooperative defense is certainly well known among many species. For example, Wilson (1971) documented the existence of self-sacrificial altruism among many species of ant. If nest walls are broken open, soldier ants pour out and engage in combat with foraging ants from other nests. Meanwhile, behind them, worker ants repair the broken walls. Many of the soldier ants will die in combat, sacrificing their lives in order to save their nestmates.

Cooperative defense occurs in other species, too. Guard bees, for example, protect their nest entrances against ants and wasps. By taking turns at guard duty, the bees can free each other for foraging trips without ever leaving the entrance untended (Wilson 1975, p. 44). Birds will cooperate to mob a predator in the hopes of driving it away from the area. In experimental studies in which a stuffed owl is presented, small birds will attack it while at the same time uttering sounds that attract other birds to the area to join in the attack. Often the bills of the birds seemed to be directed at the eyes of the owl (Wilson 1975, p. 47). On other occasions birds will emit warning calls that signal danger to other birds of the presence of a predator. These are uttered by such diverse species as blackbirds, robins, thrushes, reed buntings, and titmice. If a hawk is seen flying overhead, the bird will crouch low and emit the warning signal. This is clearly altruistic behavior because it warns other birds of the danger while at the same time attracts the possible attention of the predator to the self (Wilson 1975, p. 123). Cooperative attack, similar to that of mobbing by birds, also occurs in numerous species including deer, elephants, and chimpanzees.

Chimpanzees in particular are noted for cooperative defense. A leopard predator will attract a joint assault by dominant males who charge forward in an aggressive frenzy in an attempt to drive it away. Some of the chimps charge upright on their hind legs. Near the leopard some will seize saplings and lash them back and forth, sometimes striking it. This has been observed in both naturalistic observation as well as experimentally, by using stuffed leopards (Wilson 1975, p. 46).

A final form of cooperative defense is the "protective circle" formation, also noted by Darwin in relation to bull bisons in North America. Social ungulates often will arrange themselves in protective circular formations around calves in order to repel such predators as hyenas and wolves. Cooperative defense similar to this has been observed even among killer whales.

Rescue Behavior.

Rescue is another very altruistic form of behavior. One animal frequently mentioned in this regard is the dolphin. Dolphins belong, along with whales, to the taxonomic category *Cetacea.* They are warm blooded, air-breathing mammals, which live in the sea. They give birth to their young alive and suckle them. Biologically they are much closer to humans than to fish. The newborn infant is born tail first, unlike land-dwelling mammals in whom the position of birth is head first. The reason for this is that the infant might drown if the blow hole were exposed before the baby could come to the surface for air. Newborn infants that do not rise for air at once are pushed to the surface by their elders. Injured adults often may be supported by an assisting pair of dolphins for a considerable length of time, thus keeping its blow hole above the water level. Such instances show cooperation among several individuals and are well authenticated. Siebenaler and Caldwell (1956), for example, related the observation of what happened when dynamite went off in the sea, partially stunning a dolphin. Immediately two other adults came to its assistance by coming up alongside it and holding it afloat to breathe. This they continued to do until their companion recovered. These and other investigators have provided a number of such well-documented instances.

Similar rescue behavior has been observed among elephants. If an elephant is felled and left to lie in the sun it soon can suffocate from its own weight. Other elephants have been seen to help raise the injured one to its feet. Finally, it has been noted, a chimpanzee male often will rush to the aid of an infant that calls out when under attack by a predator, even though the infant is not , his own (Goodall 1971).

Cooperation in Hunting.

This behavior is not completely altruistic since the individual animals participating in the hunt also are gaining from it. However, it seems appropriate to review it here. Ants, for example, attack large, active insect prey in the vicinity of the nest and discharge alarm pheromones which attract other workers within distances of ten centimeters or so, with the result that the prey is more quickly subdued (Wilson 1971). Honey bees search out food and then return to the hive and by means of their "waggle-dance" tell the other bees in the hive where the food source is (von Frisch 1967). Wolves, African wild dogs, and lions also all hunt socially, fanning out and coordinating their circling attacks with almost military precision. Killer whales too hunt in packs and cooperate. Wilson (1975 pp. 54-55) cited one observation in which a pack of fifteen to twenty killer whales pursued and encircled about one hundred porpoises, gradually constricting them inwards. Then one whale charged inwards and fed on the porpoises, while its companions held the line. Eventually it traded places with another whale, who fed for a while. This procedure continued until all of the porpoises were consumed.

One set of rather important observations of cooperative hunting was made of chimpanzees at the Gombe National Park on Lake Tanganyika in Tanzania. Geza Teleki (1973) recorded her observations of the natural hunting behavior of these animals. On a hunt, for example, all the animals cooperate intelligently and purposively. They keep very quiet, which is unusual in itself, and their movements and positioning are done without regard for the normally obvious social hierarchy. Their prey consists of mammals such as rodents, infant baboons, and even baby antelopes up to about 10 lbs. in weight. Teleki's (1973) observations are important for a number of reasons. For one, the degree to which chimps were predators had not been realized previously, and because they are phylogenetically so close to humans, this has certain implications for theories of early human evolution, a topic to which we will return later in the chapter.

Food Sharing.

Food sharing is a particularly altruistic activity in which a number of species engage. Kühme (1965) observed food sharing behavior in a pack of hunting dogs in the Serengeti Plains of East Africa. He noted in detail their democratic food-sharing behavior. The pack contained six males and two females, of which one had four and the other eleven pups. All the members of the pack behaved very tolerantly towards one another, although the two females occasionally had minor disagreements, evidently because they competed in caring for the pups. During a hunt the females and a couple of males stayed behind to guard the pups while the other males went off in a pack to catch and kill baby antelope. After killing their prey, the hunters bolted down huge chunks of meat which they disgorged back at the den for the guards and pups to share. The guard dogs, too, often disgorged their food, and food passed through many stomachs before being digested.

As Kühme reported, the communal treatment of the food supply made a true division of labor possible between guards and hunters. Each dog was equally qualified to do either, and there was a total absence of rank. All combinations of working and living together occurred. Further evidence of their communal living pattern came from their apparent shows of affection for each other.

When meeting each other they pushed with the nose against the mouth of the other. Sometimes males licked the udder of a female, or a female crept under a male like a nursing pup under its mother. Kühme (1965) concluded that they all behaved rather like children of one great family. Thus evidence for altruistic behavior comes also from hunting dogs.

Food sharing also has been noted frequently among chimpanzees. One early study was carried out by Nissen and Crawford (1936) at the Yerkes Regional Primate Research Center at Emory University in Atlanta, Georgia. These investigators set up two cages, side by side, in which they put two hungry chimpanzees. One of the chimpanzees then was given a little food. The question was, would it give any of its food to its hungry companion? The answer was a definite yes. Sometimes the food was passed over without the other's request. On other occasions it was passed over rather ungraciously. Sometimes, when the chimp without food kept up its begging, the chimp with the food would hurl some scraps at the other. Begging elicited even greater amounts when the pair were friends than when they were strangers.

More dramatic evidence of food sharing in chimpanzees came from further observations made by Teleki (1973). As mentioned in the previous section, she observed chimpanzees cooperatively hunting as predators. Following a kill of, say, a baby baboon, there was the initial division of the meat. For a short period the meat was common property, and even other chimps that had not taken part in the hunt could take a piece for themselves. During this period there was a total absence of aggressiveness and again, an absence of the usual deference to dominant superiors that otherwise characterizes much chimp behavior. After this initial division of the meat, food sharing in earnest began. Chimps that now arrived on the scene arranged themselves into "sharing clusters" around one of the chimps with meat from the first food share. Sometimes these sharing clusters numbered as many as thirteen, but almost always every individual received some portion. Teleki noted an odd exception, interesting because it was one of the leaders of the troop, one of the most dominant, that was refused a share and, further, by one of the more submissive animals. The leader, at this point did not assert himself and take what he could have. Teleki herself concluded that meat sharing actually had very little nutritional value for the chimps and that it was largely for social reasons that it occurred.

That chimps are social animals sharing long-term emotional attachments to one another and spending a great deal of their time in mutual grooming and social play is now well documented. Goodall (1968, 1971) wrote much about the chimps of the Gombe Stream Reserve and provided many examples of, for instance, sons still sharing affectional association with their mothers after several years of independence and also of long-term friendship between males. Such "awareness of the other" in chimps and their obvious affectionate sociability makes it not at all surprising that examples of altruism can be found in those animals.

Empathy.

Some researchers have suggested that infrahuman animals are capable of "empathy." For example, Masserman, Wechkin, and Terris (1964) found that rhesus monkeys would consistently refrain from pulling a chain that brought them food in order to avoid giving a shock to their partners. The authors suggested that the sight of their fellows in distress produced empathic feelings in the first monkey, thus motivating the altruistic response. It should be noted, however, that the monkeys could get food on alternate trials by pulling another chain, so the amount of sacrifice was not very large. It might be interesting to know what would happen if a hungry monkey had to choose between pulling a chain that resulted in a much preferred food *and* shock to the other animal, versus a much less preferred food and *no* shock to the other monkey. If the monkey continually chose the least preferred food in order to save his partner from pain, even greater altruism might be said to have occurred.

Miller, Caul, and Mirsky (1967) also conducted a study that suggested the workings of empathy. Monkeys were paired with a partner by means of television monitors. In an initial training session both monkeys were given electric shock that, alternatingly, one of them could terminate by pressing a lever. They both were then taught to avoid the shock by pressing the lever when a warning signal came on. The next stage, which tested for empathy, gave the warning signal to only one of the monkeys and the lever to the other. Would the second monkey be able to avoid shock for them both by observing the distress of the first monkey to the warning signal which he himself could not see? The answer was yes. Signs of distress in the first monkey were seen on a television monitor by the second monkey who would then press the lever thus avoiding shock for them both. An interesting aspect of this study was that cardiac rates were measured, and it was found that the heart rate of the second monkey went up as soon as the first monkey started to show signs of distress. A second interesting finding was that this worked only for "normal" monkeys. Other monkeys that had been subjected to total social isolation in the first year of life could neither "send" the appropriate facial signals nor "receive" them. Otherwise they had no difficulty in learning the responses involved. This suggests that some degree of learning is required for empathy which the social isolate had not experienced. Unfortunately, although demonstrating the operation of empathy in monkeys, this study was concerned with cooperation rather than with more extreme altruism. The second monkey not only avoided a shock for the first monkey, it also avoided one for itself. It would have been interesting to see if it would work at lever pulling simply to avoid shock to its friend.

A study by Church (1959) is of relevance here. This research demonstrated that rats that had previously experienced shared aversive outcomes with another rat, in the form of electric shock, were markedly affected by the subsequent pain responses of other rats. Animals that had not experienced shared aversive stimulation, however, showed little empathic responsiveness to the pain cues of the other rat. Church (1959) concluded that empathy could be acquired through the learning experiences of the animals; it need not be under direct *genetic* control.

How can we determine whether the altruistic examples that we have described are largely under genetic control and have evolved through natural selection? One direct way might be selectively to breed for altruism in animals. As a rather dramatic example for purposes of illustration we might observe a group of chimpanzees in the wild, as Teleki (1973) and Goodall (1971) did in the Gombe Stream Reserve, and note over a period of time which chimpanzees showed the most altruism and which showed the least. Our measure of altruism in this case might be, say, willingness to defend other chimps when predators such as leopards arrive on the scene. (As already described, chimpanzees do this by throwing objects at the predator and emitting signals that warn others.) Then we could select five or six of the most altruistic (Group A) and five or six of the least altruistic (Group B) and breed them with like-behaved females. In turn, we could observe their offspring and take the five or six most altruistic from Group A's progeny and the five or six least altruistic of Group B's and breed them in turn. After five or six generations, if we had controlled for the upbringing environments by cross-fostering but nonetheless still had produced two entirely different populations in terms of altruistic behavior, it would be possible to say that selective breeding for altruism was possible and that therefore altruistic behavior *was* under some degree of genetic control.

This particular experiment would be exceptionally difficult to carry out. For one thing, it probably would mean interfering substantially with the natural state of the chimps (e.g., in order to stop members of Group A mating with members of Group B). This in turn might interfere with the natural occurrence of altruistic behavior thus contaminating the results of the study. A solution to this particular problem would be to breed for laboratory measured altruism, for example, the "empathy" shown in the experiments with rhesus monkeys cited earlier. There still would be problems. In terms of length of time and expense, the costs would be exorbitant. It would take years to do. It is for reasons like these that experimental psychologists interested in the genetics of social behavior prefer to use laboratory-reared animals that have a fairly speedy intergenerational turnover; that is, they are fast breeding. Fruit flies and laboratory rats are the two main experimental animals in this regard. Fruit flies have been bred for a variety of mating behaviors (e.g., speed to mate), and rats have been bred for such behaviors as intelligence (the ability to learn how to run mazes quickly), emotionality ("freezing" and being fearful in an "open field"), and exploratory behavior. Unfortunately, examples of altruism in the rat may be less easy to find—although perhaps not impossible.

THE PARADOX OF ALTRUISM

To summarize so far: A number of studies were reviewed that described behavior occurring among animals that conforms to the definition of altruism as "behavior carried out to achieve positive outcomes for another rather than for the self." These included parental behaviors, mutual defense, rescue behavior, cooperative hunting, and sharing food. The possibility of empathy operating among such animals as the rhesus monkey was considered. Finally, the possibility of conducting selective breeding experiments on animals was proposed to give us additional evidence on the genetics underlying such behaviors. It seems fairly clear that altruism does exist among nonhuman animals. The degree to which this evolved through the process of natural selection is a paradox, recognized early by Darwin (1871, p. 130). If the *most* altruistic members of the group were willing to die for others, for example, by sacrificing themselves in battle, then there would be fewer offspring of altruistic, self-sacrificing individuals to carry forward the characteristic. Indeed, it might even be expected that it would be those individuals within a group who were the most unlikely to sacrifice themselves for the group who would produce most offspring. But if this were the case then selfishness would be the trait selected, not altruism. How, then, is it possible that altruism could have arisen through the process of natural selection? The solution to such a paradox, Darwin (1859) suggested, lay in some form of *group* selection, rather than in selection on the level of the individual, that is, groups that have the trait survive better than groups that do not have it. Darwin, although he raised the possibility of group selection, did not elaborate on it. Altruism remained as something of an anomaly in his theory of evolution and thus was ignored, as was the whole question of selection at the level of the group.

It was not until 1932 that the question was raised again seriously. At this time J.B.S. Haldane wrote an important book integrating the theory of genetics (which had developed since Darwin's time) with the Darwinian theory of evolution. Haldane raised the specific question of whether there were *genes for altruism*, and if there were, how these would fare under natural selection. He asked again whether there might be some form of group selection operating. Although Haldane once again had brought up the issue, once again it was ignored.

It was Wynne-Edwards (1962) who finally brought the issue forward so as to provoke attention. He suggested that whole groups of animals collectively refrained from overbreeding when the density of population became too great—even to the point of directly killing their own offspring if necessary. The purpose of this altruistic self-constraint, Wynne-Edwards suggested, was essentially to protect the animal's ecology so that in the longer run all might benefit. The degree to which each individual imposed self-limitation was dependent on the population density at the time. This was communicated to each animal, he proposed, through such displays as flocking in birds and swarming in insects. Whole flocks that adopted self-limitation would be selected for, argued Wynne-Edwards. Those that did not adopt self-limitation died out as a group. Wynne-Edwards furthermore brought together much disparate evidence to support his views. Such an extreme form of the group selection hypothesis was immediately disputed by other biologists. In order to refute this theory, many new data had to be gathered and new ideas considered. Thus the issue of group selection finally had an impact on biologists. As it turned out, most of the new studies found evidence against the Wynne-Edwards hypothesis of group selection (Williams 1966).

Wilson (1975) pointed out that the concept of group selection can be applied on a number of different levels to various numbers of individuals. On levels just above that of the individual are groups related by common genes, as in siblings, parents and their offspring, and closely knit tribes or families. Group selection on this level, Wilson suggested, might profitably be named *kin selection*. On a higher level, the term "group" also could refer to the entire breeding population (as in Wynne-Edwards's). Group selection on this more encompassing level might be called *interpopulation selection*. It thus becomes possible to conceive of a continuum with pure kin selection at one end and pure population selection at the other. It is that end of the continuum concerned with kin selection that solves the paradox of altruism. It does so through the notion of *inclusive fitness*.

Hamilton (1964, 1972) proposed the concept of *inclusive fitness* as a major extension of the original Darwinian idea of *individual* fitness. Although individual fitness was based solely on the number of direct offspring left, inclusive fitness includes not only an individual's own offspring but also the *sum of all the offspring of relatives*. This is because it is *genes* that survive and are passed on in offspring. If an animal sacrifices its own life for its brother's offspring, it ensures the survival of *common genes*, for it shares 50 percent of its genes with its sibling and 25 percent with its nephew or niece. The percentage of genes shared therefore should be an important influence on the amount of altruism displayed. The case of the social ants makes this clear. Female worker ants tend to be sterile for most of their lives and engage in much altruistic self-sacrifice for their sisters. Indeed, they are the most altruistic species so far discovered. *They also share three fourths of their genes with their sisters.* By devoting their entire existence to the needs of others and sacrificing their lives if need be, they are in fact helping to propagate their own genes. They do this not through self-reproduction (the original Darwinian idea of *individual* fitness) but by helping the reproductive success of those with whom they share genes (the new idea of *inclusive* fitness). Thus the appropriate analysis for understanding natural selection is the gene rather than the individual organism. As Wilson (1975) dryly put it, "the organism is only DNA's way of making more DNA" (p. 3). Dawkins (1977), a popularizer of sociobiology, entitled his book: *The Selfish Gene.* Any means by which a *pool* of genes, in a number of individuals, can be transmitted more effectively into the next generation will be adopted. Here, it was suggested, are the origins of maternal behaviors, sterility in castes of worker ants, and self-sacrificial altruism. All these phenomena are means by which genes can be more readily transmitted. In this analysis altruism loses much of its mystery and some of its nobility. It is only a mechanism by which DNA multiplies itself more effectively.

It is now nearly time to consider the implications of all the above for human societies. Let us first consider some of human history to put this into proper perspective.

THE EMERGENCE OF ALTRUISM AND SOCIETY AMONG HUMANS

The best current evidence suggests that the material universe came into being some fifteen thousand million years ago in a small region of space and began to expand outwards. It suggests that four and a half thousand million years ago the planet earth coalesced from a cold dust and then was warmed by the heat of the sun. Two and a half thousand million years ago, biological evolution—the origins of life—began. Seventy million years ago, the first primitive primates emerged in the form of shrewlike creatures. Twenty-five million years ago, primates were well established and the higher primates had split into three types: the New World monkeys, the Old World monkeys, and the apes. Fourteen million years ago, apes and human beings started to move along separate evolutionary lines. *Ramapithecus*, ancestor to humans, had climbed down from the trees and had begun to explore the fringes of the forest. By five million years ago, in Africa, *Ramapithecus* had evolved into at least three different hominid types: *Australopithecus africanus, Australopithecus boisei,* and *Australopithecus afarensis.* Just over two million years ago, *Homo habilis* evolved from the *Australopithecus afarensis* line. The definitive existence for this phylogenetic taxonomy rests on only very recent fossil findings in East Africa (Johanson & White 1979; Leakey & Lewin 1977). *Homo habilis* stood 5 ft. tall, walked fully erect, had a brain size of 800 cc, and used rudimentary stone tools. The stage was set for the emergence of humans, and only one and a half million years ago, *Homo erectus* was just that. A species of human had evolved upon the earth. As depicted in Figure 2.1, it spent a long time coming.

H. erectus lived in small bands of probably no more than one hundred members, most of whom were *genetically related*. Time was spent hunting and gathering along the banks of streams or on the shores of lakes. Weapons and implements were made from bone and stone. Furthermore, he or she discovered fire. It was the discovery of fire that enabled humans to move from open encampments along the water's edge to caves. Perhaps more important still, now

Figure 2-1 The Evolutionary Origins of Homo Sapiens. From left to right: Ramapithecus (14 million to 10 million years ago); Gigantopithecus (9 million to 1 million years ago); Modern apes (gorillas and chimpanzees); Australopithecus robustus (3.5 million to 1.5 million years ago); Australopithecus Africanus (3.5 million to 1.5 million years ago); Homo habilis (at least 2 million years ago); Homo erectus (1.6 million years ago; Homo sapiens (10,000 years ago). (Source: Julian Allen, *Paths to Man.* Reprinted by permission of the artist.)

able to keep warm, ancient humans started their migrations into the chilly, often glaciated regions of prehistoric Europe. The remains of *H. erectus* have been found in Africa, Asia, and Europe.

H. erectus was a confirmed hunter, a habitual eater of fresh meat, and his or her prey included animals of all sizes and age groups. This we know from the weapons and burnt animal bones that have been found with the fossil remains of this primitive human. It also seems that both cannibalism and head hunting were practiced, although possibly more for ritual reasons than for nutritional ones. Meat from the hunt formed only part of the diet of *H. erectus*. Other edible forms of life were snakes, birds and their eggs, mice and other rodents, and many others. Many of these even children might have caught, as with present-day hunters like the Kalahari Bushmen and the Australian aborigines. Vegetable food was a particularly large part of humans' diet in the form of fleshy leaves, fruits, nuts, and roots. It is, however, the fact that *H. erectus* was a hunter that has excited the most interest.

The conditions of life in which early humans lived apparently exerted tremendous evolutionary pressures. It has been estimated that selection pressures were such that during this last million years adult cranial capacity (a rough index of brain size) increased from the 1,000 cc in *Homo erectus* to the average 1,300 to 1,500 range of modern-day humans, *Homo sapiens*. The extremely rapid growth in intelligence accompanying this enlargement constituted a great leap forward in mental evolution.

One view of humans that has emerged from our increasing knowledge of prehistory, is that offered by the anthropologist Raymond Dart (1949) and popularized by Robert Ardrey (1961) in his book *African Genesis*. Ardrey wrote:

> . . . Man had emerged from the anthropoid background for one reason only: because he was a killer. Long ago, perhaps many millions of years ago, a line of killer apes branched off from the nonaggressive primate background. For reasons of environmental necessity, the line adopted the predatory way. For reasons of predatory necessity the line advanced. We learned to stand erect in the first place as a necessity of the hunting life. We learned to run in our pursuit of game across the yellowing African savannah. . . . lacking fighting teeth or claws, we took recourse by necessity to the weapon.
>
> A rock, a stick, a heavy stone—to our ancestral killer ape it meant the margin of survival. But the use of the weapon meant new and multiplying demands on the nervous system for the co-ordination of muscle and touch and sight. And so at last came the enlarged brain; so at last came man.
>
> Far from the truth lay the antique assumption that man had fathered the weapon. *The weapon, instead, had fathered man.* (Ardrey 1961, p. 31, italics added)

In support of his thesis that humans emerged from a long line of "killer apes," Ardrey used much interesting, albeit speculative, evidence that suggested that as far back as three million years ago, *Australopithecus*, at the time thought to be a direct ancestor of *Homo erectus*, was already committing murder and killing its own kind with clubs. Such a view of human nature also was propounded by Nobel Prize Laureate and founder of modern ethology, Konrad Lorenz, in his book, *On Aggression* (1966). It also was taken up and popularized by Desmond Morris in his best-selling book, *The Naked Ape* (1967). This view of human evolution is a very distorted one, however, the veridicality of which has been severely disputed (e.g., Montagu 1968).

If killing, through hunting or battle, did provide some of the impetus for humans' evolution to a bipedal erect gait and larger brain, then the ability and desire to wield clubs certainly was not sufficient. The much more important necessity was that they learn to cooperate and work as a group. It also must be borne in mind that humans were not only hunters. They also were hunter-*gatherers*. It is quite likely that only about one third of their diet was meat, and the remaining two thirds was plant foods, as occurs among such present-day hunter-gatherers as the !Kung (Leakey & Lewin 1977, chap. 7). As these authors noted, the early human economy was based on a special *mixture* of hunting and gathering—separate activities linked together as a powerful social pattern by the sharing of goods among members of the troop. Division of labor became increasingly possible. Cooperation on a hunt, therefore, was only one aspect of coordinated behavior by a group of social animals operating in a mixed economy.

We might speculate that in order to survive, humans had to repress their immediate desires to gratify their own individuality. They had to integrate their behavior with that of their society. Language possibly developed partially as a necessity for the enhancement of cooperation. Along with cooperation might well have come group loyalty, altruism, and a range of related phenomena including strong patterns of friendship and feelings for the group, social signals, and means of communicating friendship, leadership, and social organization.

The large forebrain made symbolic manipulation possible, and this would bring forth unprecedented kinds of social behavior, most of them concerned with the maintenance and enhancement of social organization and interdependent cooperation. With the increasing complexity of social organization would have come the social rules necessary to keep the individual's personal drives and emotions concerning jealousy, fear, sex, aggression, and food, under control. Indeed, such rules were actually able to suppress such powerful urges as sex. Thus humans became religious, obedient to rules, and capable of abstract theorizing about their nature and the society of which they were part. Humans had created a society in which they were interdependent on others. They had created a society in which *altruism*, in the widest sense of that term (i.e., regard for others) was a *sine qua non* of existence. *Altruism and society both arose out of evolutionary necessity, as much as did any killer instincts.* Human nature therefore is far more complex and positive than that suggested by such terms as "killer ape." Even if killing does turn out to have been one of humans' evolutionary pacemakers, there can be little doubt that cooperation and altruism towards group members was another. A tendency toward hostility to and suspicion of outgroups, and loyalty and identification to ingroups appears to be the fuller story of this earlier development.

Evolution continued and three hundred thousand years ago, the earliest forms of modern humans, *Homo sapiens*, emerged. *H. sapiens* was quite different from its predecessors, *H. erectus*, both in brain size (1,350 cc versus 1,000 cc) and in brain organization. *Homo sapiens* has a highly developed forebrain. Increases in the size and complexity of the forebrain made symbolic thought and communication possible.

There seem to have been many types of *Homo sapiens* at first, including Neanderthal people who had brains even *bigger* than those of modern people (1,450 cc). Their prominent brow ridges, sloping forehead, chinless jaw, and robust body combined to give them a brutish appearance, but Neanderthal people gave us the first evidence for both burial and religion. The last Neanderthal people existed forty thousand years ago, and their remains have been found throughout Europe, North Africa, and Asia. Still another type of *Homo sapiens* was the Cro-Magnon who existed in Western Europe about thirty-five thousand years ago. Cro-Magnon people stood 6 ft. tall, had a high forehead and large brains, and were responsible for many of the polychrome paintings found on cave walls in France, Germany, and Spain. Nobody knows why these subspecies (Neanderthal and Cro-Magnon) disappeared. It is possible that they were exterminated or absorbed by *Homo sapiens*. In any case, by twenty-five thousand years ago; a modern form of *Homo sapiens* totally dominated the land masses of Europe, Africa, and Asia, and had even crossed the Bering Sea into the Americas.

Evolution continued and *Homo sapiens* was faced with many challenges—not least of which was the last ice age which retreated only some ten thousand years ago from a line that reached as far south as London and New York. This last ice age destroyed many forms of animals and allowed new ones to develop, one of which, largely because of the extension of grasslands, was the horse. In addition it produced enormous changes in the distribution of plants and animals, especially in the Northern Hemisphere. It was the retreat of the polar ice cap that brought the next, vitally significant, stage of human development—agricultural settlements.

The invention of agriculture, ten thousand years ago, speeded up human evolution, both biological and cultural, to a dizzying speed compared with the relatively sedate progress of the previous three or four million years. As Leakey and Lewin (1977) pointed out, it shifted humans from an essentially mobile, hunting and gathering existence, to a virtually sedentary, agricultural one. It shattered a way of life that had first emerged at least three million years earlier. As a result of agriculture, those populations that were most capable of giving up the hunter-gatherer way of life and adopting an urban, agricultural way, increased enormously in numbers, organization, and finally in military power. Many smaller bands of hunter-gatherers became either absorbed or extinct. Tribes, kingdoms, and finally states of an extremely complex and interlocking nature replaced them.

The evolutionary pressures that agriculture exerted on the human gene pool must have been enormous. Those individuals who were members of successful agricultural settlements must have reproduced themselves at a far greater rate than did those who remained outside such settlements. The greatly increased food supply and security thereof, throughout the year, allowed for a far larger population to exist. A full-time division of labor became possible, with one of the first occupational specialties being professional soldiers (to protect the food supply). Agricultural settlements made possible a complex urban society and ultimately, civilization. Agricultural settlements must have arisen all over the world at the same time as the ice age receded. It is certainly a highly adaptive system for humans to live in, and there have been independent urban civilizations in many parts of the world—in Egypt, Mesopotamia, China, Peru, India, Mexico, both East and West Africa, and Europe.

Campbell (1965) suggested that this changeover from the basically nomadic hunter-gatherer existence, increased enormously the genetic basis of moral behaviors in humans. He pointed out that urban living had three great advantages allowing for increased survival value. Each of these advantages, Campbell suggested, helped to increase the selection for certain moral behaviors.

The first advantage was shared thought. Information about cooking, weaving, building, and planting was handed down by word of mouth and later by written language, rather than each individual learning for himself or herself in a trial-and-error manner. The necessity to communicate and to use the communications of others therefore was even more essential than it was before agriculture. Campbell (1965) speculated that this required the development of both *honesty* and *trust* in an even greater form, both of which could be partially selected for on the genetic level. Certain extremes of unreliability and mistrust based on genetic mechanisms would be selected out as such individuals would be unlikely to produce societies that worked. Thus honesty and trust are presumably universal values in human society.

The second advantage of urban living is the allowance it makes for specialization of labor and subsequent increment in the complexity of the society. The specialization of labor rests to a large extent on there being a stored food surplus, and this in turn increases the selection pressure for certain necessary moral behaviors. These would include, for example, *industriousness, abstinence from indulgence, ability to save,* and *willingness to share.*

The third advantage of group urban living outlined by Campbell was mutual defense. This required, as we already have discussed, group *loyalty* and ultimately the *altruistic willingness to sacrifice the self for the group.*

This reasoning suggests that, on a priori grounds, there are no reasons for ruling out genetic factors as causes of such moral behaviors in humans as honesty, trust, abstinence from indulgence, willingness to share, loyalty, and altruistic willingness to sacrifice the self for the group. The tremendous survival value of being social makes innate prosocial motives as likely on a priori grounds as self-centered, egoistic ones. Groups genetically predisposed to behave in such ways would have a distinct advantage over groups that did not, and we have seen how the notion of kin-selection can handle the evolution of such behaviors. In addition, natural selection processes probably were operating *within* the group to eliminate those members who were particularly likely to engage in antisocial behaviors.

Humans thus have been evolving for about one and a half million years and continue to evolve, for evolution is a continual process. *Homo sapiens* evolves, both biologically and socioculturally. Indeed, these are mutually related means of evolution. For example, as early humans started to use tools or weapons, those who were physically most adroit at using them would survive, and those who were not would be eliminated. Use of tools (sociocultural evolution) affected physical adroitness (biological evolution). This in turn led to more extensive use of tools (back to sociocultural). Finally, during the last five hundred or so years, the development of science led to the most massive changes in sociocultural evolution so far observed, and the world population of *Homo sapiens* now exceeds four billion. It is expected to reach seven and a half billion by the year 2000.

There is no reason to suppose that this mutually interdependent system of biological and social evolution broke down after the discovery of agriculture ten thousand years ago. Just as hunter-gatherer groups differentially survived, so have cultures and civilizations and, very often, the gene pools associated with them. It has been estimated that in Western Europe alone, between the years A.D. 275 and A.D. 1025, there has been a war every two years on the average. Often these wars directly and substantially affected the gene pool, as when genocide was practiced (a not uncommon occurrence during the extremely bloody history of *Homo sapiens*). At other times the wars brought changes to the social structure, as when a new ideas-system or religion won out in battle against an alternative. For example, cultures that put a high premium on trade and exploration (as in Western Europe over the last several hundred years) led to a movement of the gene pools through migration. This also occurred with militarily expanding peoples who migrated into areas in which they displaced the vanquished. These processes are still going on in the twentieth century.

We already have discussed some of the provocative formulations currently being advanced in biology and zoology as in Wilson's (1975) *Sociobiology: The New Synthesis.* (For an introduction emphasizing the implications for psychology and social science, see Barash 1976 and Wilson 1978). According to these formulations, the whole purpose of ethics, social structures, economic systems, and the like are to allow for the gene pool to extend itself maximally into the next generation. Accordingly, any emerging social behavior that increases the likelihood of a group or culture surviving will itself survive into subsequent generations.

Trivers (1971) extended some of the basic ideas of sociobiology to a variety of complex human behaviors. He suggested that altruism among humans is based primarily on the idea of reciprocity. Reciprocal altruism occurs when a person who helps another is likely to be helped back at some point. Trivers proposed that reciprocal altruism also might be under genetic control. If this were the case, then altruism might arise even among unrelated individuals. All that would be required is that the species have sufficient cognitive processing ability to remember who had and who had not helped in the past. Trivers (1971) also offered a number of other genetically determined dispositions that would reinforce adherence to the reciprocity dispositions. The best example of this is *moralistic aggression* brought to bear on cheaters who do not live up to their reciprocal duties. Certainly moral outrage and a strong sense of justice (injustice?) are particularly human characteristics. On the other hand again, certain immoral behaviors among humans also might be selected for. If a human could cheat and get away with it then possibly his or her own inclusive fitness actually might be increased. Wilson (1975) quoted Hamilton: "By our lofty standards, animals are poor liars" (p. 119). Species closest to humans, such as chimpanzees and gorillas, *will* apparently lie to one another in order to obtain food or to attract company.

The ideas of sociobiology have aroused a great deal of controversy and interest. Currently a debate rages as to the status of such ideas among both behavioral and biological scientists (see, for example, Campbell 1975; Gregory, Silvers, & Sutch 1978; Lewontin 1975; and Wispé & Thompson 1976). Interestingly enough, Campbell (1972), after considerable reflection, came to doubt the views that he proposed in 1965; that is, that urban living genetically selected such moral traits in humans as honesty, trust, abstinence from indulgence, and industriousness. He now feels that human genes predispose us toward egoism and that massive socialization is required to overcome this. These controversies are likely to lead to very interesting research in the future.

Does sociobiology, as a science, have any value for us in the attempt to comprehend human altruism? It appears to organize a variety of disparate data on other species, and it provides a feeling of insight into the phenomenon with humans; it clearly also does make predictions. It predicts, for example, that we are most altruistic to those who are genetically similar to ourselves, that is, family rather than friends, and friends rather than strangers. Within families, mothers should be more altruistic than fathers to offspring. This is because mothers have a potentially larger genetic investment in any one child than does a father. A human male is biologically capable of reproducing his genes an enormously greater number of times than is a human female. Biologically he is capable of impregnating one or more women every day for several years. A human female is biologically capable of reproducing her genes at most once every ten months or so. Therefore, it follows from sociobiology that each offspring a human female produces is of potentially far greater importance to her (as a vehicle for her own genes) than the same offspring is to the father. Genetically speaking, mothers should care more for their offspring than fathers should. In the same way, parents should be more altruistic to their offspring than to their own parents. A less obvious prediction is that parents should be more altruistic to their *healthy* male offspring than to their *unhealthy* male offspring, with both healthy and unhealthy female offspring falling between the two male types. The reason is that healthy male offspring have the greatest opportunity to propagate their genes into future generations whereas the unhealthy males have the least, and females, both healthy and unhealthy, are in between. (For an interesting and popularized rendition of some of these notions, see a book by Dawkins (1976) entitled *The Selfish Gene*.)

Critics might question how behaviors such as running into burning buildings to rescue strangers from otherwise certain death are explained by such a theory. The answer lies in human history: One and a half million years ago when human altruism evolved, such dramatic behaviors did in fact propagate one's own genes because people lived within a tribe of individuals who all were more or less directly related to one another. Today our genes are still fulfilling the same function, as though the stranger were more genetically similar to us than he or she in fact is.

GENETIC DIFFERENCES
IN HUMAN ALTRUISM

It is perhaps useful to examine the theory of sociobiology with particular respect to the question of individual differences in altruistic behavior. As will be discussed in chapter 4, there is substantial evidence to suggest that there are consistent patterns of individual differences among people in how much altruism is exhibited. There are individuals who state their moral beliefs and in turn act on those beliefs, but there also are psychopaths who apparently have no concern whatsoever for other people. What determines these individual differences? It seems that sociobiology will help us to comprehend these differences between people only if we assume that some individuals are more pre-disposed genetically toward altruism than others, that is, that some people have a greater capacity to develop altruistic behavior. According to evolutionary theory, it is necessary for natural selection to have this variety in genetic material with which to work. The idea of genetic differences between people causing individual differences in altruistic behavior is a highly interesting possibility that would be difficult, although not impossible, to test adequately.

One possible approach to the question of genetic differences in altruism would be to compare monozygotic and dyzygotic twins in order to calculate heritability coefficients. Heritability scores are estimates of the percentage of variance in a set of scores from a *sample* of persons that is attributable to the genes (rather than the environment or genes X environment interaction). Comparing monozygotic and dyzygotic twins is one method of assessing heritability.

Twins are of two kinds. First, there are monozygotic, or identical, twins who, it is assumed, have 100 percent of their genes in common. Here a single sperm fertilized a single egg. During cell division, however, the cell broke into two, continued to divide and grow, and eventually furnished two genetically identical children. Second, there are dyzygotic, or fraternal, twins, which occur when two spermatozoa fertilize two separate eggs. Comparisons can subsequently be made between monozygotic and dyzygotic twins in order to estimate the amount of genetic influence on a particular characteristic. If the correlation between scores for the monozygotic twins is higher than the correlation between scores for the dyzygotic twins, the difference can be attributed to the role of genetics, assuming that the environments are equal. As Mittler (1971) described, there are many disagreements about the practicalities of computing heritability scores for humans. I shall not address this controversy except to point out its existence. It is quite possible that in the next few years major advances will be made in this area.

Notwithstanding some of the difficulties in estimating heritability scores, Mittler (1971) pointed out that the best current estimates are that, at least among white North Americans and Western Europeans, the genes account for 40 to 80 percent of the variance in human height and weight, rate of breathing, blood pressure, perspiration, pulse rate, EEG-measured brain activity, and intelligence. They also seem to have some effect on temperament (for example introversion-extroversion and anxiety level) and predisposition toward schizophrenic breakdown. They do not seem to contribute particularly to such factors as susceptibility to visual illusions, handwriting, treatment for neurotic disorders, and many other personality traits.

The question for our purposes is what are the heritability coefficients for altruistic behaviors? If reliable and representative measures of altruism could be constructed (e.g., a sensitivity to the suffering of others as measured perhaps by an individual's autonomic nervous system responses), then heritability coefficients could be computed. Similarly, we could compute heritability coefficients for the degree of selfishness and egocentricity displayed if we could find reliable and valid measures. If we could carry out such studies, it is possible that we would find that some of the variance in individual differences in altruistic behavior is attributable to heritability.

This leads to what is perhaps a major incompletion (or at least, lack of emphasis) in the sociobiological account of altruism so far presented. Essentially there has been no discussion of social learning. In fact, social learning theory is both compatible with and complementary to Wilson's theory of sociobiology.

SOCIOBIOLOGY AND SOCIAL LEARNING

Homo sapiens unlike the social insects, are altruistic primarily because we have *learned* to be so, being genetically programmed to learn from our environment. In this way we acquire both the norms of appropriate social behavior and of empathic responsivity, which are discussed in detail in the next chapter as the two primary motivators of much of human altruism. How these motivations are acquired and the process of social learning itself will be covered in a subsequent chapter. Where then do genetic differences fit?

If individual differences in human altruism are a result of differential learning experiences producing differential degrees of empathic responsivity or norms of social responsibility, why must we speak about genetic influences at all? Certainly we need not expect that genes work directly, irrespective of environmental input. It is possible, though, that genetic differences make some people more responsive to certain types of experience than others. For example, some people may be more innately predisposed to learn to respond empathically to others or to internalize moral norms. (In the same way, people may inherit nervous systems that predispose them to behave more calmly or excitedly than others, or bodies that predispose them to being more athletic.) Whether these potentials become developed, however, will depend entirely on the learning experiences the person has. In a similar manner, we all also inherit the capacity to become aroused and aggressive. Whether we deal with these feelings constructively through self-control, anesthetize them with alcohol or drugs, or engage in physical or verbal assault will depend on our previous learning experiences. Aggression is highly susceptible to control and modification through appropriate learning experiences (Bandura 1973; Baron 1977). Whether altruistic potentials become developed also will depend on the learning experiences a person has. Indeed, the thesis of this book is that our society can increase the amount of altruistic behavior engaged in through a judicious use of the agencies of socialization it has at its command.

SUMMARY

There is reason to believe that the basic nature of human beings is to be altruistic. Evidence for this view comes from studies of altruism in other animal species that, like our own, live in social groups. These vary from the social insects such as ants, bees, and wasps, through to birds, dogs, porpoises and chimps. All these species engage in considerable amounts of altruistic behavior. Examples include parental care, mutual defense, rescue behavior, cooperative hunting, and sharing food.

Altruism in animals presents a problem for theories of evolution. Darwin's theory, for example, stresses natural selection and survival of the fittest. How then do behaviors arise, such as altruism, that appear to diminish the personal fitness of individuals engaging in them? The solution to this paradox lies in the notion of kin selection. *Genes* survive and are passed on in offspring. If an animal sacrifices its own life for its brother's offspring, it ensures the survival of *common genes,* for it shares 50 percent of its genes with its sibling and 25 percent with its nephew or niece. The notion of kin-selection allows for the evolution of altruism, including altruism in human beings. Those groups of related-humans that were most capable of forming themselves into cooperative, interdependent, altruistic societies survived, whereas groups of humans who were not so capable, died out.

Specifically *human* evolution has been occurring only for about two million years. During most of that time we were hunter-gatherers. That we were hunters has led some anthropologists to describe us as "killer-apes." This however is far from true. Cooperation, sharing, rule-following, and altruism far better characterizes the behavior of even early species of human. With the invention of agriculture ten thousand years ago, there was a dramatic increase in the necessity to replace aggression and selfishness with cooperation and consideration for others.

Although evolutionary theory suggests that *Homo sapiens* are genetically disposed to altruism, it must be emphasized that most of human behavior is acquired through social learning. This is particularly necessary to emphasize when we consider the question of *individual differences* in altruism. Why are some people more altruistic than others? How can we help bring about a more altruistic society? These are important questions the solution to which lies in understanding the processes of social learning.

chapter 3

MOTIVATIONS TO BE ALTRUISTIC

Altruism was defined earlier in behavioral terms, that is, as "social behavior carried out to achieve positive outcomes for another rather than for the self." Another way of looking at the question of altruism is to examine the motivations underlying the behavior. Many motivational constructs have been suggested as explanations of altruistic behavior. These have included, among others: altruistic attitudes, beliefs, opinions, values, empathy, sympathy, role-taking abilities, moral principles, rules, norms, standards, and cognitions. Many of these constructs have been embedded within larger theoretical frameworks, for example, cognitive-developmental theory, equity theory, and attribution theory. Unfortunately, at the moment none of these theories is adequate to account for altruistic behavior. The approach to be taken in this book is that of social learning theory. Essentially it is suggested that people behave altruistically (or selfishly) in any particular situation because they have learned to do so in previously similar situations. The term "social learning" is used here to stress both the social context in which learning takes place and particular processes of learning, such as learning through the observation of others. The questions then become (a) what exactly is it that is learned; that is, is it specific behaviors in particular situations or are there basic underlying motivations and dispositions that are acquired? and (b) how exactly does the learning take place; that is, what are the "laws of learning"? This chapter will cover the products of learning; chapter 5 will deal with how they are learned.

I would like to suggest that much of the research literature and terminology concerned with the motivations to be altruistic can be usefully subsumed under one of the two motivational systems of empathy and personal norms. These motivational systems are "hypothetical constructs"; that is, they cannot be observed directly. They are postulated in order to "explain" the regularities in behavior that can be observed. As will be reiterated in each of the sections to follow, few of the experiments to be discussed measured directly the motivational system underlying the behaviors. Instead, researchers varied aspects of the environment to see whether these produce changes in altruism. Such changes are subsequently explained in terms of an underlying motivational construct. Very rarely are independent assessments made to see whether the suggested motivational construct is indeed the mediator of the behavior. As will be discussed later in the chapter, there is always a danger for hypothetical motivational constructs to be used loosely and after the fact to explain behavior and thereby to lose predictive utility. Nonetheless, hypothesizing the mediating mechanisms of empathy and personal norms has allowed for a better ordering of data. We now shall examine these theoretical constructs and some of the literature that they help to organize.

EMPATHY

Empathy, defined as experiencing the emotional state of another, is a major organizing idea in the study of altruism. A state of empathy is said to exist between A and B when A matches his or her feelings with those of B. This matching of emotion can result from either (1) cues given *directly* by B or (2) A's conscious knowledge of B's situation. Both animals and extremely young infants experience empathy on the basis of direct cues. Furthermore, direct cues undoubtedly will continue to be important to eliciting altruism throughout the life span. Among humans, however, cognitive abilities come into play as age increases, which vastly extend the capacity for empathic responding. What we refer to as "role-playing" and "perspective-taking" abilities —that is, the focusing of A's attention on B's situation and the attempt to imagine what that is like—provides the capacity to empathize, even with individuals who lived thousands of years ago or who are still to be born.

Because the notion of empathy emphasizes the feelings of others, many researchers consider it a prime candidate for an internal mediator of altruistic behavior. Some theorists (e.g., Aronfreed 1970) have even suggested that the term altruism ought to be restricted to actions controlled by empathic processes. Although it seems unnecessarily limiting to restrict an entire class of behaviors to a single motivational construct, there is no doubt that empathy is central to the study of altruism. According to this formulation, A is motivated toward altruistic behavior in order either to decrease empathic distress at the plight of B or to increase empathic pleasure at the anticipated pleasure of B.

Human infants may be born with the capacity to respond empathically. Much emotional expression in humans is innate, as was established by Ekman and Friesen (e.g., 1971), and it is therefore possible that *responses* to such expressions, including empathic ones, are built in. Preliminary evidence for this was presented by Sagi and Hoffman (1976) who found that a rudimentary form of empathy was present at birth. These investigators played a variety of tape-recorded sounds to one-day-old infants. They found that when the sound was of another infant crying, the one-day-olds were far more likely to start crying themselves. Certainly, empathic responding starts extremely early in life. Hoffman (1975), for example, described several cases of what appeared to be empathically based responses in particularly young children. One example involved Michael, who, at the age of fifteen months, was struggling over a toy with his friend Paul when Paul started to cry. Michael let go of the toy, but Paul kept on crying. Michael paused, appeared concerned, then gave his teddy bear to Paul. The crying, however, continued. Michael paused again, then ran to the next room, returned with Paul's security blanket, and offered it to Paul—whereupon he stopped crying. Hoffman's (1975, p. 141) interesting analysis of the incident suggested that Michael first assumed that his own teddy bear, which often comforted him, also would comfort his friend. When this failed, Michael had to consider alternative solutions. Michael, young as he was, somehow reasoned by analogy that Paul would be comforted by something that he loved in the same way that Michael loved his teddy bear.

Empathic behavior may not be as common as other forms of altruism in very young children. In a study of the naturally occurring altruistic behaviors of twenty-six preschoolers. Strayer, Wareing, and Rushton (1979) coded four categories of altruism: object-related, cooperative, helping, and empathic. Comforting an upset peer is an example of empathy. After thirty hours of observation, a total of 1,195 altruistic acts had been observed. Of these, only 55 were empathic (i.e., less than 5 percent of the total). On the average, an instance of empathy was observed about once every two hours, compared to fifteen examples of sharing and thirteen of cooperation (see Table 1.2). Although empathic activity certainly could, and did occur, it did not seem a frequent behavior at this stage—at least not in the relatively benign atmosphere of the University of Waterloo preschool.

In somewhat older children, external cues have been manipulated to increase the potential amount of empathy. Rosenhan (1969), for example, examined the effect of sympathy cues on children's donations to a charity. The children, aged six to ten, won gift certificates on a bowling game, which were exchangeable for prizes based on the more certificates, the better the prize. Before exchanging the certificates for a prize, the children were given the opportunity to donate some of their winnings to an "orphan's fund." A picture of ragged orphan children and a donating bowl into which the children could place their certificates stood nearby. The children were left entirely alone to decide whether or not to give, thus ruling out effects of the experimenter's presence. Furthermore, a number of certificates already lay in the bowl, so that the children would not think the experimenter would notice later on whether the child had given or not. In the "sympathy" condition, the orphans were described with heavy emphasis on their needs (no parents, few clothes, no toys, and so on). In the "nonsympathy" conditon, the orphans were described in more neutral terms. It was found that when the orphans' needs were stressed, more children shared their gift certificates. Sympathy cues were clearly working at this age.

In the study by Rosenhan (1969), just described, although sympathy cues were manipulated in the environment, we cannot be sure that the subsequent, increased generosity resulted from the motivation of sympathy. The same problem arises with the observational studies of the naturally occurring behavior cited earlier. The behavior only appeared empathic. In order to determine whether or not it is empathic, some independent evidence is required.

Empathic emotion was demonstrated in a series of experiments by Stotland (1969). A confederate of the experimenter pretended to undergo pain while taking part in an experiment. A variety of physiological measures were taken from observers who watched the "volunteer." When the volunteer showed signs of pain, the observers reacted physiologically. Their heart rates, blood pressures, and galvanic skin response scores went up. These physiological indices were positively correlated with the observers' statements of empathy for the person whom they were watching. Stotland (1969) also showed that empathy could be increased or decreased by the type of information given. The more it was suggested that they attend to the volunteer's pain, the more empathic they reported feeling. For example, subjects who were told either to imagine him or imagine themselves in the situation showed more physiological reactions than those under instructions to simply watch him. The influence of thought processes in empathic responsivity also was demonstrated by another aspect of the study: The more similar to themselves the observers had been led to believe the volunteer was, the more empathically they responded.

Aderman and Berkowitz (1970) showed another link between empathic response and helping behavior. They presented college students with tape-recorded conversations between two people; one requiring help, the other in a position to give it. The students were divided into two groups, being told to pay special attention to either the person in need or to the potential helper. In some conversations the potential benefactor gave his help and was shown extreme gratitude, in others his help was unrewarded, and in still other conversations, he refused to help. After hearing these conversations, the students were given a chance to help somebody themselves. Those students who were the most helpful had attended to either (a) a person who had not received the required help or (b) a helper who had been thanked. Having empathically experienced either the victim's distress or the pleasant feelings of the profusely thanked helper, the listener's own motivation to aid others was heightened. It should be noted, however, that empathic emotion was not directly manipulated or measured in this experiment.

A study carried out by Krebs (1975) demonstrated a correlation between empathy and altruism. The psychophysiological responses (skin conductance, blood pulse, heart rate) of observers were measured as they observed a similar or dissimilar other win money and experience painful shocks while playing a game. Subjects who believed they were similar to the performer tended to react more strongly than did subjects who believed they were different from him. Similar subjects also reported identifying more with the performer and feeling worse while he waited to be shocked. When subsequently required to choose between helping themselves at a cost to the performer or helping the performer at a cost to themselves, the subjects who previously had reacted the most empathically now behaved the most altruistically. It should be noted, though, that Krebs (1975) did not actually demonstrate a causal relation between empathic emotion and helping—only that the two are correlated. In Krebs's study, empathic emotion and helping conceivably could have been correlated because both were *independently* increased by the subject feeling *similar* to the performer.

Clearer evidence for a causal relationship between empathy and helping was demonstrated by Coke, Batson, and McDavis (1978). Subjects in two experiments learned of another person's need from taped radio broadcasts and subsequently were given the opportunity to offer their help to that person. The two experiments used quite different techniques for manipulating the emotional response to the other's plight. In Experiment 1, the subjects' observational set was varied first by asking them to focus their attention on either the plight of the victim or on the techniques being used in the broadcast. Subjects also were given a placebo pill which supposedly would result in either physiological relaxation or arousal. In the "arousal" condition this manipulation was intended to induce the subjects to attribute, erroneously, empathic arousal to the effects of the pill. These subjects should have been less likely, therefore, to label their emotional arousal as "empathic distress" and thus should have offered less help. Subjects led to expect that the pill would relax them, on the other hand, should have been inclined to attribute emotional arousal to their empathic distress at the plight of the victim and therefore should have been more willing to offer their help. These predictions were borne out, as shown in Figure 3.1.

In the second experiment, Coke, Batson, and McDavis (1978) gave subjects

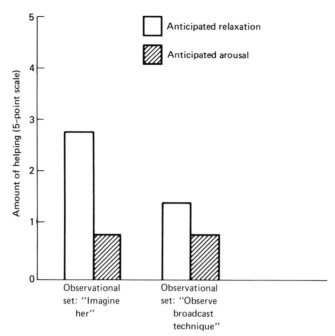

Figure 3-1 Mean Amount of Help Volunteered by Subjects in Each Condition. Source: Coke, Batson, & McDavis, Experiment 1. *Journal of Personality and Social Psychology,* 1978, *36,* 752-766. *Copyright 1978 by the American Psychological Association. Reprinted by permission.*

false feedback about their level of emotional arousal while listening to a broadcast in which a person needed help. Those subjects who were led to believe that they were experiencing the most arousal were the most likely to offer their help.

In all of these studies, sympathy cues were manipulated in the environment and occasionally in the person's direct experience of emotional arousal. It is possible that sympathy cues, in addition to activating empathic emotion, also activate personal norms, the next motivational system to be discussed. In this alternative account, persons have internalized standards for their own behavior which are activated by stimuli in the environment. Some stimuli (e.g., those connected with persons in distress) elicit these norms more than others (e.g., there is a norm to help the unfortunate more than the fortunate). It is possible, of course, that the motivational system of *both* empathy and personal norms work together.

NORMS OF APPROPRIATE BEHAVIOR

A norm may be defined as a *standard by which events are judged and on that basis approved or disapproved.* An individual might apply such standards to evaluate good from bad, right from wrong, appropriate from inappropriate, beauty from ugliness, or truth from falsehood. Standards vary in the degree to which they are internalized. Norms that are held strongly enough to be considered "oughts" are called moral principles. Those norms held more abstractly often are referred to as values, and norms held tentatively and found arbitrary may be called social rules. For our purposes, the notion of a norm, defined as an internal standard, will encompass all constructs such as rules, values, and principles.

There are many norms concerned with prosocial behavior. The discussion of these will be organized into three categories. These categories are not mutually exclusive, nor are they exhaustive. They are (1) norms of social responsibility, (2) norms of equity, and (3) norms of reciprocity. These have in common the fact that they all are internal standards against which events are judged. If one's own behavior does not match up, one censures oneself, which produces an aversive state requiring redress.

(1) Norms of social responsibility.

There is a definite norm to help one another. If we should stop a stranger in the street and ask for directions we would expect that he or she would provide the information and perhaps apologize were it not possible. If the stranger instead should say "Yes, I do know where that place is but I cannot be bothered to tell you," we would be rather surprised. The person would have violated an unspoken expectation of behavior. Berkowitz (1972) reviewed a variety of studies examining the norms that govern helping behavior. For example, people tend to be more helpful to someone who is dependent on them than to someone who is not (Berkowitz & Daniels 1963, 1964). Berkowitz (1972) explained these studies and a variety of others by invoking the norm of social responsibility.

In one experiment, university students were brought to the laboratory in pairs and told that the investigators were trying to produce a good test of supervisory ability. The students were told that one of them was to be a "supervisor" and the other would be a "worker." They would be in separate rooms, and the supervisor would communicate with the worker through written notes. The experimenter passed each of the students a note, supposedly from the supervisor, asking them to construct as many cardboard boxes as possible from a pile of material on a table. Sometimes the note stressed how dependent the supervisor was on the worker and sometimes it did not. In the most dependent condition it was suggested that the supervisor might actually win a prize, depending entirely on how many cardboard boxes the worker constructed. It should be noted that the students did not know each other and did not expect to meet again afterwards. In fact they were told that the supervisor would not even know how hard they had worked. Despite this, there were clear findings that the workers were more likely to work hard and produce more boxes if they thought that the supervisor was dependent on them. One explanation of this finding is that the other person's dependency brings the social responsibility norm into operation. The more dependent the person seemed, the more the norm of social responsibility was elicited.

Studies also have assessed the conditions that affect the amount of help offered as a result of the social responsibility norm. Dependency, for example, elicits extra help when the recipient is liked, when the benefactor him- or herself has received help in the past, and when the benefactor believes that the potential recipient is observing his or her behavior. The relationship between dependency and the norm of social responsibility is not always so straightforward as the preceding experiments suggest. Berkowitz (1969) demonstrated that the *reasons* for the person's dependence are important. Dependency perceived as caused by events beyond the person's control are viewed more sympathetically. If, however, the person's dependency appeared to be voluntary, there was little or no helping. The operation of norms depends very much on the potential helper's perception of the situation.

One way in which it is possible to examine whether there are particular norms operating is to *break* them and see what happens. If there is a norm in operation, some form of restitution might be expected to occur. A number of studies induced people to break the norm of social responsibility by causing them unintentionally to harm another person. These studies often found that such people subsequently will engage in reparative behavior. Freedman, Wallington, and Bless (1967) reported two studies that can be interpreted in this way. In the first, students were induced to tell a lie to the experimenter. A confederate of the experimenter, posing as another student, described the experiment to some of the students. When the experiment began, the students were told that it was essential that they know nothing about the test they were going to take and were asked if they had heard anything about it. Virtually all students said they had not heard anything. After taking the test, the experimenter asked for volunteers to help her out in a different study. Those who had been induced to tell a lie volunteered twice as often as those who had not told a lie. In the second experiment students were induced to knock over a table with some index cards on it. After taking part in the experiment they were there to do they were asked if they would volunteer for another experiment. Those who had knocked the cards over volunteered more often than those who had not.

A study by Carlsmith and Gross (1969) can be used to illustrate the same idea. Students were led to believe that they had delivered either shocks or only loud buzzes to a confederate of the experimenter in an experiment on the effects of learning under punishment. After the "learning" part of the study was over, the student and the confederate were asked to fill out a brief questionnaire. While they were filling out these questionnaires, the confederate turned to the student and said something like, "Hey, I wonder if you could do me a favor. I'm working on a committee that is trying to enlist support to save the California redwood trees. I'm supposed to telephone a lot of people and I wonder if you'd be interested in helping me telephone them?" The student then said either yes or no, and if he or she said yes, the confederate asked how many names he or she would take. The results are very impressive. Only one quarter of the students who had delivered buzzes agreed to take any names, but three quarters of those who had delivered shocks were willing to help. In another study Wallington (1973) found that students who were induced to lie to the experimenter administered more shocks to themselves than those not so induced did.

It is not necessary to cause harm to another oneself in order for feelings of social responsibility to motivate helping. Seeing someone else cause harm can be sufficient. In an experiment by Cialdini, Darby, and Vincent (1973), a stack of cards was knocked off a chair by the student or by the experimenter. Afterwards, regardless of whether it was the student or the experimenter who had caused the accident, persons in both conditions acted more altruistically to make telephone calls for a good cause than did those in a control group.

The above studies can be understood in terms of norms of social responsibility. By performing restitutive acts, people may be relieving themselves of self-censure as a result of having broken, or seen broken, the norm of social responsibility. In this analysis, it is the reduction of self-censure or "guilt" that is the motivator. An interpretation in terms of guilt-reduction was the one favored by Freedman (1970) for some of the earlier studies. These all are inferences, however; no independent evidence for these processes is provided in the studies. Alternative explanations also are possible. For example, when harm is done to another, empathy rather than social responsibility may motivate restitution. Other explanations are possible. As we shall see in the next section, some of these studies can be interpreted in terms of a desire to restore norms of equity or justice. If a person unintentionally causes harm to another (or sees harm caused to another), a state of inequity would exist to the degree to which the person felt his or her internal standards of what was just had been violated. The resulting negative feeling of inequity might then motivate altruistic behavior toward the wronged other in order to restore justice. The guilt-reduction hypothesis based on the norm of social responsibility gains some favor over either the empathy or equity hypothesis from findings that demonstrate if people transgress against one person, they also are subsequently more likely to give aid to persons *other than those who were harmed.*

In a field experiment, for example, Regan, Williams, and Sparling (1972) asked women shoppers to take their pictures with a camera provided for the occasion. Half of the shoppers were subsequently made to feel that they had broken the camera. Of the shoppers who thought they had broken the camera, 55 percent provided help to another shopper in a staged incident nearby; only 15 percent of the shoppers in the control group did so. Konecni (1972) found somewhat similar results by inducing people to seem to cause another person to drop valuable books. Finally, Katzev, Edelsack, Steinmetz, Walker, and Wright (1978) reprimanded individuals either for touching art objects in violation of museum rules or for feeding unauthorized food to animals in a zoo. This significantly increased the likelihood that these people would subsequently help another person pick up dropped items. Furthermore, the more severe the reprimand was, the more the person subsequently helped others.

These studies do not provide much support for the equity theory because the altruistic behavior did not repair the injustice. Rather, it benefitted another person entirely. Similarly, the empathy theory runs into trouble, for why would breaking rules in one situation lead to an increase in empathy for another person in a different situation? It seems plausible to conclude, therefore, that people were repairing their self-concept and decreasing self-censure or guilt by helping another. It is clearly not possible, however, to rule out completely the alternative explanations.

The idea of a norm of social responsibility is a useful explanation for many of the "helpful bystander" examples outlined in chapter 1. It will be remembered that data were presented showing that passersby responded overwhelmingly with help when asked for aid such as the time of day, change for a quarter, or street directions. According to the norm of social responsibility view, socialization leads people to internalize this norm. In certain situations, the norm is elicited and the individual behaves accordingly. When the norm is fulfilled, he or she will receive gratitude and self-approval. If, on the other hand, he or she fails to live up to the norm, there likely will be some degree of self-censure, guilt, or anxiety.

A series of studies conducted by Latané and Darley (1970) are relevant here. These studies were concerned with the *non*response of bystanders to emergencies. A real-life incident had occurred that triggered this, as well as a lot of other research. In March 1964, a woman named Kitty Genovese was attacked as she returned home from work at 3:00 A.M. in New York City. Although it took her assailant over half an hour to murder her, not one of what turned out to be thirty-eight witnesses came to her assistance—or even telephoned the police. This bizarre situation, which caused much social comment and speculation, led Latané and Darley (1970) to investigate emergency situations experimentally in the laboratory.

In one experiment, students were invited to an interview to discuss "some of the problems involved in being at an urban university." They sat in a small room and filled out a preliminary questionnaire while waiting to be called for an interview, either alone or in groups of three. Suddenly they were faced with an ambiguous, but potentially dangerous, situation. A stream of smoke began to puff into the room through a wall vent. It continued to jet into the room in irregular puffs, and by the end of the experimental period (six minutes), it obscured vision. The findings were quite startling. When the person was alone, he or she would report the smoke within two minutes, on the average, of first noticing it. When there were three people waiting together, however, very seldom did anyone report the smoke during the entire period, despite the discomfort it must have produced. The sheer presence of others seemed to inhibit the norm of social responsibility.

A follow-up study showed extremely similar results. In this case, a college student arrived at the laboratory and was ushered into a room from which a communication system would enable him to talk to other participants. Over the intercom, the student was told that the experiment was concerned with the kinds of personal problems faced by college students. The student had ostensibly been placed by himself in order to avoid embarrassment. Over the intercom the student heard each of the participants talk in turn. One of them found it difficult to get adjusted to New York and to his studies. Very hesitantly and with obvious embarrassment, the person mentioned that he was prone to seizures, particularly when studying hard or taking exams. Finally, growing increasingly loud and incoherent, he continued:

> I-er-um I think I-I need-er-if-if could-er-er-somebody er-er-er-er-er-er-er-give me a littler-er-give me a little help here because I-er-I'm-er-h-h-having a-a-a real problem-er-right now and I-er-if somebody could help me out it would er-er-s-sure be sure be good . . . because-er-there-er-er-a cause I-er-I-uh-uh-I've got a-a one of the-er-sei . . . er-er-things coming on and-and I could really-er-use some help so if somebody would-er-give me a little h-help-uh-uh-er-er-er-c-could somebody-er-er-help-er-uh-uh-uh (choking sounds) . . . I'm gonna die-er-er-I'm gonna die-er-help-er-er seizure (chokes, then, quiet).
>
> (Latané & Darley 1970, pp. 95-96)

The major question was: how many people would go for help? As in the previous study, the answer depended on how many other people the subject thought were present. When the subject thought he was alone, 85 percent reported the seizure before the victim's voice was cut off. Only 31 percent of those who thought that four other bystanders were present did so! As Latané and Darley (1970) demonstrated, the subjects, whether or not they intervened, believed that the victim's fit was genuine and serious. Many of the participants gasped, swore, and spoke out loud to themselves showing confusion about what they ought to do.

How do we account for findings such as these? The authors labeled this phenomenon a "diffusion of responsibility." The diffusion of responsibility findings suggest that the normative explanation be qualified. Besides a norm to help, there also must be a feeling of personal responsibility. If this feeling of personal responsibility is absent, the normative rules will not be sufficient to motivate behavior. Thus, just as Berkowitz (1972) suggested that dependency can increase the saliency of the norm of social responsibility, the presence of others can decrease it.

(2) Norms of equity.

A vitally important set of norms that governs human behavior is that concerned with justice and fairness. This often is discussed under the rubric of "equity theory." It is postulated that there is in all of us a set of finely balanced "scales" which we use to weigh the fairness of many aspects of our environment and that when the scales get out of balance, a motive to redress that balance is set in motion. Many psychologists currently are spending much research time examining the properties of this internal balance. Certainly feelings of justice and injustice form a pervasive part of human existence (Berkowitz & Walster 1976; Walster, Walster, & Berscheid 1978).

An early experiment by Adams and Jacobsen (1964) illustrated just how pervasive and deeply rooted these feelings of justice are. In their study, students were hired as proof readers at a fixed amount per hour. Some of the students were told that although they actually were unqualified, they were being paid at the same rate as qualified proof readers were. This was the high-inequity condition. Another group, the medium-inequity condition, was told that they were unqualified and were being paid less, therefore, than qualified proof readers were. A third group, the no-inequity condition, was told that they were qualified and were therefore being paid at the qualified proof reader rate. As expected, the first group, the one which had the largest "fairness" discrepancy, worked qualitatively better and made fewer errors in their proof reading than the other two groups did. Being paid more than they deserved evidently made them redress this balance with better work.

Two other studies carried out with children might be mentioned here. Long and Lerner (1974) either "overpaid" or "properly paid" ten year olds for a job. Those who were overpaid donated more than those who were properly paid to a charity. Miller and Smith (1977) either overpaid, properly paid, or underpaid eleven-year-old children: Children shared more with each other when they were overpaid, less when they were properly paid, and still less when they were underpaid. Note here that the recipients of altruism were not themselves the source of inequity.

As mentioned in the previous section, a number of studies induced people to break the norm of social responsibility by causing them unintentionally to harm another person. These studies often found that such people subsequently will engage in reparative behavior. One interpretation of this is in terms of feelings of inequity. If a person unintentionally causes harm to another, a state of inequity would exist to the degree to which the person felt he or she had violated his or her internal standards of what was just. The resulting negative feeling of inequity then might motivate altruistic behavior toward the wronged other in order to restore justice. Berscheid and Walster (1967) conducted an experiment that can be interpreted this way. Women were induced to fall short of their stated goals on a game and thus deprive not only themselves but also another person of expected rewards. In a subsequent game, the women had an opportunity to compensate the other person. In general, there was a very strong inclination to do so.

The other studies on causing or seeing harm done to another by Carlsmith and Gross (1969); Cialdini, Darby, and Vincent (1973); Freedman, Wallington, and Bless (1967); and Wallington (1973) that were discussed in the last section also can be understood in terms of norms of equity. Once again it must be pointed out that this is an inference; there is no independent evidence for equity as the motivator. The justice motive as a basis for altruism, however, allows us to organize disparate data. For example, many people are very actively engaged in social and political activity to rectify the inequities they perceive in the socioeconomic makeup of their society. Here norms of justice might be viewed as the basis of the motivation.

The studies examined in this section highlight the difficulty of trying to isolate the underlying motives for altruism. Perhaps they also emphasize the commonality of the different normative approaches to altruism being hypothesized; that is, both equity and guilt reduction explanations are deviations from an internal standard which results in an aversive state requiring redress.

When norms are violated, people have a number of choices of how to restore matters. The examples provided so far have shown how it is possible to restore matters by behaving with altruism towards somebody. There are other ways of restoring balance, however. Persons witnessing harm done to others (e.g., when they see others living in slum conditions) might restore a sense of fairness by derogating the victim by convincing themselves that the victim deserved to suffer. Alternatively they may relieve the imbalance by pointing to particular virtues present in those who are particularly well off, thus suggesting that they deserve their privileged positions.

That individuals faced with an objectively unfair situation often seek to resolve the discrepancy to themselves by derogating the victim often has been demonstrated by equity theorists. Lerner (1970, 1974; Lerner & Simmons 1966) for example, repeatedly showed that people who suffer a misfortune through no fault of their own tend to be devalued and derogated by uninvolved observers. People who have been raped, assaulted, or kidnapped, for example, often receive inquisitions and censure from their friends and family instead of sympathy. Lerner (1970) explained this phenomenon in terms of a "just-world" hypothesis. People are motivated, it is argued, to believe that the world is basically a just one. Flagrant breaches of such justice are seen as a threat. In order not to feel threatened, it is easier to derogate the victim than to perceive the world as inequitable.

In an early study by Lerner and Simmons (1966), students watched a fellow student react with apparent pain to a series of supposed electric shocks. In one condition students had an opportunity to compensate the victim by voting to reassign her to a reward condition in which she would receive money rather than shocks. Virtually all the students availed themselves of this opportunity and were told that the victim would be reassigned. In this condition, justice was able to be restored. In another condition, however, students could not reward the victim and were informed that the victim would continue to suffer. Students who knew that the victim would be compensated, rated her more favorably than those who knew that her suffering was to continue. The ratings provided in the latter condition indicated considerable rejection of the victim, suggesting that she was seen as somehow deserving her fate.

This basic finding has been replicated and extended in subsequent studies (e.g., Stokols & Schopler 1973; Stein 1973). Stokols and Schopler (1973) found that rape victims who suffered major consequences of physical pain and emotional trauma were devalued (on a rating scale) more than those with milder negative consequences. Stein (1973) found that children would negatively evaluate other children whom they nonetheless also perceived as suffering undeservedly. It would seem that injustice is often perceived as just.

There are circumstances in which the tendency to derogate victims is decreased. In a very interesting study, Sorrentino and Boutilier (1974) looked at the interaction between empathy for a victim, on the one hand, and the just-world hypothesis, on the other. Sorrentino and Boutilier (1974) reasoned that if observers were told to expect a similar fate to that of the victim, they would be less likely to derogate the victim. Subjects in their experiment observed another female undergraduate receive a series of electric shocks as a "learner" in a teaching-effectiveness project. Some of the subjects had been told that they would serve as learners later; others had been told that they would not. Anticipation of a similar fate led to significant reduction in the response of devaluing the learner.

A more direct manipulation of empathy was employed in a study by Aderman, Brehm, and Katz (1974). Subjects watched an innocent person receive a series of seemingly painful electric shocks. In one condition the subjects were told to imagine themselves in the same situation. In the other conditions the subjects were told to pay attention to the victim's emotional reaction or movements. Whereas in the latter conditions the subjects rated the victim negatively on questionnaires, in the former they evaluated her as a positive person.

Before leaving this section, it might be asked under what circumstances people come to believe in an *un*just world? Are there not many situations in which oppressed individuals believe that the world is unjust and that social and political action must be taken as a corrective? Unfortunately this is an area that has not been largely researched.

(3) Norms of reciprocity.

Reciprocity is a particularly important case of equity. Gouldner (1960) suggested that all societies have very strong reciprocity rules prescribing that people should help those who have helped them in the past. It is certainly a very widespread human behavior. On the basis of much comparative anthropological data, for example, Mauss (1954) concluded that three types of obligations are widely distributed in human societies in both time and space: (a) the obligation to give, (b) the obligation to receive, and (c) the obligation to repay. Reciprocal exchanges breed cooperation and good feelings. A failure (or inability) to reciprocate, on the other hand, breeds bitterness and dislike. Numerous studies, some of which were reviewed by Bar-Tal (1976) and Staub (1978) have demonstrated the tendency of individuals to reciprocate favors.

In a cross-cultural study, Gergen, Ellsworth, Maslach, and Seipel (1975) investigated reciprocal and nonreciprocal exchanges in Japan, Sweden, and the United States. People who were lent chips for a gambling game evaluated the donor more positively if he asked for the chips to be returned in equal amounts than when he said there was no necessity for the chips to be returned at all. In all three countries, reciprocity seemed to be the preferred condition. Several other studies also showed that people prefer conditions under which they reciprocate a favor. For example, Gross and Latané (1974) found that a benefactor is liked more when the recipient of aid is allowed to reciprocate or to offer aid to a third person. It seems that people behave in a manner that maintains equity between themselves and others.

Common experience often is in accord with these formulations as, for example, in the usual turn taking in such things as dinner invitations or corresponding with friends. Some experimental evidence also shows how a prior benefit will instigate reciprocation. It has been shown, for example, that someone who has received prior help, compared to someone who has been refused prior help, when given the opportunity, will provide more help for his or her benefactor (Goranson & Berkowitz 1966) or even for a new partner (Berkowitz & Daniels 1964).

Fisher and Nadler and their colleagues (e.g., Fisher & Nadler 1974; Nadler, Fisher, & Streufert 1974; Fisher, Harrison, & Nadler 1978) showed that receiving aid in some circumstances leads to quite a negative effect on the self-concept. For example, when there is little possibility of repaying a helper, and it is not possible to derogate the helper because of his or her status or importance then people tend to devalue themselves. The sensitiveness of persons to disruption of reciprocal arrangements also was demonstrated by their findings that it is more self-threatening to receive aid from attitudinally *similar* others than from dissimilar ones. With similar others, presumably feelings of the inferiority of the self to the other who is able to give aid is facilitated by the inevitable social comparison processes (Festinger 1954).

Reciprocal altruism appears quite early in life as was found in a study by Strayer, Wareing, and Rushton (1979). Preschoolers demonstrated in their free-play behavior an apparent relationship between the initiation and receipt of such altruistic behaviors as donating objects, helping on a task, and playing cooperatively. Indeed, a positive correlation was found between the rate of initiated and received activity for all children. Other analyses suggested that the likelihood of receiving altruistic actions was predicted better by a child's current rate of being altruistic rather than by his or her past altruistic record or future altruistic performance.

Finally, there appear to be subcultural differences in reciprocity behavior. For example, Berkowitz and Friedman (1967) found that whereas the norm of reciprocity seemed primarily to influence the helping behavior of sons of workers and middle-class entrepreneurs, the sons of middle-class bureaucrats were more likely to be influenced by the norm of social responsibility.

SUMMARY OF EMPATHY AND NORMS AS MOTIVATORS OF ALTRUISM

Postulating hypothetical constructs of empathy on the one hand and norms of social responsibility, equity, and reciprocity on the other allows for the organization of many disparate data. The danger of such constructs, though, is that they end up being postdictive rather than predictive, thus giving us only pseudoexplanations; that is, an instance of helping behavior occurs, and then we "explain" it by saying that empathy or a norm to help must have been in operation. We can break the circle, however, and solve some of these problems, in two ways. First, and perhaps most importantly, we can specify the conditions under which empathy and norms can be acquired and modified (see chapter 5). Second, and deriving from the first, we must recognize that empathy and norms are properties of *individuals*. If this is correct, it suggests that there ought to be consistent patterns of individual differences in empathy and norms; that is, some people should be either more empathic and/or have higher moral standards than others. This allows us to test the adequacy of these motivational constructs. For example, compared to people who are relatively low in empathy, people who are highly empathic should (a) register more physiological distress at the sight of another's suffering, (b) perceive themselves as more empathic, (c) be perceived by others as more empathic, and (d) behave more to reduce the unhappiness or the suffering of another. Similarly, persons who have high moral standards should (a) endorse rules based on those norms more than do individuals who have not internalized the same norms, (b) behave more in accord with those norms than do people who have not internalized them, (c) be able and willing to verbalize rules based on those norms to others, and (d) apply sanctions to individuals who violate the norms.

The question of these "personality" differences will be examined in the next chapter. It will be seen that predictions of altruistic behavior can be made from knowledge of the consistent pattern of individual differences in empathic responsivity and internalized norms. This suggests that the two hypothesized motivations for altruism do have predictive utility and are not simply circular, after-the-fact explanations. Knowledge of what the motivations underlying altruism are also is useful when we wish to teach altruistic behavior. This will be of concern in chapter 5.

The discussion so far has implicitly suggested that there is some degree of consistency in people's motivations across situations. The idea of consistency will be clarified in the next chapter when the patterns of personality that allow prediction of behavior are examined. These allow us to predict what a person will do "on the average." Occasionally we all depart from our typical behavior as a result of fluctuations in the situations in which we find ourselves. Many situational factors can affect altruistic behavior. The research on the effects of good and bad "moods" is illustrative of the importance of situational factors in influencing the amount of altruism in society. For the remainder of this chapter we shall examine how moods can temporarily alter a person's disposition to be altruistic, regardless of his or her average motivation based on the relatively enduring qualities of empathy or moral principle.

THE INFLUENCE OF THE SITUATION

Good Moods and Altruism.

Most of the experiments to be discussed do not directly measure the operation of *moods*. Instead, researchers vary the *environment* by providing people with "success" or "failure" experiences, allowing pleasant or unpleasant events to occur, and asking people to think happy or sad thoughts. They then assess the effects of these environmental variations on the amount of altruism in which people subsequently engage. Any differences in altruism are explained in terms of activated mood states. Very rarely are independent assessments made of whether it is changes in mood that mediate the effect. Nonetheless, hypothetical constructs, as we discussed in the sections of this chapter on empathy and norms, help to organize disparate data. So it is with the research on moods.

In an early series of studies summarized by Berkowitz (1972), people were given either a success or a failure experience, and the ensuing effects on altruism were observed. Although success experiences increased altruism, failure ones tended to decrease it. For example, Berkowitz and Connor (1966) gave university students an opportunity to earn money by completing a crossword puzzle within two and a half minutes. Those who were allowed to be successful then helped another person by making more boxes for him or her, when requested, than did someone who did not have the success experience. A failure experience, on the other hand, did not result in significantly less giving than did a control group in this particular study. In a subsequent study Berkowitz (1970) induced students to believe they were about to be evaluated by others. This led them to help less than others who were not concerned about the upcoming evaluation. Berkowitz (1970) suggested that it was preoccupation with self-concerns that led to the diminution in concern for others.

Many studies conducted by Alice Isen and her colleagues examined mood effects on altruism. Isen (1970), for example, paid students money to take part in a test of perceptual-motor skills. The students then were given feedback that their performances had been either extremely good or extremely bad. Those who thought they had done well donated more money to a charity than those who thought they had done poorly. Those who did well also were more altruistic on other measures when compared to those who had done less well. These other measures included: offering to help an overburdened confederate of the experimenter, picking up a dropped book, and opening the door for the confederate.

Isen and Levin (1972) investigated mood effects in two experiments. In the first experiment, a confederate of the experimenter gave cookies to one group of college students while they were studying in individual library cubicles. Another group was not given cookies. A second confederate of the experimenter then approached the students and asked them to spend some time in one of two experiments. Those who previously had been given cookies were more likely to volunteer their time in a situation that aided the experimenter—unless the experiment called for the student to annoy other students. Thus the induced increment in altruism was directed not only toward the experimenter; it also appeared to diffuse out to the population in general. In the second experiment, Isen and Levin found that people who entered a phone booth and found a dime in the tray were later more likely to pick up a folder full of papers dropped in their path than were those who found no money. Levin and Isen (1975) conceptually replicated this study. People who found a dime in a telephone booth were more likely to mail an apparently lost letter left in the booth than those who did not find a dime.

How long do such moods last? In an ingenious study, Isen, Clark, and Schwartz (1976) delivered a free sample of stationery to a person's door. A few minutes later, a confederate telephoned and asked the person if they would telephone a garage for them because they were stranded on a highway and had just used their last dime. Those people who had had free stationery just delivered to them were more inclined to help by phoning the garage than those who had not. The effects of this good mood lasted for nearly twenty minutes after receiving the stationery. Telephone calls after that time period did not elicit any greater helping from the group given free stationery than it did from a control group not given any stationery. Good moods appear to have generalized positive effects beyond increasing helping behavior. In a study by Isen, Shalker, Clark, and Karp (1978), those passersby on a suburban mall who received a small gift in the form of a free advertising sample, subsequently rated the quality of their car and television set significantly more positively than those who had not received such gifts. In a second study, winning a game led subjects to be able to recall more words that they had previously learned.

The positive effects of good moods on altruism also have been found in children. Isen, Horn, and Rosenhan (1973) found that success on a game resulted in greater amounts of money being donated to a charity for poor children than either control or failure experiences did. Moore, Underwood, and Rosenhan (1973) asked children to reminisce about happy experiences or sad experiences. Those who reminisced about happy experiences contributed more to charity than control children who were simply to count, whereas children who thought about sad experiences contributed less than the controls did.

Positive moods have been induced in children in other ways. Long and Lerner (1974) either overpaid or properly paid ten-year-olds for a job. Those who were overpaid donated more to a charity than did those who were properly paid. Miller and Smith (1977) either overpaid, properly paid, or underpaid eleven-year-old children: Children shared more with another when they were overpaid, less when they were properly paid, and still less when they were underpaid. To the degree to which overpayment results in a good mood, this might be the explanation for the findings. Note that these two studies were used previously to fit an equity explanation as well as, now, a good mood one.

Positive moods may result not only in greater kindness to others, but also in greater kindness to oneself. Rosenhan, Underwood, and Moore (1974) found that children who reminisced about happy experiences both rewarded themselves more and shared more with others. In further studies, Rushton and Littlefield (1979) and Underwood, Froming, and Moore (1977) found that children increased their donations to charity as a linear function of a good mood.

Most, but not all of the literature on moods have been able to demonstrate, fairly unequivocally, that good moods increase altruism. For a thorough review of this literature, see Rosenhan, Moore, & Underwood (1976). Less support is true for the converse, that is, that bad moods decrease helping. There is some additional evidence that this is the case. Underwood, Berenson, Berenson, Cheng, Wilson, Kulik, Moore, and Wenzel (1977), for example, found that people who had just seen sad movies were less willing to donate money to a charity than people who had just seen movies that the authors had judged to be neutral. Barnett and Bryan (1974) found that a competitive atmosphere could reduce altruistic behavior. Sherrod and Downs (1974) found that distracting background noises decreased helpfulness compared to soothing background noises. With this latter example in mind we might even offer an alternative explanation for the oft-reported finding discussed in chapter 1, that people in big cities are less helpful than people in smaller towns or suburbs (e.g., Milgram 1970; Rushton 1978). Perhaps the amount of noise and other stressors simply induce bad moods in big-city dwellers and thus decrease altruism.

How do we account for the fact that good moods tend to increase altruism, and bad ones decrease it? One view would be in terms of cognitive-processing capacity. Compatible with all the data mentioned above would be the view that good moods increase the amount of *cognitive processing capacity* (Easterbrook 1959) that an individual has at his or her disposal, thus giving the person more attention to be able to divert to the problems of others. He or she thus would be able to monitor the other person's needs, be more aware of his or her own standards of appropriate behavior for such situations, and so on. It is possible that good moods even directly increase an individual's empathic capacity. Bad moods in this view, result in a reduction of an individual's cognitive-processing capacity, restrict his or her attention to the needs of others and to his or her own moral standards, and perhaps also decrease his or her own empathic capacity. Such an explanation also would fit the disturbing findings by Darley and Batson (1973). These authors had divinity students pass by a groaning victim while on their way to deliver a short talk on the *Parable of the Good Samaritan*. The results showed that although normally 63 percent of such students would stop and give direct aid, only 10 percent would help if they were made to feel very late for an important appointment. Making people feel very rushed may serve to limit their attention to others. In such situations the needs of the victim are hardly even perceived.

The discussion of moods so far has focused entirely on their temporary state as a result of experimental interventions. It is likely that people who frequently gain successes in life and/or have good experiences will tend to develop an overall better sense of well-being than those who more often experience failure and/or bad experiences. It is likely that stable individual differences in mood and temperament may occur with some people being more optimistic and happy and others more pessimistic and unhappy. If so, the former may tend to be more empathic and altruistic than the latter. We shall return to this question in the next chapter, on personality.

THE INTERACTION
OF PERSONS AND SITUATION

Whatever the final explanation of how moods affect altruistic behavior, the data in this section demonstrate that experiences in prior situations can affect the degree of altruism. This does not mean that the motivational bases of altruism discussed earlier in this chapter are overruled. As we shall see in the next chapter, personality differences in altruism are quite predictive. What it does mean is that behavior is the result of an *interaction* between personality and situational factors. This is true of all behavior, not just altruism. Sometimes it is knowledge of the relatively enduring differences among people that enables us to predict most of the variance in the behavior of different people (e.g., Rushton & Endler 1977), but for others it is knowledge of the different situations the people are in that allows maximum prediction (e.g., Haney, Banks, & Zimbardo 1973). More often still, most of the variance in the behavior of different people is accounted for by the interaction among both personality and situational factors (Endler & Magnusson 1976).

Most theorists consider themselves to be "interactionists" when it comes to predicting behavior. As Bandura (1977b, 1978b) pointed out, however, there are at least three different ways of conceptualizing interaction, each of which requires fundamentally different assumptions. According to Bandura's social learning formulation, it is useful to analyze the interaction into three separate components. These are (a) aspects about, or events occurring within, the *person*, (b) his or her overt *behavior*, and (c) the *situation* in which the person finds himself or herself. This can be represented schematically, as in Figure 3.2.

In this formulation, encountering a *situation* such as a person in distress might cause internal factors within the *person*, such as feelings of empathy and norms of social responsibility to be elicited, which in turn might cause the *person* to engage in altruistic *behavior*. This would result in the *situation* changing as the distressed person becomes relieved of his or her suffering. In turn, this might well lead the *person* to reaffirm his or her personal norms and to increase his or her feelings of efficacy and self-worth. Indeed, just engaging in the behavior itself, regardless of whether it succeeds in alleviating the other's distress may lead to increases in the person's feelings of self-worth and efficacy. Changes in perceived self-efficacy, in turn, affect people's decisions as to whether to be altruistic or not, how much effort they expend, and how long they will persist in the face of obstacles and aversive experiences. At any point, each of the three components can be viewed as having independent effects on the interlocking causal chain. The self-regulatory systems of personal norms and empathy outlined in this chapter clearly influence behavior. They do so, however, only in reciprocal interaction with environmental events and the behavioral competencies of the individual.

SUMMARY

Two motivational systems are proposed to account for human altruism: empathy and norms. Empathy is defined as a matching of emotion between A and B and, it is suggested, this occurs either as a result of direct cues, or

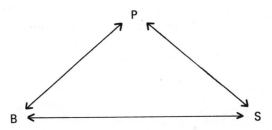

Figure 3-2 Schematic Representation of a Triadic, Reciprocal Interaction. B signifies behavior, P the person, and S the situation. Adapted from Bandura, *American Psychologist*, 1978, *33*, 344-358. *Copyright 1978 by the American Psychological Association. Reprinted by permission.*

through role-taking. Norms are defined as rules, or standards, by which events are judged and on that basis approved or disapproved. It is suggested that norms are personal in nature, having been internalized by individuals in various degrees. Three types of norms are posited to account for human altruism: (1) norms of social responsibility, (2) norms of equity, and (3) norms of reciprocity. These have in common the fact that they are all internal standards against which events are judged.

Postulating motivations to be altruistic helps to organize the data. The danger of motivational constructs is that they only "explain" behavior after the behavior has occurred. One way of testing the adequacy of these motivational constructs is to examine individual differences in them by pencil- and paper-measures and see if these can be used to predict subsequent situational behavior. This implies that there is consistency in people's motivations across situations. This is quite true, as the next chapter will document. However, many situational variables can affect altruistic behavior. The research on the effects of good and bad moods is illustrative of this. As this research evidence makes clear, people are more motivated to help when they are in a good mood and less likely to do so when in a bad one.

Altruism, then, is a product of both enduring characteristics of the person such as his or her self-regulatory system of personal norms and empathy, and fluctuating aspects of the situation. Altruistic behavior is perhaps best viewed as part of a three-way reciprocal interaction involving characteristics of the *person,* the *situation,* and the person's *behavior.* At any point, each of the three components can be viewed as having independent effects on the interlocking causal chain. The self-regulatory systems of personal norms and empathy outlined in this chapter clearly influence behavior. They do so, however, only in reciprocal interaction with environmental events and the behavioral competencies of the individual.

chapter 4

THE ALTRUISTIC
PERSONALITY

In the previous chapter two major motivations for altruism, empathy and personal norms were discussed. The question now becomes, are some people more empathic and/or normatively altruistic than others; that is, is there such a thing as "the altruistic personality"?

In order to answer this question we first must ask ourselves a preliminary question: Is there any consistency in altruistic behavior? Do people who tend to be altruistic in one situation also tend to be altruistic in others? If we find that there is no consistency in people's altruistic behavior in different situations, then there will be little reason to look for the personality correlates thereof. If it turns out that there are consistent patterns of individual differences in altruism, it then becomes possible to investigate what the personality characteristics associated with these individual differences are. The preliminary question to be addressed, then, is whether there is any consistency in altruistic behavior in different situations.

GENERALITY VERSUS SPECIFICITY
IN ALTRUISTIC BEHAVIOR

For several decades there have been two opposing viewpoints on the question of whether human behavior is generally consistent in different situations. Known as the "specificity versus generality" controversy, the question has loomed particularly large in the area of personality and moral behavior. The classic study of this problem was the enormous "character education inquiry" carried out by Hartshorne and May in the 1920s and published from 1928 to 1930 in three books: *Studies in Deceit, Studies in Service and Self Control,* and *Studies in the Organization of Character.* These investigators gave eleven thousand elementary and high school students some thirty-three different behavioral tests of their altruism, self-control, and honesty in home, classroom, church, play, and athletic contexts. At the same time, extensive ratings of the children's reputations with their teachers and their classmates were made in all these areas. By intercorrelating the children's scores on all these tests it was possible to discover whether the children's behavior was specific to situations or generalizable across them. If the children's behavior is specific to situations, then the correlations across situations should be extremely low or even nonexistent. If the children's behavior is generalizable across situations, then the correlations should be substantial. There is, thus, a crucial test of the generality hypothesis. This study will be discussed in some detail for it is the largest study of the question ever undertaken, raises most of the major points of interest, and has been seriously misinterpreted by many investigators.

Altruism

Consider first the tests of altruism in which the students were given opportunities to help others. Five tests were given, making up a battery that Hartshorne and May called the "service" tests. These included:

1. The self or class test. A spelling contest was set up in which each student could compete for one of two sets of prizes, one for the winning class and one for the winning individual. No one could enter both contests. Each had to choose whether his or her score was to count for himself or herself or for the class.

2. The money-voting test. In this test, the class had to decide what to do with some money that might be, or actually had been, won in the previous contest. Scoring was in terms of the altruistic nature of the choice, ranging from "Buy something for some hospital child or some family needing help or for some other philanthropy," to "Divide the money equally among the members of the class."

3. The learning exercises. This test attempted to measure the amount of effort that would be expended to work for the Red Cross, for the class, or for oneself, on a mental abilities test using as scores, gains from the basic, un-motivated score obtained on the first day.

4. The school-kit test.   Each child was given a pencil case containing ten articles which came "as a present from a friend of the school." It was then suggested to them that they might give away any part or all of the kit in an inconspicuous way, in order to help make up some kits for children who had no interesting things of this kind.

5. The envelopes test.   The children were asked to find jokes, pictures, interesting stories, and the like, for sick children in hospitals and were given envelopes in which to collect them. The number of articles collected by each child was scored according to a complex scoring system.

Honesty

Techniques similar to those used in the study of altruistic behavior were used in the study of honest behavior. Here the students were tempted to cheat, lie, and steal in a variety of circumstances. A few of the techniques will be outlined.

1. The duplicating technique.   Students were given, for example, paper-and-pencil tests of knowledge in a school subject; the papers were collected and a photocopy made of the answers. At a later session of the class, the original papers were returned, and each student was told to score his or her own paper according to an answer key provided. Cheating consisted of illegitimately in-creasing the score by copying answers from the key. By comparing changes in the student's answer booklet with photocopies of the original booklets, such deception could readily be ascertained.

2. The improbable achievement technique.   This consisted of giving a test under conditions in which achievement above a given level was almost certain to be an indication of deception. Thus when a student was asked to put dots in the center of a number of irregularly spaced circles on the blackboard with his or her eyes closed, and he or she succeeded in doing so well beyond the capacity of the other students, it could reasonably be supposed that the student had cheated by opening his or her eyes.

3. The double-testing technique.   With this method, students were tested twice on alternate versions of a given test. On one of the occasions, they were given the opportunity to cheat, and on the others there was strict supervision and no opportunity to cheat. Any differences found between the scores made on the two occasions served as the measure of cheating. This particular tech-nique was used to demonstrate deception in work done at home as well as in the classroom. It also lent itself to testing in a quite different context, namely, athletics. The achievement of the student on such activities as pull-ups, chinning, and broad jumping could be measured when the test was self-administered and again when administered by the examiner.

4. Stealing.   In connection with the administration of a test, a box containing several puzzles, not all of which were used, was given to each student. In each box was a coin, ostensibly belonging to another puzzle which the examiner showed to the students but did not ask them to perform. Each student returned his or her own box to a large receptacle at the front of the room. It was possible to check which students had taken the coin before they returned the box by means of a system of numbering and distributing the boxes according to the seating plan of the class.

5. Lying.   Lying could be detected by asking the students whether or not they had cheated on any of the tests. It was, of course, known whether they had cheated or not.

Self-Control, Persistence, and the Ability to Inhibit Behavior.

Similar procedures were used to measure self-control. Over a dozen different techniques in all were tried. In the first of these each student had a copy of a story that was read aloud by the examiner up to the climax. The ending was very difficult to read because all the letters of the words were run into one another. The students could try to finish the story or could start a new one. The self-control measure was the approximate time the students really worked on deciphering the ending. In a second test, several candies were put on each child's desk. The children were told that the experimenter would prefer them not to eat the candies for a lengthy period, during which a paper-and-pencil test was given. Self-control consisted of inhibiting the tendency to eat the candy. In a third test, a box was passed to the students containing a peg test as well as five small puzzles attractive to children but with which they were asked not to play. Self-control consisted of inhibiting the tendency to touch and play with the puzzles. In a distraction test, an arithmetic test was set out on a page covered with interesting drawings. Self-control consisted of not giving way to the temptation to look at these. In a series of "wooden-face" tests, children were told to try not to make any change in their faces while the examiner tickled them with feathers, showed them jokes and placed bad odors under their noses. Self-control was not showing any change of expression.

Questionnaires.

In addition to all the above situational tests, a number of questionnaires were given to the students assessing such things as their knowledge of moral rules. For example, they were asked their opinion as to (a) whether it was a student's duty to engage in such activities as helping "a slower child with his lessons" and (b) whether another child should be punished for "taking a few apples from a fruit stand." These were given on different occasions in different settings. One battery of such tests was called the "information tests." They included, for example:

1. The Cause-effect Test.   This consisted of true-false forced answers to items such as "Good marks are chiefly a matter of luck" and "Ministers' sons and deacons' daughters usually go wrong." Criteria of what constituted the "correct" answer was that more than 75 percent of graduate students thought it to be correct.

2. The Recognitions Test.   Various items such as "Copying composition out of a book but changing some of the words" had to be rated to the degree to which it was recognized as an example of cheating.

3. The Social-ethical Vocabulary Test.   Students had to pick from a multiple-choice answer format that which they thought was the best definition of various words denoting moral virtues (e.g., "bravery," "malice").

4. The Free-response Foresight Test.   Students wrote down as many consequences as they could think of for such transgressions as "John accidentally broke a street lamp with a snowball."

5. The Probability Test.   The student had to rank the probability of various outcomes for such behaviors as "John started across the street without looking both ways."

Reputational Ratings.

In addition to the batteries of tests already described, both the students' teachers and their classmates were asked to make ratings of all children as to their altruism, honesty, self-control, persistence, and the like. Some of the reputational measures were quite elaborate. The ones concerned with altruism, for example, included:

1. Recording of Helpful Acts.   For six months teachers were to record the number of helpful acts performed by their students in various categories. It was stressed to the teachers that these should be actual acts only and *not* attitudes or motives, which were to be assessed elsewhere.

2. The Portrait-Matching Device.   Ten paragraph-length descriptions of people and their motives for helping others were ranked by a number of judges by the degree of helpfulness they entailed. Teachers then matched each of the portraits with the children in their classes.

3. The "Guess Who" Test.   Very short descriptions of people were provided (e.g., "Here is someone who is kind to younger children, helps them on with their wraps, helps them across the street, etc." and "Here is the class athlete . . ."). The children were asked to write down the names of any boys or girls in their class who fit each description. This test was given to both children and teachers.

4. The Check List.   Teachers were to rate each child on several adjectives such as kind, considerate, and stingy.

What were the results from this extremely large and intensive study? First, let us consider the measures of altruism. The behavioral measures intercorrelated a low average of +.23 with each other, thus suggesting support for the specificity viewpoint. However, if the five measures were combined into a battery, they correlated a much higher +.61 with the measures of the child's altruistic reputation among his or her teachers and classmates. Furthermore, the teacher's perceptions of the student's altruism agreed extremely highly (r = +.80) with that of the student's peers on the "Guess Who" test. These latter results indicate a considerable degree of generality and consistency in altruistic behavior.

Virtually indentical results to the above were found for the measures of honesty and self-control. Any one behavioral test correlated, on the average, only a lowly +.20 with any one other behavioral test. If, however, the measures were combined into batteries, then much higher relationships were found with either the teachers' ratings of the children or with any single measure taken alone. Typically these correlations were on the fairly high order of +.50 and +.60. Thus, depending on whether the focus is on the relationship between just two of the behavioral measures or whether it is instead on the broader relationship between averaged groups of situations, the notions of both specificity *and* generality are supported. The question then becomes, which of these two focal points is the more useful or accurate?

Hartshorne and May (1928-30) concentrated on the specific correlations of +.20 and +.30 rather than those of +.50 and +.60 gained from combining the individual tests. This led them to conclude in favor of the doctrine of specificity. For example, they stated:

> . . . neither deceit nor its opposite, 'honesty,' are unified character traits, but rather specific functions of life situations. Most children will deceive in certain situations and not in others. Lying, cheating, and stealing as measured by the test situations used in these studies are only very loosely related. (1928, p. 411)

Other writers sided with Hartshorne and May. For example, Mischel (1968) extolled again the notion of specificity in behavior, pointing out that the average validity coefficient of personality is +.30. Persons, therefore, are said to exhibit "discriminative facility" between situations. Mischel (1968) selectively reviewed some of Hartshorne's and May's work in order to demonstrate how behavior changed from situation to situation. Thus, if children took alternate forms of one of the paper-and-pencil tests in diverse social settings—such as at home, in Sunday school, at club meetings, as well as in the classroom—the test-retest correlations fell from a relatively high +.70 in the *same* situation to +.40 in a *different* situation.

This doctrine of "specificity" is correct in what it argues, that is, that situations are important, that people acquire different ways of dealing with different situations, and that the old idea of a trait as some "inner entity operating independently of the situation in which the individual is placed" (Hartshorne & May 1928, p. 385) is quite incorrect. Unfortunately, some have interpreted this as meaning that consistency does not exist. This is quite wrong. The evidence is very solid that there are quite stable and consistent patterns of individual differences across situations. Hartshorne's and May's conclusions were much too suggestive of specificity. By focusing on correlations of +.20 and +.30 between any two tests, rather than those of +.50 and +.60 based on a battery of items they created a very misleading impression. A much more accurate picture of reality is found by looking at the predictability achieved from sampling a number of behavioral examples. This greater predictability occurs because there is always a fair amount of randomness in any one situation. By combining and averaging over situations the randomness (called "error variance") itself is averaged out leaving a clearer view of a person's true behavior. These expectations are made explicit in psychometric theory in which, for example, in educational and personality testing, the more items there are on a test, the higher the reliability is. Thus any one behavioral test ought to be considered similar to any one item on an educational or personality test. It would be quite inappropriate to assess a person's educational attainment on the basis of just one question. Taking the person's answers to several questions together, however, allows a truer picture to emerge. This also is true in measuring altruism, and, as we have seen, combining individual tasks, in the Hartshorne and May (1928-30) studies led to substantial predictability. Correlations of +.50 and +.60 allow for the accounting for 25 percent to 36 percent of the variance in a set of scores. This is really quite high and supports the view that *there is a degree of generality in altruistic behavior.* Much further evidence for this conclusion is found in Hartshorne's and May's data. Indeed, examination of the relationships among the total scores on the battery of altruism tests to those of the batteries concerned with honesty, self-control, persistence, and moral knowledge, suggest that the generality of behavior is not limited to altruism. There is, instead, *evidence for a general moral trait.* We shall return to this point at the end of this chapter.

Since the pioneering work of Hartshorne and May (1928-30), many other studies also have provided data that speak directly to the "specificity versus generality" of altruism. As has been reviewed elsewhere (Rushton 1976), the typical correlation between any two behavioral indices is about +.30. Combining measures, on the other hand, again led to a substantially greater degree of predictability. Let us consider briefly some of this additional evidence.

To test the hypothesis that generosity was part of a pattern of prosocial moral characteristics including kindness and cooperation, Rutherford and Mussen (1968) initially sampled sixty-three middle-class, four-year-old boys. A generosity score was found for each child based on the number of candies given away to a friend. On this basis, the initial sample of sixty-three was divided into fourteen nongenerous children who gave no candies away at all and seventeen highly generous children who gave away a large proportion of their candies. These extreme groups then were found to differ in a variety of ways. Specifically, teachers rated the generous children as more generous, more kind, less competitive, less quarrelsome, and less aggressive than the nongenerous children. Highly generous children also were more generous and less hostile in objectively scored, semistructured, projective doll play. In addition, a behavioral measure of competitiveness based on a car-racing game showed the generous group to be less competitive than the nongenerous group.

Rushton and Wiener (1975) gave the following assessments of altruism to sixty children, half seven-year-olds and half eleven-year-olds: donating tokens to a charity, sharing candy with a friend, and a competitive car-racing game. These last two measures were the same as those used in the study just mentioned by Rutherford and Mussen (1968). Those children, of both ages, who were generous to a friend tended to be the ones who were generous to the charity ($r = +.24$, $p < .001$). In a later study, Rushton and Wheelwright (1979) replicated these relationships and showed that all three measures were related to teachers' ratings of the children's generosity. Thus, support for the generality of prosocial behavior was found in these studies, too.

Dlugokinski and Firestone (1973) took four measures from 164 children aged ten to thirteen: a pencil-and-paper measure of how one understood the meanings of kindness; a pencil-and-paper measure of the relative importance of altruistic as opposed to selfish values; judgments from their classmates of how considerate or selfish they were viewed to be; and a behavioral measure concerned with donating money to a charity. The six possible correlations were all positive and ranged from $+.19$ to $+.38$. Further, the authors reported, multiple correlations of any three variables as predictors of the fourth ranged from $+.42$ to $+.51$. In a later paper, Dlugokinski and Firestone (1974) replicated these relationships. Rubin and Schneider (1973) took two measures of altruism from fifty-five children five years old. One, a measure of generosity, consisted of donating candy to a charity. The other, a measure of helping behavior, was the amount of work done for a peer. These two measures were positively intercorrelated ($r = +.40$, $p < .01$).

Recent studies have examined the relations among children's naturally occurring altruism. Krebs and Sturrup (1974) reported a study of twenty-three children aged seven and eight. Three altruistic coding categories were used: offering help, offering support, and suggesting responsibly. Offering help was found to correlate +.21 with offering support and +.09 with suggesting responsibly, which in turn correlated +.24 with offering support. A somewhat higher correlation was obtained when a composite behavioral altruism score was calculated on the basis of the three preceding measures. This composite score correlated +.47 ($p < .01$) with an independently derived, teacher's rating of the child's overall altruism. In an extensive study of children's free-play behavior in a natural setting, Strayer, Wareing, and Rushton (1979) studied twenty-six children over a thirty-hour period. These authors found relationships of +.50 and +.60 among such coded altruism as donating and sharing objects, cooperation, and helping.

On the basis of this evidence it would seem that there is a "trait" of altruism. Some people are consistently more generous, helping, and kind than others. Furthermore, such people are readily *perceived* as more altruistic, as is demonstrated by the several studies showing positive relationships among behavioral altruism and peers' and teachers' ratings of how altruistic a person seems (Dlugokinski & Firestone 1973, 1974; Krebs & Sturrup 1974; Rushton & Wheelwright 1979; Rutherford & Mussen 1968). It may be remembered that Hartshorne, May, and Maller (1929) also found a solid relationship between the students' reputations for being kind and considerate and how altruistic they actually were on behavioral tests.

We now have answered the preliminary question posed at the beginning of this chapter; that is, "Is there any consistency to altruistic behavior?" with a "yes." People who are altruistic in one situation tend to be altruistic in others. If there is some consistency in the pattern of individual differences in altruistic behavior, we now can ask what personality and other characteristics are associated with this consistency. One characteristic of altruistic behavior is that it appears to increase reliably with age.

AGE AND ALTRUISTIC BEHAVIOR

Although Hartshorne, May, and Maller (1929) found no relationship between altruism and age, several other studies have. Beatrice Wright (1942) was the first to provide evidence for this phenomenon. In her study she found that eight year olds were more generous than five year olds when asked to choose between letting their friend play with the more attractive toy or playing with it themselves. Ugurel-Semin (1952), in another early study, gave Turkish children nine nuts to share between themselves and a friend. The question was, what would the children do with the odd nut? There were three possibilities: (a) to keep the extra nut for themselves, (b) to discard the extra nut so that they would have exactly the same number, and (c) to give the extra nut to their friend. In terms of behaving selfishly and keeping the extra nut for themselves, Ugurel-Semin (1952) found a dramatic decrease as the children became older. The percentage being selfish, by age, was as follows:

4 to 6 years old	67%
7 to 10 years old	23%
11 to 16 years old	0%

Many other studies, some more recent, also found that children's generosity increases with age (Dreman 1976; Elliott & Vasta 1970; Emler & Rushton 1974; Green & Schneider 1974; Handlon & Gross 1959; Harris 1971; Hull & Reuter 1977; Iannotti 1978; Midlarsky & Bryan 1967; Rosenhan 1969; Rushton 1975; Rushton & Wiener 1975). In several of these studies the procedure was as follows: Children, aged six to thirteen, played a bowling game from which they could win tokens. These tokens could be exchanged for prizes at the end of the game on the basis of the more tokens won, the better the prize given. The tokens, therefore, were of some value to the children. Before playing the game the children were shown a picture of an unhappy-looking child depicted on a "Save the Children Fund" charity poster. This child was described as "poor little Bobby" who has "no mummy or daddy or anybody to look after him." Below the poster was a charity box. The children were told that if they wanted to they could share some of their winnings with Bobby by putting some of their tokens into the donation box. The children then were left entirely alone in the room to play the game and give to Bobby if they wanted to. Unknown to each child the bowling game was programmed in such a manner that each child won exactly the same number of tokens, that is, sixteen. In this way it was possible to specify exactly how generous each child was. The percentage of the child's winnings donated to Bobby in these studies is shown in Table 4.1 as a function of age. From this table we can see that on each and every measure the eleven year olds gave away a greater percentage of their winnings than did the seven year olds. The column on the right gives the Pearson-product-moment correlation between age in months and number of tokens shared. It also indicates the sample size on which each of these studies was based.

In one of the studies reported in Table 4.1 (Rushton 1975), the children were brought back two months later to play the bowling game a second time. This was to see if the children's behavior would remain consistent over time. Once again they were given the opportunity of donating to "poor little Bobby" if they wanted to. There was considerable consistency in the two testing occasions and, as can be seen in the table, the differences between older and younger children became even clearer.

In another of the studies reported in Table 4.1 (Rushton & Wiener 1975), a second and quite different measure of children's generosity was made in addition to the number of tokens they donated to Bobby. After the children had played the bowling game and had had the opportunity to give to Bobby, they each were given twenty-four candies as a prize. The children then each were given two paper bags. On one was written his or her name and on the other the name of his or her best friend. They were told that they could put all the candies in their own bag if they wished, it really did not matter, but if

TABLE 4-1

Generosity in Children: Percentage Shared as a Function of Age

Study	Measure of Generosity		Age							Correlation
		7	8	9	10	11	12	13	
Emler & Rushton (1974)	Valued Tokens Donated to a Charity on Immediate Test	14%	37%	24%	31%	29%	34%	36%	r = .22* (N = 60)
Rushton (1975)	1) Valued Tokens Donated to a Charity on Immediate Test	19%	26%	28%	25%	33%			r = .18* (N = 134)
	2) Valued Tokens Donated to a Charity on 2-Month Retest	17%	14%	26%	23%	41%			r = .41*** (N = 134)
Rushton & Wiener (1975)	1) Valued Tokens Donated to a Charity	19%				38%			r = .47*** (N = 60)
	2) Candies Shared with Best Friend	21%				42%			r = .68*** (N = 60)

(*p < .05, ***p < .001).

they wished to give any to their friend they could do so in the bag provided. The experimenter then left the room so that the children were entirely alone to divide their candies. As the children came to leave the room with the two bags of candies, the experimenter suggested that they leave the bags on a nearby shelf until the end of the day. This allowed the experimenter to count the number of candies each child had given to his or her friend. As can be seen from Table 4.1, this measure of children's generosity also yielded the expected age difference. Eleven year olds shared 42 percent of their candies, but seven year olds shared only 21 percent.

It is not only generosity that increases with age. Green and Schneider (1974) found evidence that children's *helping behavior* also increased with age. In one situation, the experimenter "accidentally" dropped a number of pencils on the floor, thus providing the children with an opportunity to help pick them up. The results of the study showed that helping to pick up the pencils increased over the age range of five to ten years, at which time virtually all the children helped. Friedrich and Stein (1973) coded the naturally occurring free play behavior of three- to five-year-old children attending a preschool into several categories of prosocial behavior. In their sample they found that both cooperation and nurturance increased with age. Finally, Eisenberg-Berg (1979) found that the measure of altruism in her study increased with age during adolescence (Grades 9, 11, and 12). Her measure involved subjects helping the experimenter with a dull task.

Not all studies found consistent increases over this age range. Staub (1970), for example, found a curvilinear relationship to age in helping behavior. While a child sat alone in a room waiting for the experimenter to come back, he or she heard sounds of distress coming from a girl in the next room. The question was, would the child go and investigate the situation? Although "rescue behavior" in general increased over the age range of four to nine, it tended to fall off sharply at age eleven. Staub (1970) explained these findings by suggesting that as children grow older, their social behavior is more likely to become inhibited by fear of disapproval. Staub's (1970) results, therefore, basically agree with those already cited.

There were more discrepant results from a series of studies that showed that competitiveness rather than cooperation increases with age, at least in Anglo-American cultures (Kagan & Madsen 1971; Madsen 1971; Madsen & Connor 1973; Rushton & Wiener 1975).

In summary, it would appear that children's altruism reliably increases with age, at least over the range of six to eleven.

SEX

In his major review of the data, Krebs (1970) reported that out of a total of seventeen studies, including some unpublished material, no sex differences were found in eleven of them. But when sex differences were found, they

tended to favor females. This remains the general finding. An absence of sex differences in altruistic behavior was reported in a number of recent studies mostly, but not entirely, concerned with children (Eisenberg-Berg 1979; Emler & Rushton 1974; Grusec 1971; Grusec & Skubiski 1970; Harris 1970, 1971; Presbie & Coiteux 1971; Rubin & Schneider 1973; Rushton 1975; Rushton & Wiener 1975; Staub 1971; Staub & Baer 1974; Yarrow, Scott, & Waxler 1973; Yarrow & Waxler 1976; Krebs & Sturrup 1974). Mussen and others (1970) did find sex differences, although not in any systematic manner. Dlugokinski and Firestone (1973, 1974) and Midlarsky and Bryan (1972) reported some tendency for females to be more altruistic than males on some of their measures. Hartshorne, May, and Maller (1929) found that girls scored higher than boys on measures of helpfulness and service, and O'Bryant and Brophy (1976) reported that eleven-year-old girls helped a younger child with a task significantly more than eleven-year-old boys did. Finally, Ahlgren and Johnson (1979) in a survey of over 2400 students found consistent sex differences in cooperative and competitive attitudes from the 2nd through the 12th grades. Females showed consistently more positive attitudes toward cooperation in school, and males showed consistently more positive attitudes toward competition.

Among adults Latané and Darley (1970) and Schwartz and Clausen (1970) found that women came to the rescue less frequently than did men in emergency-helping situations. Neither Latané and Darley (1970) nor Rushton (1978), however, found any sex differences in aiding passersby on the street who made such minor requests for assistance as asking for directions and for change for a quarter. Piliavin, Rodin, and Piliavin (1969) found no differences between men and women in going to the aid of people who had apparently collapsed on the New York subway.

Before leaving the question of sex differences in altruistic *behavior*, it might be noted that Hoffman (1977b) suggested that sex differences might emerge in empathy, a *motivation* for altruism. Hoffman reviewed data from several studies suggesting that women were more responsive to affective states in others than were men. Furthermore Sagi and Hoffman (1976) demonstrated this with one-day-old babies who were found to cry readily at the sound of another infant crying. Sagi and Hoffman (1976) suggested this "empathic response" was innate and that female infants were more responsive than were males. In a quite different review, however, Hoffman (1977a) found no sex differences in role-taking abilities. The possibility that females are more altruistic than males is interesting and clearly warrants further research attention.

INTELLIGENCE

Few studies have reported the effects of IQ on altruism. Krebs and Sturrup (1974) found positive relationships among both IQ tests and teachers' ratings of intelligence and different measures of naturally occurring, free-play altruism,

as well as with teachers' ratings of altruism. Seven other studies, however, failed to find such a relationship using donating, helping, and sociometric measures of altruism. (Eisenberg-Berg 1979; Friedrich & Stein 1973; Grant, Weiner, & Rushton 1976; Harris, Mussen & Rutherford 1976; Hartshorne, May & Maller 1929; Rubin & Schneider 1973; Rushton & Wiener 1975).

EMPATHY

In the last chapter it was suggested that empathy and personal norms were the two main motivational systems underlying altruistic behavior. One way of testing the adequacy of this formulation is to see if independently measured individual differences in these motivations (e.g., as assessed by pencil-and-paper measures) would predict situational altruism. Several studies have supported the view that this is the case.

Liebhart (1972), for example, assessed the "sympathy orientation" of 102 male, high school students in Germany using a modified version of a projective technique devised by Lenrow (1965). At the same time, the students' dispositions to take instrumental action for the relief of their own distress was assessed. The students then were given an opportunity to intervene in a staged emergency (an apparent fainting). Those who were both high in sympathy orientation and willingness to take instrumental action intervened significantly more than those who were not.

Mehrabian and Epstein (1972) found that university students' empathy scores predicted both a refusal to administer high levels of electric shock to another person and agreement to volunteer time to help an emotionally upset confederate of the experimenter. These authors gave a thirty-three item questionnaire with such positively keyed items as "It makes me sad to see a lonely stranger in a group," "I really get involved with the feelings of the character in a novel," and such negatively keyed items as "I find it silly for people to cry out of happiness" and "I often find that I can remain cool in spite of the excitement around me." One week later their aggressiveness was measured. The students acted as teachers who could use various levels of shocks to punish learners. The average intensity of shock delivered by a student served as the dependent measure of aggression. The immediacy of the pain feedback from the victim was of two levels. In the immediate condition, the victim was in the same room with the student. In the nonimmediate condition, the victim was in the adjacent room. The findings indicated that the highly empathic students aggressed less, at least in the immediate-feedback condition. No such differences were found in the nonimmediate condition. In a second experiment, female college students who had been administered the empathy scale, were paired with confederates of the experimenter. According to a standardized script, the confederates acted emotionally upset about a personal problem and asked the students to volunteer time for a class assignment. Empathy correlated positively and significantly with helping.

Eisenberg-Berg and Mussen (1978) used Mehrabian's and Epstein's (1972) empathy scale in a replication attempt with high school students and found that those who both volunteered and actually helped the experimenter by serving as subjects without pay in a dull, hour-long task two to three weeks later, had higher empathy scores than those who did not help. This result, however, held only in the case of males.

House and Milligan (1976) demonstrated individual differences in empathy among psychopathic and nonpsychopathic prisoners. On the basis of scores on the Minnesota Multiphasic Personality Inventory's (*MMPI*) Psychopathic deviate (*Pd*) scale, these authors showed that groups characterized as high in psychopathy were far less autonomically responsive (as measured by heart rate and skin conductance) to modeled emotional distress than those low in psychopathy. This study therefore supported the often-stated proposition that psychopaths are indifferent to the feelings of others.

Three other studies have demonstrated relationships between empathy and altruism with quite young children. Barnett, Matthews, and Howard (1979) administered the Feshbach and Roe (1968; see Feshbach 1978) measure of empathy, to 84 six- and seven-year-old children. High empathy scores on this measure are gained according to the degree to which the children were accurately able to identify the emotion of another child depicted in a sequence of slides. Boys rated by teachers as highly competitive were found to be less empathic than boys rated as less competitive; no difference was found for girls. Marcus, Telleen, and Roke (1979) studied both boys and girls from three to five years of age and found that empathy scores on the Feshbach measure predicted both teachers' and others' ratings of the children's cooperativeness. Finally, Buckley, Siegel, and Ness (1979) measured empathy on a sample of 41 children aged three to nine years old using a test developed by Borke (1971). This required the child to choose from among four pictures the face that correctly depicted the emotion experienced by a child in the story. Altruism was assessed by the degree to which the child either helped another person in an experimental situation, or by whether he or she shared a cookie with this other person. The results showed that children of both sexes who exhibited altruistic behavior had higher empathy scores than did the children who did not display altruistic behavior.

Role-Taking.

Another ingredient, often suggested as a condition for generalized empathy, has been cognitive role-taking ability. It is argued that in order to empathize with another, one first must be able to role-take the position of the other. All of the studies in this section have been carried out with children.

According to a number of descriptive studies, very young children are quite limited in their ability to role-take. They see the world from only one very limited and egocentric perspective—their own. As they grow older, however, their role-taking skills improve markedly. Flavell, Botkin, Fry, Wright, and Jarvis (1968) devised a series of games to play with children aged four to fourteen to test their role-taking abilities. For example, there is the *board game* (Flavell and others 1968, pp. 82-102). Here the children are shown nonverbally how to play a snake-and-ladders type of game. The children's task is to explain in their own words the rules of the game first to a person sitting opposite and then to the same person sitting opposite blindfolded. The children are told to modify their explanation on the second occasion to account for the fact that the person can no longer see the board and counters. The degree to which the children are able to do this is used as the score of role-taking ability. Scores are based on the difference between the amount of worthwhile information given on the first occasion and that given on the second. In a second test, the cylinders task (Flavell and others 1968, pp. 55-70), children are shown a series of four stimulus displays and are asked to reconstruct each one as it would look to another person seated at different points vis-a-vis the display. Yet another test presents a series of seven pictures depicting a story that children are asked to tell. Three pictures then are removed from the sequence, and the children are asked to tell the story depicted by the remaining four as a second person would tell it, the children being told that the second person had never seen the seven together. The version attributed to the second person provides an indication of the degree to which the children have freed themselves from the perspective initially imposed by having seen the story depicted on seven pictures.

A number of researchers have used these and similar tests to see whether they predict altruistic behavior. Rubin and Schneider (1973) found that, indeed, as egocentricity in children went down and role-taking ability went up, so the children's altruistic behaviors increased. These investigators had fifty-five seven-year-old children take part in a test of their role-taking capacities by having them attempt to describe low-encodable, graphic designs to the experimenter so that he could pick up the same card at which the child was looking. After completing the role-taking task, the experimenter measured the child's altruistic behavior in two different situations. In the first one, the child was given the opportunity to donate boxes of candy to a group of poor children. In the second, the child was given the opportunity to help a younger child put tickets into small piles. The results of this study showed that the less egocentric the child was, the more altruistically he or she behaved.

Several other studies, however, failed to find the predicted relationship between role-taking ability and children's generosity. Emler and Rushton (1974) gave sixty children aged six to thirteen two different role-taking tasks as devised by Flavell and others (1968) and one measure of altruism (tokens donated to a charity). No relationships were found among the three measures. A study by Rushton and Wiener (1975) with sixty children aged seven and eleven failed to find relationships among two different measures of role-taking capacity, again taken from Flavell and others (1968), and three different measures of altruism. On the other hand again, Krebs and Sturrup (1974), using the same Flavell and others (1968) role-taking tasks as Emler and Rushton (1974) did, found that role-taking ability correlated with a composite altruism score derived from two months of observation of nine- and ten-year-old children's naturally occurring altruism. More significant correlations were found between the role-taking tasks and teachers' ratings of the children's prosocial and cooperative behaviors. Unfortunately, in Krebs's and Sturrup's (1974) paper, intelligence, as measured by both IQ tests and teachers' ratings, correlated with all measures, thus confounding the relationship between role-taking and altruism.

These measures of role-taking have stressed jointly the conceptual and perceptual sides of this skill. Two recent reviews, however, suggested that there is very little generality across these particular measures of role-taking ability and that researchers ought to distinguish among different kinds of role-taking ability (Kurdek 1978; Shantz 1975). When Waxler, Yarrow, and Smith (1977) attempted to do this with three- to seven-year-olds using four "perceptual" perspective-taking tasks and six "conceptual" perspective-taking tasks and relating them to six tests of prosocial behavior, they did not obtain positive results. In an attempt to measure role-taking in quite a different way, Barrett and Yarrow (1977) showed videotapes to five- to eight-year olds and asked them about the motives of the actors. This "social inferential ability" also failed to predict naturally occurring prosocial behavior.

Just to confuse the picture, some other studies produced positive results. Iannotti (1978) measured role-taking ability using procedures from both Flavell (1968) and Selman and Byrne (1974) in which high scores were given to a child based on the degree to which understanding of the motives behind the behavior of others was shown. Using these procedures, Iannotti was able to predict the number of candies that six- and nine-year-old boys would share with a needy child. Buckley, Siegel, and Ness (1979) found that a test of perceptual perspective-taking predicted either how much helping on a task or whether sharing of a cookie would be engaged in by three- to nine-year-olds. The perspective-taking task was based on one developed by Borke (1975) in which children were required to rotate a display of toys in order to view it in a similar way to that of a *Sesame Street* character viewing a similar display from another vantage point. Finally, Johnson (1975) found, with twenty-four nine-year-olds, that while perceptual perspective-taking failed to predict cooperative behavior in an experimental setting, a measure of "emotional perspective-taking" did so. This measure consisted of having the child listen to a tape recording and attempt to identify how the actor felt and why he felt the way he did. The similarity of this measure to some of the measures of empathy previously described suggests that it could have as readily been discussed in that section. It suggests that empathy and emotional role-taking are similar constructs.

In summary, there is evidence that individual differences in empathy and affective perspective taking among both children and adults lead to altruism. The studies linking individual conceptual and perceptual role-taking ability to altruism, however, have met with mixed success.

NORMS

Norms were defined in the last chapter as "standards by which events are judged and on that basis approved or disapproved," and it was suggested that there were a number of norms for prosocial behaviors such as altruism. In this context, norms of social responsibility, equity, and reciprocity were mentioned. It is highly likely that some people have internalized such norms more fully than others. Perhaps the most direct test of this hypothesis is to see whether observed individual differences in altruistic behavior are correlated with paper-and-pencil measures of a person's knowledge of, and agreement with, moral norms.

Using children as subjects, Hartshorne and May (1928-30) found a correlation of around .30 between different measures of children's prosocial behaviors and their knowledge of general moral rules. Turner (1948) used a rating scale to measure altruism among adolescents and found that those rated the most altruistic also were the ones rated independently by parents and social workers as having knowledge of "social standards." They also were the ones who engaged in less antisocial behavior.

More recently, researchers have attempted to measure the norm of "social responsibility" using a questionnaire composed of such items as "I am the kind of person people can count on" and then seeing whether this predicts whether the person will engage in altruism. Berkowitz and Daniels (1964) found that high scorers on their Social Responsibility Scale (a revised version of one by Harris, 1957) behaved more altruistically than low scorers did. Their measure of altruism consisted of the number of cardboard boxes made for another person who was allegedly dependent on the subject for his or her help. Midlarsky and Bryan (1972) used Harris's (1957) scale of social responsibility with children and found it predicted both donating money to a charity on an immediate test and donating candies on a subsequent test. In another study Willis and Goethals (1973) measured individuals' social responsibility with the Values Scale of Allport, Vernon, and Lindzey (1960) and found that although 80 percent of the subjects high on social responsibility made an altruistic donation, only 43 percent of the subjects low on social responsibility did so.

In a program of research Schwartz (1977) measured an individual's "acceptance of responsibility" for the welfare of others by using a scale with positively loaded items such as "If a good friend of mine wanted to injure an enemy of his, it would be my duty to stop him" and negatively loaded items such as "When a man is completely involved in valuable work, you can't blame him if he is insensitive to those around him." Schwartz (1968a) found that such measures predicted how people's peers would rate them on scales of considerateness, reliability, and helpfulness. The measure also allowed for prediction of actual situational behavior. Schwartz (1968b) found that it predicted voluntary participation in social service work by undergraduates, and Schwartz and Clausen (1970) found that high scorers helped a victim in a faked epileptic seizure situation more often, more quickly, and more directly than did low scorers.

Staub (1974), in a major undertaking, had his students fill out a large number of scales, including the measures of "acceptance of responsibility" by Schwartz (1968a) and "social responsibility" by Berkowitz (Berkowitz & Lutterman 1968), just discussed. He also gave (1) a measure of social *irresponsibility*: Machiavellianism (Christie & Geis 1968). Sample items include (1) agreement with "Anyone who completely trusts anyone else is asking for trouble" and disagreement with "Most men are brave"; (2) a measure of how high a person rank ordered such values as "helpful" and "equality" in a long list of alternative values (Rokeach 1973); and (3) a measure of moral reasoning based on Kohlberg's (1969) dilemmas. In a test of whether any of these measures predicted helping behavior, Staub (1974) gave all the subjects the opportunity to intervene in an emergency situation some weeks after completing all the questionnaires. While sitting in an experimental cubicle doing a task for the experimenter, each subject encountered a person in the next cubicle apparently suffering from progressively worsening stomach cramps. First, sounds of distress were heard emanating from the adjoining cubicle. Next, the distressed person mentioned the extent of his pain, then offered to go to another room so as not to disturb the worker, and finally directly requested the subject to go to the drugstore and get him some pills. The subjects were observed during all this time through a one-way screen, and their degree of helpfulness was recorded. The results of this study were very interesting. All the different questionnaire measures—that is, social responsibility, Machiavellianism, high levels of moral reasoning ability, and having "helpful" values—grouped significantly and positively together on a single factor in a factor analysis, along with high scores on measures of helping behavior. Thus, a broad, prosocial orientation emerged that had manifested itself in a variety of ways.

Of particular interest in the Staub (1974) study was the finding that an individual's level of moral reasoning correlated both with the more traditional questionnaires of moral attitudes and with measures of altruistic behavior. Most researchers in the area of moral reasoning usually see "reasoning" as "content free" and not requiring particular attitudes or behaviors to follow. However, this is certainly not the case with current measures of moral reasoning.

Piaget (1932) is the classic beginning reference in this area. Piaget's research methodology was to tell children a variety of stories and then to ask them what they thought. For example:

One afternoon, on a holiday, a mother had taken her children for a walk along the Rhone. At four o'clock she gave each of them a roll. They all began to eat their rolls except the youngest, who was careless and let his fall into the water. What will the mother do? Will she give him another one? What will the older ones say?   (Piaget 1932, p. 267)

Two boys, a little one and a big one, once went for a long walk in the mountains. When lunch time came they were very hungry and took their food out of their bags. But they found that there was not enough for both of them. What should have been done? Give all the food to the big boy or to the little one, or the same to both?   (Piaget 1932, p. 309)

On the basis of responses to stories such as these, Piaget (1932) described three broad stages of development in norms of justice. The first was the *authority* stage in which there is no idea of justice as distinct from the arbitrary demands from elders. Children at this stage of development would be likely to respond to the first story in terms of the mother punishing the child and to the second in terms of the older child having most, simply "because he's the biggest." Next comes the stage of *equality* in which authority is subordinate to the requirements of the strict equality of treatment. Thus, in the first of the stories, the child would argue that the mother ought to give her child another roll so that "everybody would have the same amount." Likewise, in the second story, "both children should have equally." Finally, the *equity* stage sees a shift from a norm of strict equality toward recognition of the relativity of individual needs and circumstances. Thus, in the first story the child might be excused and given another roll because he was "the youngest and it was an accident," and in the second either the older "because he would have a bigger appetite" *or* the younger "because he couldn't manage as well as the other."

This tripartite stage-theory of the development of norms of justice overlaps with Piaget's (1932) views of the wider aspects of morality in which the child is viewed as progressing from a stage of egocentric morality based on authority and punishment to one based on cooperation, mutual respect, and the awareness of others' needs. According to Piaget, the morality of cooperation begins to emerge around the age of seven and increases until around the age of twelve when mutual respect and consideration of others are firmly established.

Piaget's ideas about the development of moral judgment have given rise to much research. Most of this has examined the development with age of specific dimensions of moral judgment, confirming movement from "immature" to "mature" responses with chronological age and, within age, with IQ and social class.

Since then, Lawrence Kohlberg (1964, 1969, 1976) has advanced a more extensive scheme of stages of moral development. In his scheme there are six stages (grouped into three levels), and development extends into adulthood.

Many individuals never reach the higher levels of moral reasoning. Kohlberg also formulated his theories on the basis of presenting moral dilemmas in the form of stories to listeners and then asking them what they thought.

For example:

> In Europe, a woman was near death from cancer. One drug might save her, a form of radium that a druggist in the same town had recently discovered. The druggist was charging $2,000, ten times what the drug cost him to make. The sick woman's husband, Heinz, went to everyone he knew to borrow the money, but he could only get together about half of what it cost. He told the druggist that his wife was dying and asked him to sell it cheaper or let him pay later. But the druggist said, "No." The husband got desperate and broke into the man's store to steal the drug for his wife. Should the husband have done that? Why?   (Kohlberg 1969, p. 379)

The classification of possible responses to this moral dilemma uses the six stages shown in Table 4.2.

It might be interesting for the reader to attempt to provide rationales *against* Heinz stealing the drug from the perspective of each of the stages and compare these with those of Kohlberg (1969, pp. 379-80). Examples of arguing *in favor*, from each of the stages, are the following (based on Kohlberg 1969, pp. 379-380).

Stage 1.   It's okay to steal because the drug is worth only $200. It's not as though he's stealing a $2,000 drug.

Stage 2.   It's all right to steal because she needs it and he wants her to live.

Stage 3.   He should steal the drug. He was doing only what was natural for a good husband to do.

Stage 4.   If you did nothing you'd be letting your wife die, and it's your responsibility if she dies.

Stage 5.   The law wasn't set up for these circumstances. Taking the drug in this situation isn't really right, but he's justified to do it.

Stage 6.   In choosing between the two evils of stealing and letting your wife die, it becomes morally right to steal because preserving life is more important.

Theses stages are said to be qualitatively different from one another, invariant in sequence, hierarchical in nature, and universal across cultures. Each successive stage is an advanced "structural whole" incorporating previous stages and providing a comprehensive way of thinking. One of the important implications of such a view of cognitive stages is that expressed by Kohlberg (1969): "A given stage-response on a task ... represents an underlying thought-organization ... which determines responses to tasks which are not manifestly similar."

TABLE 4-2
KOHLBERG'S STAGES OF MORAL DEVELOPMENT

Level 1: Preconventional

Stage 1: The punishment and obedience orientation

Rules are there and must be obeyed. Whoever is stronger, older, or in authority must be right. Obey the rules and avoid punishment. In general, the seriousness of a violation of a rule depends on the amount of objective damage done.

Stage 2: The instrumental relativist orientation

Do whatever results in rewards or pleasures. Reciprocity conceptions are limited to "You scratch my back and I'll scratch yours."

Level 2: Conventional

Stage 3: The "good boy"-"nice girl" orientation

The orientation here is to win approval from others. Actions are judged in terms of intention. The goal is to be thought of as a nice person.

Stage 4: The "law and order" orientation

The belief here is that everybody should do one's duty to maintain social order. This is more important than satisfying egoistic desires.

Level 3: Post conventional, Autonomous, or Principled

Stage 5: The social-contract legalistic orientation

The orientation is to values and principles that are valid beyond the authority of the persons or groups holding them, or beyond one's own identification with such groups. Right actions are those a society has agreed on; but society can change such agreements on the basis of higher values.

Stage 6: The universal ethical principle orientation

The orientation is to the self-chosen ethical principles of one's own conscience. Principles must be applied universally i.e., one must intend that everyone act on the same principle.

(pp. 352-353). Such a viewpoint often is found in the literature on cognitive development. For example:

> . . . a child of eight who possesses the grouping structure will, by implication from the structure, show reversibility of thought, a relative lack of egocentrism, a capacity for synthesizing rather than simply juxtaposing data, and a number of other characteristics. (Flavell 1963, p. 18)

The transitions with which we shall be concerned are interesting in their own right as a documentary on development. More interesting still is the picture of the underlying form of organization in thought that is revealed.

(Olver & Hornsby 1966, p. 69)

The overall assumption is that children who differ in their underlying cognitive structure (stage) should show systematic, corresponding differences in their intellectual and social behaviors.

Many studies have found that individuals with "high" levels of moral judgment as assessed on the type of moral reasoning tasks just outlined also are the ones who are the most altruistic (Anchor & Cross 1974; Eisenberg-Berg 1979; Eisenberg-Berg & Hand 1979; Elmer & Rushton 1974; Haan, Smith, & Block 1968; Harris, Mussen, & Rutherford 1976; Krebs & Rosenwald 1977; Rubin & Schneider 1973; Rushton 1975; Staub 1974). These studies differed considerably from each other in the age range tested, the measure of moral judgment used, and the indices of altruistic behavior assessed. For example, Rubin and Schneider (1973) gave fifty-five children seven years old six moral judgment dilemmas as adapted by Lee (1971) from Kohlberg (1964) and two opportunities to behave generously. The first measure of generosity was donating candy to poor children, and the second was helping a younger child complete a task. These authors found that there was a significant, positive relationship between the child's level of moral judgment and the degree of altruism shown in both tasks.

Emler and Rushton (1974) used the two moral judgment stories from Piaget (1932), described above, and found that predictions of 60 seven- to thirteen-year-old children's anonymous donations to a charity could be made with better than chance results with knowledge of the children's level of moral judgment. Furthermore, this finding was maintained when the effect of age was covaried from the analysis. In a subsequent study, Rushton (1975) replicated the Emler and Rushton (1974) findings with 140 seven- to eleven-year-olds and, furthermore, showed that the relation between moral judgment and altruism held up over a two-month retest.

The findings are not limited to laboratory measures. For example, Harris, Mussen, and Rutherford (1976) used *peer ratings* of the children's prosocial disposition and found correlates with moral judgment. These authors gave thirty-three boys, ten and eleven years old, the Kohlberg test of moral judgment and found that maturity of moral judgment was significantly correlated with IQ and, even with intelligence partialled out, with resisting a temptation in a situational test as well as a reputation among their peers for being concerned with the welfare of others.

Finally, there are the studies with adults. The most extensive of these was that already mentioned by Staub (1974). He found, consistently, that adults at higher stages on Kohlberg's test engaged more frequently in helping and rescue behavior in laboratory situations than did those at lower levels. Krebs and Rosewald (1977) demonstrated a significant, positive relationship between the moral reasoning of adults as measured by Kohlberg's (1964) test of moral development and their altruism. The test of altruism was whether subjects would mail a questionnaire back to the experimenter at some minor inconvenience to themselves. Although over 90 percent of those at Stages 4 and 5 helped in this way, only 40 percent of those at Stages 2 and 3 did so. Eisenberg-Berg (1979; see also Mussen & Eisenberg-Berg 1977) found that high school students' responses to prosocial moral dilemmas predicted their subsequent altruistic behavior. For males such scores predicted their completion of a dull experimental task two to three weeks later, while for females they predicted humanitarian sociopolitical attitudes. Finally, Anchor and Cross (1974) found a relationship between Kohlbergian moral judgment and an unwillingness to engage in gratuitous aggression on a Prisoner's Dilemma game. This study had been carried out with both institutionalized male psychiatric patients and a group of college students.

In almost a dozen studies, therefore, it was found that there is a degree of relation between how a person makes moral judgments (to either Piagetian or Kohlbergian stories) and how he or she subsequently responds to situations requiring altruistic actions. The higher the individual's level of moral judgment is, the more altruistically he or she behaves. This is a most interesting finding and one that still requires a full explanation. For example, the question arises as to whether or not this relationship is a causal one. Rushton (1975) attempted to examine the causality of moral judgment with 140 seven to eleven year olds using an "interaction approach." He reasoned that if high moral judgment was the cause of the child's generosity, then it might be expected to interact with and affect the reception of other determinants of altruistic behavior, especially those derived from the environment. Rushton (1975) suggested that what another person did might be perceived and evaluated differently depending on whether the child had a high or a low level of moral judgment. Specifically, it might be expected that high moral reasoners would react differently to a person behaving selfishly than low moral reasoners would. The study showed that high moral reasoners devalued a model who preached selfishness more than low moral reasoners did, thus providing some support for the notion of causality. People's judgments of what is appropriate conduct appear to guide their subsequent behavior.

THE ALTRUISTIC PERSONALITY

The evidence reviewed so far in this chapter warrants two conclusions. First, individual differences in altruism are quite consistent across different situations. Second, they are related to many of a person's characteristics. Those people who donate most to charity are the ones who cooperate the most, share the most with their friends, and help people out when they need it. They also were those who were judged to be altruistic, kind, and considerate by both their classmates and their teachers, thus providing evidence for a consistent "altruistic personality." Further, the probability of a person engaging in altruistic behavior can be predicted from the manner in which a person endorses or responds to items on a number of paper-and-pencil measures of empathy, moral judgment, social responsibility, and moral knowledge. There is, indeed, evidence for the operation of a general factor of morality across diverse measures. Let us return to some of the data from Hartshorne's and May's (1928-30) study to illustrate just how pervasive this is.

Hartshorne and May examined the relationship among their batteries of tests of altruism, self-control, honesty, and persistence, and found that these four intercorrelated at an average of +.31. Furthermore, measures of moral knowledge intercorrelated at an average of +.37 with the four batteries of behavioral tests. Thus, knowledge of how children endorse items such as "most of the things you learn in school never do you any good anyway," "clean speech is a sign of being a 'goody-goody,'" and "I feel it is a student's duty to help a slow or dull child with his lessons," allows a greater than chance prediction of such diverse behaviors as: voting to give money to a charity rather than to oneself; not cheating on either a game or on an exam when given the opportunity; controlling the tendency to make a face when smelling a bad odor or being tickled with a feather; and not being distracted from an arithmetic test by a page full of interesting drawings. All the above could also be predicted by better than chance by knowledge of whether the students were rated as conscientious by their classmates. All of this supports the idea of a pervasive general factor of "moral character." This also has been the conclusion of many subsequent researchers. Burton (1963), for example, reanalyzed much of the original Hartshorne and May data and subjected them to more sophisticated statistical analyses. A factor analysis revealed a first general factor that accounted for between 35 and 40 percent of the common variance, a figure strongly suggesting the existence of "moral character." This has since been replicated using other children and other tests (e.g., Nelsen, Grinder, & Mutterer 1969) and reviewed by Burton (1976).

Despite the conclusions of Hartshorne and May themselves about the specificity of behavior, they carried out several analyses that almost necessarily assumed that there was consistency across situations. They studied, for example, *individual differences in consistency* across situations, arguing that such differences suggested integration of personality and, I even suggest, "integrity." Integrity would exist when a person's behavior could be predicted from both his or her past behavior and from knowledge of his or her moral principles. Hartshorne and May found a distinct relationship between "integrity" and acting in a prosocial manner. For example, although altruism and honesty were characteristics that could be predicted from one situation to another, dishonesty, lying, cheating, and the whole range of antisocial activities tended to be unpredictable and unintegrated. Thus, the behavior of the person lacking in integrity tended to be inconsistent, undependable, unpredictable, and even contradictory. Such a person would be at the mercy of the varying temptations of every situation. It is interesting too that Hartshorne and May found distinct relationships between integrity and emotional stability, and also among both of these and persistence and resistance to suggestion. There appears to be a general prosocial, moral person characterized by what has often been labeled, rather vaguely elsewhere, "ego strength."

There is further evidence for this in a personality dimension called "locus of control" (Rotter 1975). People who feel that they can influence their lives and that they have some degree of control over the reinforcements that occur to them are described as having an "internal" locus of control. Those, on the other hand, who feel that the reinforcing events in their lives are caused by chance, other people, or to in general forces over which they have little control, are described as having an "external" locus of control. Those with an internal locus of control have been found to have greater overall emotional stability than externals do, to have better self-concepts, and indeed to feel (and be) generally more competent in both academic and nonacademic situations. They also tend to engage in more altruistic behavior.

Midlarsky (1971), for example, provided male students with the opportunity to help another student engage in, under stress, a motor-coordination task, even though an electric shock occasionally accompanied the helping behavior. It was found that those with an internal locus of control helped more than those with an external locus of control. Two subsequent studies replicated these findings (Midlarsky & Midlarsky 1973, 1976). Fincham and Barling (1978) investigated locus of control and generosity in three groups of children varying in academic achievement, namely, the learning disabled, normal achieving, and gifted. Thirty-four boys, nine and ten years old, took part in the study. Internal locus of control increased with academic ability and predicted the number of candies donated to a charity. Perhaps those individuals with an established sense of personal control are more likely to feel self-efficacious and assist others, than those without this sense.

This discussion now dovetails with that at the end of the previous chapter. There over a dozen studies were examined that demonstrated how good moods increase altruism. By combining the evidence from the locus of control literature with that from moods, it can be suggested that some people have a generally better sense of overall personal efficacy and well-being than do others and that these are the people who are most altruistic overall. Staub (1978) elaborated on these ideas and reviewed the work of a Polish investigator, Reykowski (1975), and his colleagues, which provide some support for this notion. As Staub summarized:

People who tend to have positive moods, high self-esteem and a positive sense of well-being may be less preoccupied with themselves, have a greater sense of potency or strength, and perhaps feel more benevolent toward others than individuals characterized by more negative moods, low self-esteem, and a poor sense of well-being. Consequently, the former may tend to be more helpful, on the whole, than the latter. (1978, p. 308)

There is certainly extensive evidence that there are consistent individual differences in overall self-esteem that remain stable over a period of years (Wylie 1974). Many people (e.g., Bandura, 1977a) have also described the importance of feelings of self-efficacy to the centrality of most people's everyday lives and pointed out its wide-ranging implications for their behavior in diverse settings.

It would seem that there is an altruistic personality and that it can be described as follows: This person is more motivated to engage in altruistic acts. He or she has internalized higher and more universal standards of justice, social responsibility, and modes of moral reasoning, judgment, and knowledge, and/or he or she is more empathic to the feelings and sufferings of others and able to see the world from their emotional and motivational perspective. On the basis of such motivations, this person is likely to value, and to engage in, a great variety of altruistic behaviors—from giving to people more needy than themselves, to comforting others, to rescuing others from aversive situations. Altruists also behave consistently more honestly, persistently, and with greater self-control than do nonaltruists. As a result of his or her altruistic activity, this person will have a *reputation* for being altruistic among his or her peers and colleagues. Furthermore, the consistently altruistic person is likely to have an integrated personality, strong feelings of personal efficacy and well-being, and what generally might be called "integrity."

SUMMARY

For several decades there have been two opposing viewpoints on the question of whether human behavior is generally consistent in different situations. Known as the "specificity versus generality" controversy, the question has loomed particularly large in the area of personality and moral behavior. Hartshorne and May (1928-30) carried out the classic study in this area. They gave eleven thousand elementary and high school students some thirty-three different behavioral tests of their altruism, self-control, and honesty in home, classroom, church, play, and athletic contexts. At the same time, extensive ratings of the children's reputations with their teachers and their classmates were made in all these areas. By intercorrelating the children's scores on all these tests it was possible to discover whether the children's behavior was specific to situations or generalizable. If the children's behavior is specific to situations, then the correlations across situations should be extremely low or even nonexistent. If the children's behavior is generalizable across situations then the correlations should be substantial. Thus, there is a crucial test of the generality hypothesis.

Hartshorne's and May's results show that the average intercorrelation between any two of the behavioral measures was of the order of $r = +.20$ to $+.30$. When the individual measures were combined into a five item battery they correlated a much higher $+.60$ both with other batteries of behavioral tests and with the measures of the child's altruistic reputation among his or her teachers and classmates. Furthermore, the teacher's perceptions of the students' altruism agreed extremely highly ($r = +.80$) with that of the students' peers. These results indicate a considerable degree of generality and consistency to altruistic behavior. They support the view that there is an "altruistic personality."

Several characteristics of the altruistic person have been found. First, altruism increases with age, at least up to the age of eleven or twelve. Second, it appears as though altruism might be sex-related, with the female being a little more altruistic than the male, except perhaps in emergency rescue situations. Further, the probability of a person engaging in altruistic behavior can be predicted from the manner in which a person endorses or responds to items on a number of pencil-and-paper measures of empathy, moral judgment, social responsibility, and moral knowledge. Altruists also behave consistently more honestly, persistently, and with greater self-control than do nonaltruists. Furthermore, the consistently altruistic person is likely to have an integrated personality, strong feelings of personal efficacy and well-being, and what generally might be called "integrity."

chapter 5

LEARNING TO BE ALTRUISTIC

How do we account for the development of the empathy and norms that in chapter 3 were named as the prime motivators of altruism? How do we account for the fact that both of these abilities, along with altruistic behavior itself, increase with age, as was suggested in chapter 4? And how do we account for the consistent patterns of individual differences that also were observed in that chapter? One common-sense view would be that as children grow older they *learn* to develop better role-taking abilities, to be more empathic, to adhere to moral principles, and to be more altruistic. This view also would hold that differences among people are a result of differential learning experiences. This will be the view advanced here. It should be noted that there are other accounts. For example, the "structuralist" theories of such cognitive-developmentalists as Piaget (1932), Kohlberg (1969, 1976), and Krebs (1978) are far more "maturational" in nature and see behavior as emerging in inevitable, sequential, and irreversible order (given the right "interactions" with the environment). For such theorists, role taking, moral reasoning, and motives for altruistic behavior differ at different ages because of fixed developmental sequences in the hypothetical stages, or structures, thought to underlie behavioral phenomena.

As we shall see in this chapter, much can be accounted for by using increasingly well established learning processes. Indeed, these processes explain many data with which more structuralist views have difficulty, for example, reversibility of behavior, and moral judgments, and the speeding up of behavioral and cognitive functioning beyond the ages that most structuralist models would predict. This chapter will examine the growth of empathy and role-taking ability and the internalization of moral norms from the perspective of social learning theory (Bandura 1969, 1977b). Four categories of learning will be studied: classical conditioning, reinforcement learning, observational learning from models, and learning from such verbal procedures as instructions and preachings.

CLASSICAL CONDITIONING:
THE LEARNING OF EMOTIONAL RESPONSES

Initially, most stimulus events in a child's environment are emotionally "neutral" to him or her. By the time the child is an adult, however, the range of significant emotional stimuli has increased considerably. The simplest procedure by which this might come about is through classical conditioning (Pavlov 1927). In this analysis, positive or negative associations are formed between stimuli presented together. For example, an initially neutral stimulus (conditioned stimulus, CS) comes to acquire a particular valence as a result of having been associated in time with an already valenced stimulus (unconditioned stimulus, US). If the US elicits a response (unconditioned response, UR) then the CS also will tend to elicit that response (conditioned response, CR). For example, a dinner bell, or the aroma of cooking (CS), itself will result in the digestive juices flowing (CR) as a result of previously having been associated with delicious food (US). Even the sight of good food (CS) in a shop window can make the mouth water (CR). A similar situation could occur in which the unconditioned stimulus was unpleasant. Thus, some smells of cooking elicit odious expectations as a result of having been associated with burnt rather than delicious food.

The process of positive and aversive classical conditioning helps to explain the acquisition of emotional reactions to previously neutral stimuli. In an early demonstration of this, Watson and Raynor (1920) conditioned a fear response to a rabbit in a very young child by banging a loud gong (US) directly behind the child whenever the rabbit (CS) was presented. In another early study, Jones (1924) showed how such procedures also could be used to *eliminate* unwanted fears. Jones (1924) used food as a US to elicit digestive processes incompatible with anxiety to decondition a fear response to a rat (CS) in a young child.

Through classical conditioning procedures many of the objects in our environment acquire an emotional significance to us. A previously neutral stimulus, once associated by contiguity to an unconditioned stimulus, can be the basis for further, *higher order conditioning*, by itself being paired with other neutral stimuli. It is suggested that through higher order conditioning, words and symbols also become potent stimuli able to elicit autonomic responses.

A study by Staats and Staats (1957) illustrated this latter process. They wanted to find whether it was possible to condition the meaning of regular English words to syllables that had no meaning. To do this it was necessary to use a method of measuring meaning. They chose to use the semantic-differential technique which assumes that much of the total variation in persons' judgments of meaning can be explained in terms of three factors: evaluation (good-bad), potency (powerful-weak), and activity (active-passive). A word such as *church* might be viewed as very good, mediumly powerful, and very passive, whereas a word like *bullet* might be seen as very bad, very powerful, and very active. Their experiments paired syllables such as *xeh* and *yof* with English words high or low on the evaluative dimension (*pretty, insane*); potency dimension (*hard, quiet*); and activity dimension (*excited, calm*). The subjects were instructed to remember as many of the syllables as possible. Before testing the subjects on the memory task, the experimenter told them that it would be necessary to find out how they felt about the syllables since that might have affected how they had been learned. Each of the nonsense syllables were rated by the subject on the semantic differential. Essentially it was found that nonsense syllables that had been consistently paired with highly positive, highly active, or highly powerful English words were themselves subsequently perceived as more positive, more active, and more powerful than were control syllables that had been paired with neutral English words. Similarly it was found that syllables paired with very negative, very passive, or very weak English words were themselves subsequently seen as more negative, passive, and weak than were control syllables. Thus, it is suggested that classical conditioning processes can give meaning to words.

The classical conditioning paradigm also has been used to explain attitude change. In this formulation, attitudes are typically conceptualized as an evaluative response (e.g., Staats 1967). Staats and Staats (1958, 1963), for example, paired national names (Swedish, Dutch) and familiar masculine names (Tom, Bill) with either positively evaluated words (sacred, happy), negatively evaluated words (ugly, failure) or words having little evaluation (e.g., chair). The results indicated that the person's attitude toward both the national and personal names altered in a positive or a negative direction depending on with which words they had been paired. In this way, national and ethnic groups (or new consumer products, for that matter), can acquire powerful positive and negative valences even before we have any direct experience with them.

The basic ideas of classical conditioning have been elaborated upon by a number of theorists. One of the most encompassing of these elaborations is the *reinforcement-affect* model outlined by Byrne. Expressed simply, this theory states that we like stimuli associated with reward and dislike stimuli associated with punishment. This idea has been applied successfully to account for a number of social psychological phenomena including interpersonal attraction (Byrne 1971) and human sexual behavior (Byrne & Byrne 1977).

It is perhaps worthwhile to note that associating two stimuli results in *both* acquiring some of the valence of the other. For example if a person we admired, liked, and whose opinion we trusted, were to make very positive statements about an event that we did not regard highly, our estimation of the event might rise, but our estimation of our friend also might drop a little.

Particularly dramatic applications of the classical conditioning paradigm to social functioning are found in psychotherapy, in which classical conditioning is sometimes called counterconditioning. There are essentially two possibilities: to alter the valence of a stimulus from an inappropriately negative one (e.g., snakes) to a neutral or even positive one or to alter the valence of a stimulus from an inappropriately positive one (e.g., heroin) to a negative one. The first process often is referred to as *desensitization therapy* and the second, *aversion therapy.*

Words and symbols that conjure up strong affective reactions also can condition physiological arousal. For example, Gale and Jacobson (1970) demonstrated that after insulting comments were paired with a neutral tone, the tone alone began to elicit emotional reactions as measured physiologically. Previously neutral stimuli, as a result of being paired with potent stimuli, acquire the capacity to elicit physiological arousal. This leads directly to the question of whether classical conditioning procedures can be used to develop *empathy*. The answer appears to be yes.

Aronfreed and Paskal carried out the relevant experiments, one based on positive affective empathy and the other on empathic distress. Their first experiment, with six- and eight-year-old girls, was the attachment of positive affective empathy (CR) to the expressive cues (CS) of an adult (Aronfreed & Paskal 1965). In the critical experimental condition, the adult pressed a lever resulting either in a 60 percent likelihood of candy or one resulting in a 60 percent likelihood of a red light. Whenever the red light came on, the adult both vocalized the expressive cue "There's the light" (CS) and at the same time joyously hugged the child (US). On testing trials, the CS "There's the light," was sufficient reinforcement for the child for her to press the lever resulting in the light more often than the lever resulting in candy. By contrast, in control conditions in which the expressive cue (CS) and hug (US) had not been paired, the children subsequently pressed the lever resulting in candy more frequently than that resulting in the red light.

Midlarsky and Bryan (1967) replicated Aronfreed's and Paskal's (1965) study and extended it to demonstrate (1) that the pairing contingency of CS (expressive cue) and US (experience of affection) could occur backwards (i.e., US-CS), as well as the more usual Pavlovian pairing of CS-US, and (2) that the girls who sacrificed candy also donated to a charity in the absence of the adult.

In a subsequent study, Aronfreed and Paskal (1966) conducted an experiment on negative empathy based on shared distress cues, rather than on the positive empathy of their previous study. The subjects again were seven- and eight-year-old girls. The CS consisted of expressions of distress by an adult (clutching her head and grimacing while listening to noise over earphones). The US was a loud aversive tone over the child's own earphones. Subsequently the adult terminated the child's own earphone noise by pressing a special lever, thus demonstrating an instrumental response to alleviate the distress of another. In a series of test trials, the child was faced with a child confederate of the experimenter who emitted the distress cues (CS) that the experimenter had previously. When this happened, the children who had gone through the appropriate conditioning trials, helped the child confederate more often than the other children did. Aronfreed and Paskal (1966) argued that their experiment thus demonstrated altruism motivated by reduction of empathic distress.

LEARNING THROUGH REINFORCEMENT AND PUNISHMENT

One of the best established principles in all of psychology is that behavior is under the control of its consequences (Skinner 1953). According to Skinner's formulation, most human social behavior may be viewed as voluntary instrumental response patterns or operants. Operants may include such behaviors as an infant's smiling response, social interaction in the nursery school, criminal delinquency, and adult sexual behavior. The central principle of operant learning is that when an operant is followed by reinforcement (rewards or avoidance of punishment), the probability of its later occurrence is increased. Similarly, when an operant is followed by a punishment, the probability of its later occurrence is decreased. Rewards can consist of an almost endless myriad of events and include: information, sensory change, money, social approval, removal of aversive stimuli, and opportunities to engage in preferred behavioral activities. Punishments, too, may vary widely and may consist of such events as physical pain, verbal reprimand, time out from reinforcement (e.g., removal of a positive reinforcer), or the substitution of less preferred behavioral activities (e.g., washing dishes instead of watching TV).

Reinforcement theory is quite simple to understand on this level and fits in with common sense. If one rewards a response, it will increase the probability of the future occurrence of that response. If one punishes a response, it will decrease the future probability of the occurrence of that response. Our knowledge of this basic principle gives us useful psychological procedures for helping people to change their behavior.

One study might be outlined to demonstrate the uses of the operant paradigm. Allen, Hart, Buell, Harris, and Wolf (1964) went to a nursery school to study social interaction among children. One child, Ann, a bright four year old, seemed to be isolated from the others. She preferred to play by herself and rejected social advances made to her by the other children. They decided to see if Ann's increasing isolation behavior could be changed using the power of positive reinforcement. Whenever Ann spontaneously happened to play with one of her friends, the teachers immediately gave her much attention and approval. But whenever she chose to play by herself, the teachers ignored her. After several days of such reinforcement, Ann's sociability had increased significantly and eventually remained high even when the teachers no longer gave her special attention. Presumably there were now sufficient rewards operating in the inter-action with other children to maintain the behavior. Positive reinforcement in the form of attention and approval had changed Ann from being the social isolate of the nursery school to a quite normal, socially interacting child.

The effects of positive reinforcement often are much more complex than the foregoing suggests. For example, the patterning of reinforcements are crucial to determining their effectiveness. If a behavior that usually meets with "continuous reinforcement" suddenly is not met with reinforcement, then that behavior will "extinguish." Thus parents have to wean their children away from the expectation that every time they behave properly they will get approval. Parents can do this by instead of rewarding every example of good behavior, they reward only every fifth example. Eventually parents can decrease the frequency of their approval to such a degree that the behavior will be maintained afterwards in the absence of reinforcement. Now and again reinforcement can be reinstated to consolidate the behavior. Such "partial reinforcement" procedures have different behavioral effects depending on its particular patterning. For example, "fixed-ratio" schedules (i.e., providing a reward for every so many responses, e.g., every hundredth) result in a very high level of responding as employers who use the piece-work system of payment know. "Variable-ratio" schedules (i.e., providing one reward for an average number of responses, e.g., an average of every hundredth response) result in behaviors that appear particularly resistant to extinction. Schedules of reinforcement that took place in the past thus can explain why many behaviors still persist even in the absence of current reinforcers.

To what extent can reinforcement principles be applied to altruistic behaviors? A number of experimental studies have rewarded children for either sharing or helping behaviors within well-defined laboratory situations and have found that at least while the reinforcement was maintained the amount of sharing behavior increased. Fischer (1963) found, with four-year-old children, that candies, made contingent upon marble sharing, produced more sharing than social reinforcement consisting of "that's good, that's nice" did. This was an interesting study in that it demonstrated that verbal approval is not always an effective modifier of behavior. Other incentives, like money or material reinforcers, can be used to motivate the behavior that we desire to be increased.

Studies with older children *have* demonstrated that social approval increases the amount of prosocial behavior. Midlarsky, Bryan, and Brickman (1973) showed that an adult's social approval of twelve-year-old children's donations to charity led to an increase in such donating over no such approval. Interestingly, if the approval came from a previously selfish model, the approval appeared to become aversive and led to a reduction in giving. Gelfand, Hartmann, Cromer, and Page (1975) studied children individually and found that by first instructing the child and then giving social praise, the child became more generous. Finally, Rushton and Teachman (1978) provided evidence that the effects of reinforcement endured over time. These authors also showed the effects of punishment on generosity. In their study, children first were induced to behave altruistically by having generosity modeled to them. This resulted in a high level of donating by the children in the model's presence. The model, then seeing the child behaving generously either rewarded or punished the child for his or her imitative generosity. The child then was left alone to play the game again, this time entirely by himself or herself. As can be seen from Figure 5.1, the reinforcement condi-

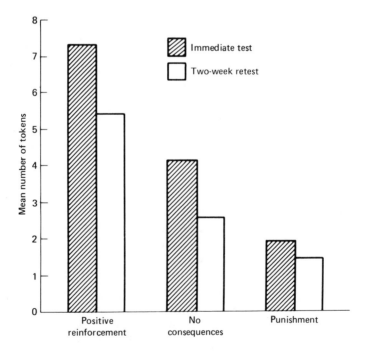

Figure 5-1 Tokens Donated on Immediate and Two-Week Retest as a Function of Reinforcement. Source: Rushton & Teachman, *Personality and Social Psychology Bulletin,* 1978, *4,* 322-325.

tions had strong effects, not only on the immediate test but also on a two-week retest.

The main finding of these studies is clear. If children are reinforced for behaving generously, their generosity will increase.

But what about adults? Is there any evidence that reinforcing helping behavior in adults leads to increments in such behavior? One study, carried out in a natural environment, is pertinent. Moss and Page (1972) set up the experiment on the main street of Dayton, Ohio. The procedure went as follows: An attractive young woman approached a passerby and asked for direction. In one condition she provided the passerby with positive reinforcement for his help (a smile and a "Thank you very much, I really appreciate this"), whereas in another condition she effectively punished him for his time and effort ("I can't understand what you're saying, never mind, I'll ask someone else"). After such reinforcement the passerby was given, seventy-five feet further down the street, a second opportunity to behave in an altruistic manner. A second confederate of the experimenter was waiting. As the target passerby approached, this second woman would drop a small bag and continue to walk down the street as if she did not know she had dropped the bag. The question was whether or not the passerby would help on this second occasion. Overall, while Moss and Page (1972) did not find that positive reinforcement in the first situation led to increases in helping in the second situation, they did find that a bad experience in the first situation significantly *decreased* the amount of helping in the second.

These studies of the reinforcement of altruism were more to increase the frequency of behavior that already had been acquired than to produce new behavioral repertoires. In this sense, reinforcement, although it may have some direct response-strengthening properties, functions primarily in terms of its informational and incentive value. From information about what is likely to be valued socially, people construct norms of appropriate social behavior. According to this formulation, if people see others valuing altruistic consideration for others, then this will become internalized as an appropriate standard of behavior. If the reinforcement contingencies change and altruism becomes socially devalued, then the norms might be expected to alter. This, of course, does not always happen. Indeed, sometimes individuals attempt to convince their society that the society's values are wrong.

Prior to leaving the section on reinforcement, it will be useful to briefly consider the role of *punishment* in bringing about internalization of standards. The effects of punishment have not been studied as extensively as the effects of other variables, but the study by Rushton and Teachman (Figure 5.1) shows that punishing generosity decreases it. Usually, however, punishment is delivered for antisocial behavior in an attempt to decrease the frequency of cheating, stealing, and being selfish, for example. While it seems that punishment is effective in suppressing such behavior and in producing long term anxiety to stimuli, the conditions that maximize its effectiveness are far from clear (see Walters & Grusec 1977, for a review). Some theorists, such as Eysenck (1977), have suggested that punishment is so effective that "conscience" can be conceptualized as a "conditioned reflex." According to this view, if a person is punished for engaging in such antisocial behavior as cheating, stealing, and being selfish, he or she will subsequently act in a prosocial manner in order to avoid the anxiety experienced as a result of the earlier punishment. Other theorists have taken the opposite view and suggested that punishment should not be used because it is ineffective, inhumane, or both. This seems extreme, however. From the punishments delivered, people undoubtedly construct appropriate rules of social conduct which then serve to guide their behavior in the future. Mild punishment can be effective in aiding children to generate their own self-regulatory controls. Both social norms and their internalization into personal standards require judgment of what is wrong as well as what is right.

OBSERVATIONAL LEARNING

The overwhelming majority of human social behavior is learned from observing others. This has been well documented in numerous studies (see Bandura 1969, 1977b). Consider the excellent example of language. Modeling procedures have been shown to be powerful influences on language and verbal behavior (see Rosenthal & Zimmerman 1978). Not only do we learn much of our grammar and vocabulary from observing others, but also our accent and styles of delivery. Whether we use a wide range of facial expressions and hand gestures when we talk also will depend on the particular "models" to which we were exposed when we were learning the language. Models are important throughout the life cycle. Continuing with our language example, parents often will acquire a whole range of new phrases associated with a teenage culture when their children become teenagers, and adults who start new occupations will acquire a whole new technical vocabulary for the job from workmate and supervisor models. More dramatically, the individual who moves to new geographical regions will often, over the years, modify his or her old accent to one more closely approximating that of the new geographical locale. Interesting in this latter situation are the instances in which people fail to modify their accent. Some of the relevant conditions determining when new learning from models will or will not take place will be cited below.

Most often learning from models need not be under conscious control in order to occur. We do not have to strive to be influenced. As with language acquisition, much social learning from models takes place relatively automatically. Neither does the model always have to be a live person in direct interaction with us. We shall discuss later how symbolic models, as represented in stories told to us, books that we read, events that we hear on the radio, or actors that we watch on the television screen, provide us with a continual barrage of observational learning experiences. It is only in recent years that the behavioral sciences have given much attention to learning through modeling. Much of the credit for this must go to Albert Bandura—whose work (e.g., Bandura 1965, 1969, 1977b) has been influential in making behavioral scientists realize that the importance of various modeling processes to social behavior is far greater and more general than was previously assumed.

So far we have considered only language acquisition, but before we move on we might underline the importance of models in this regard by mentioning the kind of therapy that this knowledge allows us to use on children with defects in their language acquisition. Armed with the knowledge of the power of modeling, speech therapists now, for example, often will attempt to get children to imitate directly specific sounds and phrases to gain mastery of sound production. Later, modeling can be used to increase systematically children's use of particular parts of speech and vocabulary (e.g., Bandura & Harris 1966). There is no question that learning from models is dramatically effective in these cases.

It is not only the rules and styles of language that are learned from the observation of models. Rosenthal and Zimmerman (1978) reviewed many studies and demonstrated that abstract concepts and principles, problem-solving strategies, and creative thought all can be effectively modified by observational learning. More important to our purposes is the knowledge that the whole repertoire of a person's *social* attitudes and behavior can be influenced in this way. Thus, one's religion and politics, one's conception of appropriate sex-role behavior, one's vocational and leisure activities, one's expectations of the behavior of others who fill certain positions, and one's own internalized set of moral codes and values can be acquired, modified, and influenced by observing the attitudes, behavior, and life styles of others.

Consider first the evidence that models are extremely potent transmitters of normative standards. In the prototypic experiment, Bandura and Kupers (1964) had children observing a model playing an electronic bowling game and rewarding himself with tokens which later could be exchanged for a prize. In one condition the model adopted a high standard of performance in which he rewarded himself only when he got a high score. When his performance fell short of his standards, he denied himself available rewards and reacted in a self-derogatory manner. In another condition the model adopted a low standard of performance in which he rewarded himself for relatively mediocre scores. Later the children performed the same task, during which they received a predetermined range of scores, and the scores for which they chose to reward themselves were recorded. The results revealed that the children's norms for self-reinforcement closely matched those of the model they had observed. Confirmatory studies have been carried out by, among others, Bandura and Whalen (1966) and Mischel and Liebert (1966). Mischel and Liebert (1966), for example, showed (a) that the behaviors would endure over a four-week retest period, and (b) that the children imposed on their peers the same standard that they had adopted for themselves, hence transmitting their own learned self-reward criteria to others. Thus, there is considerable evidence that internal standards can be acquired by watching others.

Norms of moral judgment.

One set of norms, discussed in the previous chapter, are those measured by persons' responses to the moral dilemmas created by Piaget (1932) and Kohlberg (1976). As described, these theorists espoused a structuralist view of the sequence of qualitatively distinct stages of moral reasoning. Piaget suggested that there were two basic stages (three with reference to generosity and sharing), and Kohlberg suggested that there were six. The social learning view to be reviewed here appears to account for most of the data even better than the more traditional cognitive-developmental approach does. For example, Bandura and McDonald (1963) showed the influence of modeling (and reinforcement) on five- to eleven-year-old children's moral judgments. First the children's base-line moral judgments were assessed by giving them pairs of stories to which to respond such as the following:

Story 1:
  A girl who is named Susan is in her room. She is called to dinner. She starts to go into the dining room, but behind the door there is a chair. On the chair is a tray with 15 cups on it. Susan doesn't know that all of this is behind the door. She pushes on the door, the door knocks against the tray, and bang go the 15 cups! They are all broken.

Story 2:
  A girl named Mary wants to get some biscuits. But her mother tells her she can't have any more biscuits, and she leaves. But Mary wants a biscuit, so she climbs up on a chair and reaches up to the shelf. But she knocks over one cup and it falls to the floor and breaks!

Question:
  Which of the two children is naughtier? Why?

Children with "low" levels of moral judgment think that Susan is naughtier because she broke fifteen cups rather than only one. Such children are basing their judgments on the *consequences* of the act. Children with "high" levels of moral judgment think that Mary is naughtier because her *intentions* were wrong, regardless of the consequences. According to Piaget (1932), these represent two quite distinct stages of development which he named "objective" and "subjective" morality, respectively. For Piaget, the transition from the low to high level occurred roughly around the age of seven when children acquire the capacity to "decenter" (i.e., to be able to see the world from a vantage point other than with themselves as the center point).

manner. One situation used widely has children playing a bowling game, winning tokens (or marbles or gift certificates), and having the opportunity to share some of these winnings with another (see Bryan 1975; Rushton 1976). Although details differ from study to study, in principle most of the situations are similar to the one described in Rushton (1975). A child comes alone to the experimental room where the experimenter meets him or her and establishes rapport. If the investigator is interested in the child's personal characteristics these are measured at this point. The child might be given moral judgment stories, role-taking tasks, personality questionnaires, or questions about his or her home background. The child then is shown a number of prizes ranging from comics and small puzzles to games suitable for both boys and girls of the age range being studied and is asked if he or she would like to win one. When the child answers yes, he or she is shown the bowling game. This is usually about three feet long with an upright panel at one end to indicate scores. Every time the player gets a winning score he or she takes two tokens from the table exchangeable for prizes on the basis of the more tokens, the better the prize. On a nearby table is a bowl beneath a "Save the Children Fund" poster depicting a poorly clothed child that the experimenter refers to as "poor little Bobby." A caption reads "Please Give." A number of tokens already are in the bowl. The children are told that they can donate some of their tokens to Bobby if they wish. The number of tokens that the child donates constitutes the measure of generosity. Although the amount that six- to eleven-year-old children give depends on their age; on the average, 25 percent of their winnings are given to Bobby.

Knowing this, it then becomes possible to alter aspects of the situation to see what will increase or decrease the children's generosity over this base-line. For example, modeling variables can be introduced. Before playing the game themselves, children may be introduced to an adult who "would like to play the game too." The adult then is allowed to play the game while the child watches. Sometimes the model behaves very generously and gives half of his or her winnings away. On other occasions the model behaves very selfishly and gives none of his or her tokens away. After the model has finished playing he or she leaves the room, ostensibly to trade the remaining tokens in for a prize. The child now has an opportunity to play the game. The question is, will having observed the model influence his or her behavior? The answer is definitely yes. If children have seen another person behaving generously, they will become more generous themselves. If, on the other hand, they have seen another person behaving selfishly, they will become more selfish themselves. This general finding has been replicated over and over in this and similar situations (see, e.g., Bryan & Walbek 1970a, 1970b; Grusec 1971, 1972; Grusec & Skubiski 1970; Hartup & Coates 1967; Presbie & Coiteux 1971; Rosenhan & White 1967; Rushton 1975; Staub 1971). Interestingly enough, although both generous and selfish models are imitated equally, they are not equally liked. If children are subsequently asked how much they liked the model, generous models are evaluated more positively than are selfish ones (Bryan & Walbek 1970b; Rushton 1975). In the Rushton (1975) study, for example, children made judgments about the selfish model similar to the following: "I didn't like Mr. Wilson at all . . . I hope he's not going to be a teacher in this school . . . he's stingy and mean . . . he's a horrible man." Despite these negative evaluations, children replicated the model's selfish behavior when they were presented with the opportunity to be generous. Evidently, negative evaluations of models do not always serve to moderate the model's power to guide behavior!

Other studies showed that a model's behavior determines not only the amount but also the *direction* of children's subsequent altruism. Harris (1970) found that ten- and eleven-year-old children shared with the model if the model had shared with them, donated to charity if the model had done so, or retained their winnings if the model had. In a subsequent study, Harris (1971) also found that children were influenced by the model in how they distributed their winnings among different charities.

Several studies revealed evidence that speaks to the critically important question of whether the behavior change found in children after exposure to an altruistic model endures over time and generalizes across situations. Rosenhan (1969) reported that the effects on six- to ten-year-olds of observing a model and being able voluntarily to rehearse generous behavior lasted for seven days and, furthermore, generalized on a three-week retest to produce more generosity in a quite different situation. Unfortunately, he failed to provide complete details of the sample, significance tests used, or the generalizable effects of the other conditions. Other studies, however, confirmed that modeling can produce both durability and generalizability. In regard to durability, for example, White (1972) reported a somewhat similar study to Rosenhan's (1969) with nine- to ten-year-olds in which five-day retests showed that those children exposed to a generous model were still more generous than children who had not seen a model at all. Rice and Grusec (1975) and Rushton (1975) showed that altruistic modeling was still affecting children's generosity on retests carried out *months* later. Thus, there is little doubt that such modeling can have durable effects.

In regard to *generalizability*, Elliott and Vasta (1970) showed generalizability from the modeled sharing of candy to the very similar situation in which the child had the opportunity to share pennies. Midlarsky and Bryan (1972) demonstrated that an adult donating tokens to a charity affected children's donations of candy to the same charity ten days later, even when the candy donations were solicited by a different experimenter in a different setting; and Rushton (1975) showed that the modeled behavior, whether generous or selfish, generalized across changes in the retest situation such as a different experimenter in a different locale.

If modeling affects children's generosity, as these studies seem to show, then another variable of interest might be the *amount* of modeling to which the child is exposed. Rushton and Littlefield (1979) examined this hypothesis in a study that gave children an opportunity to observe a model donate either none, two, or eight of her tokens to "Bobby." The observing children then were tested to see how generously they behaved, both immediately and again two weeks later. As can be seen in Figure 5.2, there was a noticeable effect of the amount of modeling. Although there was some decrement, the results still were evident two weeks later.

There is strong evidence that *adults* also are influenced by what they see others doing. Several of the studies with adults have been made in naturalistic settings. Schachter and Hall (1952) showed that modeling could increase the amount of volunteering in class for a psychology experiment. Rosenbaum and Blake (1955) and Rosenbaum (1956) also found that a model who volunteered for an experiment increased volunteering among those who saw him or her. These latter investigators also found that a model refusing to volunteer for an experiment decreased the amount of volunteering compared to a group who saw no model. Bryan and Test (1967) carried out a series of experiments to assess the impact of observing helping models on subsequent helping behaviors. In the first it was found that the base-line for the number of passersby stopping their vehicles to help a woman motorist with a flat tire was seventeen per one thousand cars. But if the passersby had, a quarter of a mile earlier, seen another car raised on a jack with a woman watching a man changing the tire, the fre-

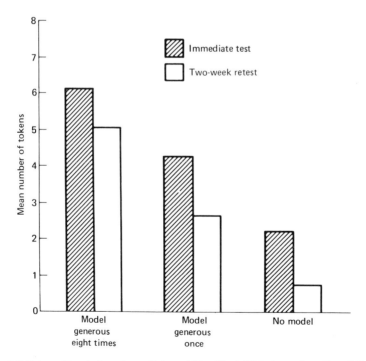

Figure 5-2 Tokens Donated on Immediate and Two-Week Retest as a Function of Number of Times Generous Behavior was Modeled. Source: Rushton & Littlefield, *Journal of Moral Education* (in press).

quency of helping almost doubled and rose to twenty-nine per one thousand. In a second experiment, Bryan and Test (1967) found that the base-line for the number of passersby donating money to a Salvation Army kettle at Christmas time was approximately twenty-two per hour. If, however, a model gave and the observation period was limited to the twenty seconds following that modeled donation, then the rate of donating increased to thirty-five per hour. In a third experiment, Bryan and Test (1967) replicated the findings of the second experiment in a different locale and with a different procedure.

All these studies showed that modeling altruism to adults causes at least an immediate increase in the altruistic behavior of those adults who witnessed the model. To what extent will such effects endure over time and situations? Rushton and Campbell (1977) carried out a quasi-field experiment to investigate this question. Forty-three occupational therapy students, eighteen- to twenty-one-year-old women, came to the social psychology laboratories to participate in an experiment on social interaction. Once there they were introduced to a confederate of the experimenter—the future model—who was described as a "visiting lecturer" who was "helping in this study just like you are." The students and the model then were asked to sit in the chairs provided and get acquainted by talking to each other about their plans for the forthcoming summer. This social interaction was videotaped without the students' knowledge. During the interaction the model acted in a friendly and interested manner toward the student. After ten minutes, the experimenter reentered the room, informed them that their part in the study was now concluded and then debriefed both the student and the model regarding the fact that they had been recorded. After the debriefing, the student's permission was sought to use the videotapes. Finally the experimenter thanked both the student and the model, handed them a petty-cash slip to cover their expenses, and directed them to an office where they would receive payment.

On the floor above the laboratories and near the general offices, elevators, and mail boxes (i.e., in a setting quite dissimilar to the social laboratories) there was a table surrounded by "Give Blood" posters. A second female experimenter wearing a large "Give Blood" badge sat at the table. As the model and student passed by the table they were approached by the canvasser and asked if they would be willing to donate a pint of blood. In one condition the canvasser approached the model first and in a second, control condition, she approached the student first. If the model was asked first, she always agreed to donate and went to the nearby table to fill out the form. If the student was asked first, the model always stepped out of the way and engaged in conversation with another passerby. Thus, each student either had or had not observed a female model volunteer to donate blood. The results of the experiment: Modeling significantly increased the number of female observers who agreed to donate (67 percent versus 25 percent).

Of even more importance, this study used a follow-up measure. All the completed donation forms were forwarded to the regional transfusion center which then mailed appointment cards to each of the potential donors. For those who failed to attend on the first occasion, four additional separate appointments were mailed over the next three months. Again a clear result. In the model condition, nine of the original twenty-seven students actually donated, whereas none of the original eight students in the no-model condition gave (i.e., 33 percent versus 0 percent).

After reviewing the findings from some of the studies of the modeling of altruism, it is evident that even relatively brief exposure to highly salient models *can* produce durable and generalizable change in observers. Furthermore, such modeling effects are not limited to children in the laboratory but also influence behavior in adults in the natural environment.

Neither is the power of modeling limited to the altruistic behaviors described here. Modeling has been applied successfully to increase several other behaviors requiring self-control. These include the delaying of gratification in both children (Bandura & Mischel 1965) and eighteen- to twenty-year-old prisoners (Stumphauzer 1972), courage in the presence of fearsome snakes, again with both children and adults (Bandura, Blanchard, & Ritter 1969), resisting temptation (Grusec, Kuczynski, Rushton, & Simutis 1979), and the imposition of high standards of self-reward (Lepper, Sagotsky, & Mailer 1975).

Factors associated with the effectiveness of modeling.

Characteristics of the model.   People do not, of course, model themselves on just anyone. Characteristics of the observer (e.g., his or her age, sex, intelligence, and previous learning history) will determine *which* models are likely to be influential. The characteristics of a model also are important. Generally, and depending on the situation, successful people will be imitated rather than unsuccessful ones, powerful rather than nonpowerful, prestigious rather than nonprestigious and similar rather than dissimilar. Generally, models who are seen as possessing indices associated with reinforcing outcomes for a particular individual are more likely to elicit imitative behavior than models who do not possess such qualities. One study found, for example, that an apparently high-status pedestrian, well dressed in a suit, who crossed the road against the red light produced more imitative pedestrian traffic-signal violations than the same transgression performed by the same model when dressed in old and patched clothing (Lefkowitz, Blake, & Mouton 1955).

Two principle characteristics of models have been studied in the experimental laboratory: nurturance and power. Grusec and Skubiski (1970) proposed the provocative hypothesis that although nurturing models may facilitate the acquisition of expressive behaviors in children, they actually may hinder the acquisition of behaviors such as altruism which have some costs for the individual engaging in them. Nurturing models, then, may simply lead children to become self-indulgent. That high nurturance may convey permissiveness for self-indulgence in situations entailing exercise of personal control had been shown in a study by Bandura, Grusec, and Menlove (1967a). Children who had had an indulgent relationship with adult models set for themselves more lenient performance standards for self-reward. Grusec and Skubiski (1970) wondered whether, instead of nurturing models, powerful ones would be effective in producing imitation of those behaviors involving costs for the individual. In a study to test this idea, Grusec (1971) did indeed find that a powerful model induced more sharing than a nonpowerful one did, while nurturance in a model actually tended to decrease the child's imitation of altruism. These results have since been replicated. Weissbrod (1976) demonstrated the diminishing effect of model nurturance and Eisenberg-Berg and Geisheker (1979) found the enhancing effect of model power and competence.

These brief laboratory studies have been criticized as tests of the effects of nurturance because the interaction was usually of a very brief duration. Some investigators have provided more extensive interactions between socializing agents and children. Yarrow and Scott (1972) offered two and a half hours of either high- or low-nurturant interactions to each of 118 three- to five-year-old nursery school children. During these interactions, besides modeling high or low nurturance, these socializing agents also modeled: (1) *task-related behaviors* consisting of a particular mixture of nurturing and aggressive behaviors toward toy animals that were the objects of attention in the play task (e.g., fondling and stroking the toy sheep but treating the toy pig roughly), and (2) *incidental behaviors* in the task, consisting of idiosyncratic gestures and examining a rock collection. Then the behavior of the children was observed. It was quite obvious that both the nurturing and the non-nurturing models were imitated in almost all their behaviors. Children, it seems, have a remarkable facility for modeling themselves on the adults to whom they are exposed. Of particular interest was the finding that the children who had been exposed to the nurturing models performed a greater percentage of nurturing acts toward the toy animals than aggressive ones did, whereas the children exposed to the non-nurturing models performed a greater percentage of aggressive acts toward the toy animals than the nurturing ones did. No differences were found between the two groups on measures of peer interaction in which the children later were observed engaging.

In another study, Yarrow, Scott, and Waxler (1973) again provided nursery school children with nurturing or non-nurturing adult socializing agents who spent much time interacting with the children and building up a constructive relationship. These socializing agents then spent some time modeling altruistic behavior for the children. This included making sympathy statements about pictures of distress, making sympathy statements and providing help during dramas enacted with miniature dolls, and providing sympathy and help in real-life situations. The effects of this modeling were then assessed two days and two weeks later. Generalization to alternative forms of the training session occurred in all training methods and showed some durability. There were quite dramatic transfer effects among those children with nurturing caretakers who had modeled helping and sympathy in both symbolic and real distress situations. Those children showed increased real-life helping during a two-week retest in a situation with personnel other than those experienced during training.

At first glance it would appear that the findings from these more extended laboratory studies suggest that nurturance by socializing agents does increase the likelihood that children will imitate the altruistic behavior being modeled. Yarrow, Scott, and Waxler discuss the role of nurturance at some length and tentatively conclude that it will be most influential "when (a) it is a meaningful, warm relationship that has been built up over time, (b) when it has included some withholding of nurturance, (c) when it not only precedes the adult's modeling but is continuous throughout the entire modeling sequence" (1973, p. 258). Unfortunately, this analysis and their study confound nurturance as such (noncontingent warmth) with positive reinforcement (contingent warmth and approval) as in Items (b) and (c) above.

Several other laboratory studies have failed to find an effect of either nurturant or powerful models over "neutral" ones (Bryan & Walbek, 1970a; Grusec & Skubiski 1970; Rosenhan & White 1967). On the balance of this evidence, therefore, it appears that it is still an open question as to whether nurturance by a model diminishes, enhances, or has no effect on the effectiveness of that model in increasing altruism among the observing children. Nonetheless, the findings of Bandura, Grusec, and Menlove (1967a), Grusec (1971), and Weissbrod (1976) do suggest that some caution be exercised in regard to providing too much nurturance in the sense of being noncontingently accepting of all a child does. It may, for example, result in the setting of too low standards for a child. Mischel and Liebert (1966) found that models who set high standards of reward for themselves but who demanded less in the way of achievement from the children observing them, caused the children to adopt the lower standard for themselves. We will return to the question of nurturance when child-raising in the family context is discussed in Chapter 6 (see especially pages 123 to 126).

Consequences for the model.

If an individual behaves in a particular way (e.g., altruistic) and then expresses pleasure at his or her action, it might be imagined that he or she is "feeling good" about the behavior. Observing such positive consequences is referred to as "vicarious reinforcement" (Bandura 1971, 1977b), and if we see them accruing to another, we are more likely to imitate that other than if we see either no consequences or negative ones accruing to the individual. Do such considerations affect altruistic behavior that is modeled by another? The results suggest that they do.

Two earlier studies failed to find an effect. Elliott and Vasta (1970) showed children a film of a six-year-old boy giving three quarters of the candy he had won to a charity box. Following this, in one condition, the experimenter went up to the film model and said, "That was very nice, Johnny, here's a toy to keep." Such vicarious reinforcement failed to produce an increment in the observing child's subsequent altruism—at least not over the condition involving a generous model who received no reinforcement. Harris (1970) also failed to find that observation of an experimenter praising a generous model increased the donation behavior of observing children.

Three other studies did demonstrate vicarious reinforcement effects. Bryan (1971) showed that a generous model expressing positive affect ("This is fun" or "I feel wonderful") immediately after behaving generously produced more subsequent imitative generosity than a model making the same statement after a short delay. Presbie and Coiteux (1971) found that praise to a model for his behavior, whether provided by the model himself or by the experimenter, induced more subsequent imitation of the model by children than when the model was not so praised. This effect was demonstrated for both a generous model and a selfish model. Midlarsky and Bryan (1972) also showed vicarious reinforcement effects for both generous and selfish models. Their models smiled happily and said, "It feels good to give money."

Two other studies found effects from a model's verbalizations of positive affect *before* the model behaved. Rushton (1975) revealed that a (powerful) model making positive affect statements such as "This is really fun" or "I like this game," before actually behaving, produced the most imitation. This finding emerged on both an immediate test and a two-month retest and occurred regardless of whether generous or selfish behavior was modeled. These models also were *evaluated* most highly by the children. These findings were replicated by Rushton and Owen (1975) using a four-minute television film instead of a live model.

A study by Hornstein, Fisch, and Holmes (1968) strongly supported the notion of vicarious reinforcement. It was particularly strong because the subjects in the experiment were adults in a naturalistic setting who did not know that they were in an experiment. Even more striking is the fact that the "model" consisted of a scrap of paper with some writing on it. Hornstein and others (1968) dropped wallets all over downtown New York City. In the wallet was a short, typed letter, apparently written by somebody else who had found the wallet, intended to return it to its owner, and lost it a second time. The letter consisted of either a positive or negative message. In the positive condition the letter read:

Dear Mr. Erwin:
   I found your wallet which I am returning. Everything is here just as I found it. I must say that it has been a great pleasure to be able to help some-

body in the small things that make life nicer. It's really no problem at all and I'm glad to be able to help.

In the negative condition the letter read:

Dear Mr. Erwin:
   I found your wallet which I am returning. Everything is here just as I found it. I must say that taking the responsibility for the wallet and having to return it has been a great inconvenience. I was quite annoyed at having to bother with the whole problem of returning it. I hope you appreciate the efforts that I have gone through.

To make comparisons more significant there also was a neutral condition in which the letter just said that its author was returning the wallet. The rate of wallet returns by Manhattanites showed a pattern strikingly affected by the messages. Fifty-one percent of the wallets were returned in the positive message condition, 43 percent in the neutral message condition, and only 25 percent in the negative message condition. This was remarkable evidence of the effects of modeling and consequences on the model.

Empathy and role-taking.

Can empathy be acquired through the observation of models? Unfortunately, there have been no direct attempts to test this experimentally. It certainly is predicted by social learning theory that seeing a salient model whom we admire and would like to emulate, express deep concern and distress cues upon the distress cues of another, would lead us to feel similar empathic responses. The opposite also would be expected to occur; that is, prestigious models expressing unconcern and callousness in the face of another's obvious distress would lead observers to reduce their natural tendencies toward empathy and helping. Support for this latter notion was documented, for example, in Milgram's obedience studies (Milgram 1963, 1965). In these studies the experimenter remained undisturbed by the agonized screams of protest from a person apparently "learning" under conditions of electric shock. (Actually the person is a confederate of the experimenter and does not receive any shocks.) Instead, the experimenter orders people who have volunteered to participate in the experiment to disregard the protestations and to increase the shock level. The majority of people will continue to deliver shocks even designated as "extremely dangerous" if ordered to do so by the apparently calm and insensitive experimenter. While doing so, however, they exhibit great uncertainty and distress.

Vicarious emotional arousal of an empathic nature has been investigated in a number of laboratory studies. Stotland (1969), for example, found that when adults watched another adult undergoing apparent pain, they showed a great deal of physiologically measured emotional arousal. Such results have been well replicated (e.g., Yamaguchi, Harano, & Egawa 1978). Other studies have demonstrated that once emotional arousal has been instigated, it can be conditioned to environmental stimuli through observing the affective responses of others to those stimuli (e.g., Berger 1962; Craig & Lowery 1969). In these studies observers see another person exhibit emotional arousal (usually of pain) at hearing a tone. After this sequence of events has been repeated several times, the observers themselves begin to respond emotionally to the tone, even though they themselves have never experienced any pain in conjunction with it. Presumably such emotional arousal also could become conditioned to the sight of a third person's plight or even to that person's plight as depicted abstractly in words and stories. As noted by Bandura (1969, 1977b), observers also can attenuate the emotional impact of modeled pain through their thoughts and attention. For example, Bandura and Rosenthal (1966) discovered that observers who were moderately aroused displayed the most rapid and enduring acquisition of autonomic responses, whereas those who were either minimally or markedly aroused achieved the weakest vicarious learning. Modeled pain reactions proved so upsetting to those observers who were beset by high arousal that they diverted their attention from the sufferer with distracting thoughts. Those with low arousal were people who were presumably unresponsive to pain from others. Taken together these studies strongly implicate the role of observational learning in the development and modification of empathic responsivity.

When we turn to role-taking ability there is definite experimental evidence that this can be learned. Chandler (1973), for example, had one group of delinquent elementary school children take part in a film-making and acting project which required them to interact with one another in a manner that required much role-taking and cooperative activity. Compared to controls, these delinquents later demonstrated higher role-taking skills on measures of affective role taking and a greater decrease in antisocial behavior. Iannotti (1978) administered perspective-taking tasks as pretests and posttests to a group of children (aged six and nine). The training was similar to Chandler's (1973) in that the children, in skits, played the roles of various characters. The training methods increased the children's role-taking scores on the two tasks. For six-year-olds (but not for nine-year-olds) they also increased scores on a measure of altruism (donating candy to charity).

Burns and Brainerd (1979) argued that since the two previous studies employed children from the elementary school age range, which is also the age range during which performance on traditional perspective-taking tasks is rapidly improving, it is conceivable that the "learning" effects observed in those experiments were primarily "performance" effects: hence their study. Four- and five-year-old children were given pretests and posttests on five perspective-taking tasks including one perceptual, two cognitive, and two affective tasks. The training consisted of several sessions of either (1) *cooperative constructive play* in which children worked interdependently on a cooperative project such as constructing a wagon out of provided materials or (2) *sociodramatic play* in which the children engaged in prolonged, make-believe role playing such as being in a doctor's office. The results were impressive. First, obvious improvements in preschool children's perspective-taking performance were produced by both training procedures. Besides being statistically significant, the learning effects were great in an absolute sense. The average pretest to posttest improvement was 54 percent for the cooperative-constructive condition and 70 percent for the sociodramatic condition. Second, these improvements were produced by general cognitive experiences rather than by directly training the children in the specific skills that were to be tested.

From these three studies, it would appear that role-taking skills can be increased readily, even among preschoolers, by appropriate training procedures. Theoretically this is very necessary for altruism, because being able to role-take the position of another is generally considered a necessary requisite of much altruistic behavior.

PREACHING, INSTRUCTIONS, AND ATTRIBUTIONS

Besides modeling and reinforcing generous behavior, socializing agents also spend much of their time preaching the virtues of various actions. According to the results of several experiments, preaching has considerably less effect than either a model's behavior or his or her praise does. In one set of experiments, Bryan and Walbek (1970b) had a model behave either generously or selfishly. At the same time the model preached the virtues of either generosity ("We *should* share our tokens with Bobby") or selfishness ("We should *not* share our tokens with Bobby"). The results of this series of experiments revealed that whereas what the model *did* had a strong effect on the observer's behavior, what the model *said* had no effects whatsoever. In a somewhat similar study, Grusec and Skubiski (1970) showed that although a model's behavior was an evident source of behavioral change in observers, the model's preachings were not. The preachings in these two studies, though, were fairly mild and innocuous.

When the preachings were made stronger, more positive effects were obtained (Grusec 1972; Midlarsky & Bryan 1972; Rice & Grusec 1975; Rushton 1975). For example, Rushton (1975), although finding no immediate effect from preaching, did discover that it had substantial impact on children's donations eight weeks later in a somewhat different situation. Rice and Grusec (1975) found that preaching about what was expected produced just as much generosity from children as modeling did. These effects also lasted over a four-month retest period. Grusec, Saas-Kortsaak, and Simutis (1978) gave children both modeling and different kinds of moral exhortation, including *specific* preaching ("It's good to donate marbles to poor children to make them happy") and a *general* exhortation ("It's good to help them in any way one can"). Grusec,

Saas-Kortsaak, and Simutis (1978) also provided a range of behavioral tasks for the children in order to assess their effects. These included (1) an immediate and a three-week retest of *donating* to charity; (2) an immediate test of *helping* the experimenter pick up paper clips; (3) an immediate test of *sharing* pencils with children in the school who had not been able to take part in the study; (4) a test five weeks later which was *making* drawings and *collecting* craft articles for the Hospital for Sick Children. Although the exhortations did not have much effect on the immediate donation test nor on the helping test, it appeared to be more successful in other tests. Boys in the specific preaching conditions shared more than those in the other conditions (although there were no effects for girls). Girls and boys collected more craft items for the Hospital for Sick Children in the general preaching condition. This study therefore provided evidence that preaching can have generalizable effects, even weeks later.

It is still uncertain under what circumstances preaching is likely to affect behavior. Nor is it at all certain how they work. Inasmuch as these experiments have been conducted in laboratory situations, it might almost have been thought that children would take them as *instructions*. This, however, cannot have been the case or much stronger effects would have ensued. When direct instructions *are* given, as in a study by Grusec, Kuczynski, Rushton, and Simutis (1978), then just as much donating on immediate, delayed, and generalization tests is found as with modeling. Other studies also have revealed strong effects from direct instruction (Lepper, Sagotsky, & Mailer 1975; White 1972).

Walters and Grusec (1977) examined how *reasoning* can socialize children. As with preaching, moral exhortation, and direct instruction, reasoning relies on a form of verbal persuasion. This is what Walters and Grusec (1977) concluded about reasoning in the context of punishment.

> Children respond to reasoning either to reduce anxiety or to not be punished. A parent who relied solely on reasoning as a disciplinary technique would not be very successful in obtaining response suppression. *Reasoning becomes effective only when it is supported by a history of punishment.* (Walters & Grusec 1977, p. 207, italics added)

Perhaps all methods of verbal persuasion are effective to the degree to which they are supported by predictable consequences (positive as well as negative). Certainly if parents preached but paid little subsequent attention to how their children behaved, it is doubtful that their verbalizations would have any impact.

A conceptualization of normative internalization that might also be useful here is attribution theory. Recently, Dienstbier, Hillman, Lehnoff, Hillman, and Valkenaar (1975) proposed that although the negative emotional states associated with punishment remain much the same over an individual's life span, the causal attributions made to these states can change; and they feel that it is these attributions that determine subsequent behavior. Thus, if children attribute anxiety after deviation to fear of being found out and punished, they should be less likely to suppress deviation when there is no chance of detection than if the anxiety is attributed to the knowledge that personal standards of behavior have been violated. Walters and Grusec (1977) suggested that individuals who perceive that they have behaved in a certain way independent of external coercion and who therefore attribute the behavior to their own morality rather than to external pressure, will be more inclined to continue behaving in the same way than those who attribute their conformity to external pressure. Thus, to the extent that preaching minimizes the perception of external pressure and leads the children to adopt the standards as their own, attribution theory might fit rather well. Attribution theory, in combination with self-standards, creates a powerful mechanism for handling the problem of internalization. It should generate expectations of the self and others that would guide behavior and reactions to the behavior of others in a variety of situations. Two studies attempted to test this idea by altering attributions experimentally.

Grusec, Kuczynski, Rushton, and Simutis (1978) first induced children to donate winnings from a game to charity, either by having seen a model donate, by being instructed to donate, or by a combination of the two. It was then suggested to them that they had donated either because they were the type who must enjoy helping others or because they thought they were expected to do so. (A third group was not given any reason for its behavior.) The study demonstrated that there was more donation both immediately and two weeks later in the modeling group given an internally oriented attribution. Attributions had no effect on the two influence procedures using direct instruction. On a generalization test, children in the self-attribution group shared more pencils with other children than either those in the no-attribution or in the external-attribution group, regardless of training condition. Attributions were having an effect. A study by Rushton and Teachman (1978), however, failed to find effects for their alterations of the children's expectancies of why they behaved as they did. These latter authors suggested that this was because the lavish positive reinforcement that occurred in all attribution conditions already had led the children to make the internal self-attribution (i.e., "I must be a nice person for this adult to be standing here praising me like this and, furthermore, I must be nice because I'm giving to charity").

SUMMARY

Four processes of social learning have been used to account for the development of both altruistic behavior itself and the motivations that give rise to it. These processes are: (1) classical conditioning; (2) response-contingent reinforcement and punishment; (3) observation of the behavior of others and the consequences accruing to it; and (4) verbal preaching, instruction, and attributional labeling.

Empathic feelings of arousal can be acquired through classical conditioning procedures. In these, pairing of pleasant or unpleasant feelings in the observer is made with pleasant or unpleasant expressions of feeling in the observed. Standards of what is appropriate behavior in any setting are acquired through the reinforcement or punishing consequences that the behavior earns. For example, generous behavior that results in approval increases in frequency, whereas generous behavior that meets with a rebuke, or punishment, tends not to be repeated. Much learning of appropriate standards, as well as of empathy, is acquired from watching others. Indeed, observational learning is a particularly human way of learning and is extremely important. If people see attractive others engaging in helping, and behaving compassionately, they too are likely to emulate this way of behaving. If, on the other hand, people see attractive others behaving selfishly and callously, then these are what the observer comes to feel are appropriate. Finally there is evidence that preaching and giving verbal instructions to people as to how they ought to behave can also affect their later altruism.

chapter 6

THE FAMILY: THE PRIMARY SOCIALIZER

In virtually every society in human history it is the family that is the pivotal institution, the building block of society. The family, like religion, is a universal human institution that dates back to the dawn of prehistory. The family has been found everywhere presumably because it performs certain vital functions that help maintain the survival of the society's members. Of these functions the most vital are the reproduction of the next generation. Under this rubric would occur (1) the actual biological reproduction of the next generation, (2) the status placement of the child, (3) the maintenance of the child, (4) child training or socialization, (5) the provision of sexual controls, and (6) the burial of the dead. This chapter will be concerned with the family's role in training the child to be a socialized member of his or her community, with particular concern for his or her regard for others.

Chapter 5 outlined some of the most important principles of which we are aware so far by which human behavior changes. A number of laboratory studies were discussed that exemplified these principles, showing how they influenced altruistic and prosocial behaviors. This chapter will examine a quite different set of studies—those which examined socialization processes directly in the family.

The studies reported in chapter 5 were laboratory studies. Such studies are extremely useful for investigating directly the processes felt to govern human social learning—analogous perhaps to physiologists studying cardiovascular functioning in the laboratory. Since, however, the whole purpose of doing laboratory studies is to generalize the principles discovered there to the real world (just as physiologists studying heart functioning in the laboratory wish to generalize their findings to the real world), it becomes of interest to see to what extent this does occur. Can the processes discovered in the laboratory also be found in studies carried out with real families? This chapter will consider this question and will conclude that (a) learning through the observation of what others do, found in the experimental studies, also is observed in the correlational studies about to be described; and (b) that parental discipline has very powerful effects on how altruistic the children grow up to be. On the other hand, it is also evident that many techniques found in the correlational studies in the naturalistic setting of the family are not readily confirmed by studies in the laboratory. For example, the use of reasoning techniques, which are a part of the child-rearing practices of most parents, are not always found to be as efficacious in the well-controlled laboratory experiment. It is not always the case, therefore, that the results from laboratory and naturalistic studies will neatly complement each other.

The second part of this chapter will examine whether the family can continue to remain the primary socializer of children it still is, perhaps, even today. Many data will be studied that suggest that the family is beginning to break up. Indeed, the strong claim shall be made that the family is increasingly no longer an effective socializer of children in North American society. Furthermore, unless we take active steps in the immediate future to compensate, we are in danger of producing a generation of undersocialized adults who may have many problems in keeping our society together.

SOCIALIZATION IN THE FAMILY

For the moment let us turn to naturalistic studies of family socialization influences on children's moral and prosocial behavior. Such studies perhaps can be usefully divided into two types. The first is that in which the investigator gains his or her information about parental practices from the parents and information about the children's altruism from the children. In other words, these data sources of parental discipline, on the one hand, and children's altruism, on the other, are independent of each other. The second type of investigation obtains both sets of data from the same source, and that is the child himself or herself. Let us consider the evidence from the first type of investigation.

Altruism and Parent Discipline
Assessed Separately.

One very important series of studies of the effects of parental discipline techniques on children's consideration for others was done by Professor Martin Hoffman at the University of Michigan. One early study carried out at a nursery school in Detroit was reported in two separate papers (Hoffman 1960, 1963). The naturally occurring play behavior of twenty-two working-class and middle-class children was observed over three separate half-hour periods and coded into two categories of altruism. The first, *consideration for others,* was showing concern for the feelings of others in a variety of ways while interacting socially. The second, *giving affection,* was directly hugging and kissing others and making friendly greetings. At the same time, three measures of "antisocial" behavior were scored: *hostility, power-assertiveness,* and *resisting influence.*

Having measured the prosocial behavior of the children toward their peers, the next step was to see what the parental disciplinary techniques were that accompanied these behaviors. In order to do this Hoffman (1960, 1963), interviewed the mothers in depth about their typical interactions with their children by asking them what had happened on the day before the interview. Intensive probing elicited highly detailed material on a number of parent-child interactions. A three-part scheme was used: (1) what did the child do that differed from the mother's desire? (2) what was the mother's technique for dealing with this discrepancy between her desires and her child's behavior? and (3) what was the child's reaction to the mother's influence technique? From these interviews it was possible to code the mother's disciplinary techniques into a number of categories: power assertion (use of threats and physical force), consequence oriented ("Don't do it because . . .") and other-oriented consequences ("Don't do it because of the hurt it will cause another"). In addition, a score for the mother was obtained concerning how much she accepted the child. This was based on the percentage of time spent playing with the child and engaging in other nondisciplinary interactions.

What were the findings from this study? The clearest was that parents who "accepted" their children as measured by playing games with them and giving them lots of affection, produced children who in their play behavior gave lots of positive affection to their peers—a relationship that held for both the middle-class and working-class samples (Hoffman 1963). A number of interpretations of this finding are possible, but perhaps the most obvious and straightforward one is based on observational learning: Those parents who model affection and acceptance for their children produce children who have learned that showing affection and acceptance toward others is the appropriate way to act toward others in nonconflict situations. A second finding from these studies was that parental use of aggression toward their children through unqualified reactive power assertion (parents shouting and physically abusing their children) produced children who were aggressive toward their peers (Hoffman 1960)—another clear modeling effect. Behaving affectionately toward children (and, therefore, modeling affectionate behavior) results in children who are affectionate toward others, and behaving aggressively toward children (and, therefore, modeling aggressive behavior) produces children who are aggressive toward others. These initial findings dovetail perfectly with those from the laboratory studies described earlier and strengthen our conclusions about the importance of modeling to children's social development.

Power assertion did more than just produce aggressive children. It also seemed to make the children view the parent negatively and to attempt to escape from him or her. It also made parental use of other techniques such as reasoning much less effective. Hoffman (1963) divided the children into those whose parents used a lot of reactive power assertion and those who used only a little. After splitting the sample in this manner he then looked at the effects of parental use of the consequence-oriented and other-oriented reasoning techniques mentioned earlier on the children's consideration for others in the naturally occurring play situations also described earlier. For those parents who had a low frequency of use of power assertion, use of both reasoning strategies correlated very highly with the children's consideration for others. Such reasoning strategies did not work with mothers who frequently used power assertion. The importance of modeling suggests that by not reacting assertively to the child's transgressions but rather reasoning to the child about the consequences of his or her actions for others, the parent presents a model of both self-restraint and consideration for others. Once such consideration for others has been instituted, inasmuch as it is rewarding to others, positive reactions are likely to result from the child's peers, and thus the considerate behavior will be maintained by peer approval. In other words, the child's behavior then can become independent of the original parental socialization techniques.

Later studies tended to confirm these earlier findings in regard to the positive effects of modeling and reasoning on the child. In a large study conducted by Hoffman and Saltzstein (1967), more than four hundred working- and middle-class boys and girls, twelve years old, were assessed on a variety of moral characteristics including, for example, how much guilt they typically showed after they had done something wrong, and how developed their sense of moral judgment was. Of more direct concern here is that they also were assessed on how considerate of others they were. This was measured by asking all the children in the class to nominate the boys and girls "most likely to care about other children's feelings" and "most likely to defend a child being made fun of by the group."

Data on parental discipline were assessed by asking both children and parents to imagine a variety of transgressions by the child (for example, the child delaying doing what the parent requested, or the child being careless and destroying something of value) and then reporting how the parent was likely to react to such a situation. The disciplinary techniques then were coded into three main categories. The first, *power assertion*, as before, refers to control by physical power such as using threats, physical punishment, and directly depriving the child of material possessions. The second, *love withdrawal*, included isolating the child and ignoring and refusing to speak to him or her. The third technique, which Hoffman and Saltzstein (1967) called *induction*, consisted of reasoning with the child and, in particular, explaining the painful consequences of the child's act both for him- or herself and for others.

In general, for guilt and moral judgment, Hoffman and Salzstein (1967) concluded that for these older children, too, advanced moral development was associated with infrequent use of power assertion and frequent use of induction among the middle-class sample. These relations did not hold for the children from the working-class homes. For consideration of others, however, we must qualify the results even further. First, they held primarily for girls (of both classes) rather than for boys. Second, the disruptive effects of power assertion found in the Hoffman (1963) study were not found here. Indeed, for boys (again of both classes), power assertion by parents was *positively* related to consideration for others. It is the results from this latter study that are the most suspect. Here children and parents responded to hypothetical transgressions rather than to actual ones. Responses to hypothetical situations raise serious questions about their representativeness.

A much more directly linked and clear effect of the role of parental modeling was demonstrated in a subsequent investigation. Hoffman (1975a) studied eighty ten-year-old boys and girls. This time they all were affluent, middle-class children from a suburb of Detroit. Again they were rated by their peers on measures of altruism. This consisted, once more, of asking each child which children would (a) care about how other children feel, and (b) stick up for a child of whom the others were making fun. The child's altruism score consisted of the sum of his or her scores on both of these questions. Interestingly enough, this composite score also was significantly related to a teacher's rating of considerateness, thus indicating that the perception of which were the most altruistic children was shared by both the children and the teacher. Hoffman (1975a) then interviewed both of the child's parents. The first measure taken from the interviews was of parental modeling of altruism. Parents were asked to rank eighteen values in order of importance in their own value systems. These included values like "showing consideration of other's feelings," "putting work before play," and "going out of one's way to help other people." The assumption was that parents who placed a high value on the altruistic items would be the ones who provided good models of altruism for their children. A second measure was taken of how parents handled their children's transgressions that caused harm to others. Of primary importance here was the degree to which the parent used "victim-centered discipline," pointing out the negative consequences for others. A final measure was taken of the amount of parental affection provided.

The results of this study were quite evident. Those parents who espoused or modeled altruistic values were the ones whose children were judged by both their teacher and their peers to be the most considerate of others. Once again, parental use of inductive reasoning or pointing out the negative consequences for the victim was associated with altruistic behavior in children.

The three studies discussed so far studied the child-rearing practices of the parent and the altruistic behavior of the children independently and found positive *correlations* between the two that suggested that parents who provide reasoning, restraint, and altruistic values serve as models of altruism for their children. This conclusion fits with the laboratory experimental research discussed earlier. As is widely known, however, it is not strictly possible to infer a causal relationship from a correlation. Thus, if altruistic children are found to have altruistic mothers, it is logically quite possible to conceive of the causality as being either (a) that children who behave altruistically cause their mothers to behave more nurturingly, affectionately, and reasonably with them (rather than the other way around), or (b) that there is some third, uncontrolled factor that accounts for both the mother's and the child's altruism, for example, a loving, affectionate father who induces good moods in both of them. Strictly speaking, one cannot infer causality from these correlational relationships between parental disciplinary techniques and children's behavior. Hoffman (1975b) argued forcefully that it makes far more sense, in these studies at least, to see the causal line stemming from parent to child than any of the other possibilities. First, parents usually have much more power to influence their children rather than the other way around. Second, there is no actual evidence for "third factors" operating (although this does not rule them out as possibilities). Finally, it is in accord with theoretical predictions that the causal relation runs from parent to child, and this final argument, especially when combined with all the laboratory experimental research findings, must hold if it becomes necessary to make a judgment. It is not necessary, though, to assume an extreme, undirectional view of familial interactions. In earliest phases of development, parents may exercise substantial influence over infants, but most interaction patterns reflect the operation of reciprocal influences between parents and children.

Even if we do decide that there is a direct causal link between the use of, say, inductive reasoning techniques and altruism, it still is not clear what the "active ingredient" in the disciplinary technique is. Hoffman (1975b) argued that by using induction and by pointing out the consequences of behavior for others the child's attention is focused on the distress of others, thus eliciting natural (unlearned?) empathy. But it also is possible that if induction techniques do include a punishment component they then will work by providing the child with a classical conditioning situation in which his or her own distress at receiving parental disapproval is paired ideationally with negative consequences for another. This would eventually lead to the observing of negative consequences of another resulting in unpleasant feelings in the child that he or she then could try to alleviate in a number of ways. Responding altruistically would be only one; derogating the victim would be a second. Such a paradigm was expounded by Aronfreed (1970), and experimental analogue evidence was provided. A third possibility is that by reasoning with the child the parents affect how the child comes to view himself or herself, which in turn affects the child's behavior by influencing how he or she then evaluates himself or herself for living up to such a view. Certainly attributions about the self and one's motives for altruism have been shown to affect children's sharing behavior (Grusec and others 1978). A fourth view is that it is mediated by modeling and reinforcement. Parents who point out the harmful consequences of actions for others are those who themselves behave altruistically and who reinforce altruism in their children. Certainly the disciplinary technique they use is showing concern for others. It is unfortunate that Hoffman (1975a) did not report the intercorrelations between his measure of having altruistic values and using other-oriented induction. Although the active ingredient in the three studies discussed so far has not been isolated, and in any case causal relations here can be inferred less well than from experimental studies, it is clear in these studies that parents *do* influence their children's behavior. Additional evidence is gained from a consideration of the next set of studies. These are the studies from which the investigator infers the parental disciplinary techniques only from the children's responses.

Altruism and Parent Correlates
as Seen by the Altruist.

Rutherford and Mussen (1968) carried out a study to test two hypotheses: (1) that boys' generosity would be related to perceptions of their fathers as warm, nurturing and altruistic toward them, and (2) that generosity was part of a pattern of moral characteristics, including altruism, kindness, and cooperation. A generosity score was found for each child based on the number of candies given away to a friend. On this basis the initial sample of sixty-three middle-class four-year-old boys was divided into fourteen nongenerous children who gave away no candies at all and seventeen highly generous children who gave away a large proportion of their candies. Generally, teachers rated the generous children as more generous, more gregarious, less competitive, less quarrelsome, more kind, and less aggressive than the nongenerous children were. In addition, a behavioral measure of competitiveness based on a car-racing game showed the generous group to be less competitive than the nongenerous group was. Twenty-two of these children (twelve generous and ten nongenerous boys) then responded to a number of objectively-scored, semistructured, projective doll-play situations administered by an experimenter using a standardized set of instructions. An example of these situations is the following:

Scene—In the house, parent dolls are in their bed, and the child doll is in his. *Instructions*—It's late at night. Everyone is asleep. Suddenly the boy has a bad dream and wakes up frightened. What do you think he will do? Show me.

In this situation it is assumed that how the child portrays the father doll as behaving reflects his own father's actual behavior, and that the child who describes the doll father as nurturing considers his own father to be nurturing, and so on. Each of 154 situations was then scored on a number of dimensions, the most important of which was the father's or the mother's nurturance. This required the doll child receiving help, attention, or reassurance from the father or the mother. Other indices scored were how much sympathy the father or mother doll gave directly to a child in distress and how much generosity and hostility the doll-child hero showed in his interactions. It now was possible to test directly the hypothesis that the highly generous boys (as measured earlier in the candy sharing) would have fathers who were perceived as behaving nurturingly and altruistically toward them. The data supported that view: The mean father-nurturance score of the highly generous boys was significantly higher than that of the nongenerous boys. Still another finding from the doll-play data is pertinent to the hypothesis. Only six subjects told stories in which the father comforted a child in distress (e.g., holding a hurt child). All six of these boys were in the highly generous group. Although based on only a few subjects, the data indicate that fathers of generous boys, in addition to modeling help, attention, and reassurance for their children, also were more likely to model sympathy and comforting for the child. In other words, the father-dolls were portrayed by the highly generous boys as models of altruistic behavior. It must be remembered that no assessments of the real father's actual behavior were made, so it is impossible to tell whether the generous boys' fathers were, in fact, more nurturing and generous.

Dlugokinski and Firestone (1974) studied 164 children aged eleven and fourteen attending a suburban Catholic school in the Detroit area. Data collection was from three contacts over a one-month period. In the initial session, scales assessing parental styles of discipline were administered. This was the same as used in the Hoffman and Saltzstein (1967) study discussed earlier. Children were asked to imagine how their mothers would handle a number of disciplinary situations (e.g., the child carelessly destroying property), and the child's responses were coded into the perhaps now familiar styles of either power assertion or induction (reasoning to the child about the consequences of his or her actions for others). In the following two sessions the children completed four tasks that measured their "other centeredness." One of these was a peer-rating measure in which the children nominated each other as being the kindest and most considerate. A second was a behavioral measure of how much money (out of fifty cents they had earned for taking part in the experiment) they donated to a charitable organization. A third measure was of how the children understood the meaning of kindness, and a fourth was a self-report scale on values, ranking in order of personal importance twelve statements, such as "having a beautiful home and car" and "getting a job that helps other people." From such a ranking it was possible to see how other-centered as opposed to self-centered the person's values were. From these measures it appeared as though there was a trait of altruism operating, because the children who were high on one measure tended to be high on the others. Of more importance, however, is the fact that on each age level studied and for both sexes, the children who reported that their mothers frequently used induction in discipline were regarded as more considerate by their classmates, attached greater importance to other-centered values, and donated more of their earnings to charity. By contrast, the perceived use of power assertion by the mother was associated with predominantly self-centered values and stinginess in donations.

London (1970) studied twenty-seven very real adult altruists—twenty-seven Christians who risked their lives during World War II in an effort to rescue Jews from the Nazis. Although somewhat anecdotal in nature, the data left the investigators with three quite definite impressions of the characteristics of these rescuers. The first two such characteristics were a spirit of adventurousness and a feeling of being socially marginal. Of more importance was the third characteristic. Almost all the rescuers tended to have a very strong identification with a parental model, not necessarily of the same sex, and this model tended to be a very strong "moralist." London (1970) described the contents of an interview with one of the German rescuers, which makes this clear:

"I come from a poor family. My mother came from Hesse which was mainly small farmers . . . I believe that is part of my personality. You inherit something from your parents, from the grandparents. My mother said to me when we were small, and even when we were bigger, she said to me—she ran the family, my mother, and my father was number two; he could not speak so much in front of people—'Regardless of what you do with your life, be honest. When it comes the day you have to make a decision, make the right one. It could be a hard one. But even the hard ones should be the right ones.' I didn't know what it means . . ." He went on to talk about his mother in glowing terms, about how she had told him how to live, how she had taught him morals, and how she had exemplified morality for him. Asked if she was a member of a church, "Sure, we had to be," he said. "Protestant?" we asked. "Lutheran Protestant—that is another thing. Protest is Protestant. I protest. Maybe I inherit it from way back . . . my mother . . . always in life she gave me so much philosophy. She didn't go to high school, only elementary school, but so smart a woman, wisdom, you know. It is born in you . . ." When he later described his father at greater length, he said his father was weak and incapable of raising the children, that his father did not set the moral standards for the family, and that his father's moral posture was not significant for the family, only his mother's. (London 1970, p. 247)

Interestingly, Rosenhan (1970), who analyzed in depth thirty-six American civil rights activists of the late 1950s obtained findings very similar to London's. First, it will be good to remind ourselves that times have changed greatly since the late 1950s in the area of civil rights for American minority persons. At that time, for either black or white activists to drive hundreds of miles into the Deep South on behalf of the blacks living there in an attempt to end segregation —the "freedom riders" and the "sit-ins"—was a highly dangerous undertaking, resulting often in violence against the civil rights workers. Many civil rights workers were beaten; some were murdered. What motivated the activists to expend the effort and energy and often money as well, to lay their lives on the line for the cause in which they believed? Rosenhan (1970) divided his activists into two types, the *fully committed* who were active for a year or longer, and the *partially committed* who limited their activities to only one or two freedom rides or marches.

There were two major differences in the socialization histories of the fully committed as opposed to the partially committed civil rights workers. First, the fully committed were more likely to report a very warm, emotionally positive bond with one or both of their parents than were the partially committed. Second, one or both of the parents of the fully committed were themselves fully committed to an altruistic cause during some extended period of the respondents' formative years. This latter was much less true of the partially committed. Even greater support for the modeling effect comes from the finding that the types of altruism in which the parents of the fully committed engaged also were very often of a sociopolitical nature—indeed of a left-liberal sociopolitical nature, for example, anti-Fascist fighters during the Spanish Civil War.

Studies of student activists in the anti-Vietnam War movement of the 1960s also reveal that the activists were largely modeling their behavior after the values of their parents who often exhibited humanitarian concerns. This is quite contrary to the popular belief that student protesters were rebelling *against* their parents' values. In comparative studies of political orientation, for example, nonactivists and their fathers were typically found to endorse conservative political positions, whereas activists and their fathers tended to espouse liberal views (Flacks 1967). In addition, there was evidence from the same study that students who were disposed to militant action had received greater parental reinforcement for the self-expression of strong self-assertive behavior. The five studies discussed in this section, therefore, support the conclusions from the three studies discussed in the previous section: Parental practice, and particularly modeling, is a forceful determinant of the acquisition and development of prosocial behavior in offspring.

The Importance of Parental Love.

Before leaving this section of natural socialization in the family, we should examine the effects of parental nurturance. It very often is suggested in child-development literature that warm, loving parents are necessary for the child's adequate growth. Frequently love and nurturance are seen as almost like vitamins or mother's milk, whose absence will produce children in some way deficient in their psychological functioning. It often is suggested, for example, that loving nurturance in parents is necessary for adequate moral development in children and, in the context of altruistic behavior, necessary to produce altruistic children who feel concern for others. What is the evidence for this idea? And, if it is true, what are the mechanisms by which it works?

One set of laboratory studies was discussed in the last chapter (pages 103 to 105). In those studies, children were exposed to either a nurturing or a non-nurturing model for a few minutes before seeing the model acting generously or not. The results were equivocal. Indeed, it was suggested that nurturance may lead to "permissive" behavior such that the child does just what he or she feels like doing, and what he or she feels like doing can just as easily be selfish as generous.

Let us now turn to the studies of socialization in the natural setting. First, let us consider the studies that assessed the parent's disciplinary styles independently from assessing the children's altruism. Hoffman (1963) found that maternal affection had an effect on how affectionate toward others the nursery school children were. Such affection did not, however, influence children's nonaffectionate, altruistic behavior toward other children. Hoffman and Saltzstein (1967), on the other hand, discovered that maternal affection did relate to their thirteen-year-old children's consideration for others as judged by peers. At least, this relationship held in the middle-class sample but held for lower-class children only when parental affection was measured by the children's reports. Finally Hoffman (1975a) found that maternal affection was related to ten-year-old boys' altruism, although not to that of the same-age girls. From these studies, then, there is evidence for a link between maternal affection and the offspring's altruism. (We should note that an absence of relation was found between *father's* affection and the offspring's altruism in both Hoffman and Saltzstein 1967 and Hoffman 1975a.)

When we examine the studies in which altruistic persons themselves are asked to report on how affectionate or nurturing their parents were, we find that in almost all cases they report that their parents were affectionate and nurturing (Hoffman & Saltzstein 1967; Rosenhan 1970; Rutherford & Mussen 1968). The one exception was the Christians who rescued Jews from the Nazis (London 1970).

Considering all the data together it seems reasonable to conclude that there *is* a relationship between nurturing parents and altruistic offspring. The question then becomes: What are the mechanisms by which they are related? There appear to be at least six possibilities. The first is to imagine that the nurturance is contingent upon behavior. Once love becomes contingent upon behavior, however, we have gone past the concept of nurturance and are into the realm of positive reinforcement. One of the confusions over the effects of "mother-love" might well be clarified by considering a distinction between contingent and non-contingent effects. Certainly the more affection there is, the more powerful the reinforcement will be (being hugged and kissed might generally be thought more reinforcing than just a verbal "well done"). It might also be that totally noncontingent warmth, in the absence of any disciplinary encounters, will lead to highly self-indulgent offspring. Inasmuch as all behaviors by the offspring lead to love and approval (even selfish behaviors), then no socialization pressures are occurring to select some behaviors over others. Of course, it is very difficult to imagine such totally noncontingent warmth being given, although the author has personally seen lay therapists attempting to smile and "love" autistic children who were smashing valued objects on a table and then kicking the therapist. (When questioned the therapist asserted that the child was acting disruptively because it was afraid of her love and that the answer was to give more unwavering love, not less!)

A second possibility to explain the relationship between maternal affection and children's altruism is to view the provision of nurturance and affection as modeling altruism to the child. The way in which a parent behaves toward a child may well be the first examples of "altruism" that the child receives. Being kind, affectionate, and sympathetic is showing consideration for others. One of the implications of such behavior is that it is likely to be imitated by the child in dealing with others, and the research evidence seems to support this (see especially Hoffman 1963).

A third effect of nurturance, it might be argued, is to make the socializing parent a more acceptable figure to the child when the parent disciplines the child. Knowing that the parent basically loves him or her presumably causes the child to listen more to what the parent is saying, for example. Thus, techniques based on reasoning can be effective. Hoffman (1975b) elaborated upon this view at some length, pointing out how reasoning, unlike other techniques, leads the child to focus his or her attentions on the consequences for others rather than on the punitive consequences for him or herself. It has also been argued that for reasoning to be effective it must be backed up by fear of punishment (Walters & Grusec 1977). By this account, nurturance of a noncontingent sort might well result in reasoning techniques being *less* effective. The evidence in favor of this argument is not complete, although many studies (e.g., Baumrind 1975) support the Walters and Grusec position. In a review of many of her studies, Baumrind (1975) concluded that "authoritative" mothers (i.e., those who would use power assertion when it became necessary to gain compliance), produced more socially responsible, self-controlled and independent offspring than mothers who were either "permissive" or "authoritarian."

A fourth mechanism would be that nurturance has positive effects upon the child's conception of him- or herself. In this analysis, children learn to view themselves as worth loving because others love them. Evidence discussed in chapter 4 suggested that people who felt good about themselves were more likely to show consideration for others than those who did not. In this view, parental nurturance leads to a positive self-concept which then leads to an increment in altruism.

Finally, there are two quite indirect possibilities for the positive correlations. Both of these deny the causal relationship of maternal nurturance leading to children's altruism. They are included here for the sake of completion. The first possibility is that the link is genetic. Genetically altruistic parents behave nurturantly, and their genetically related children engage in altruism. Both behave similarly because of the genes they have in common. The second possibility is that there is a causal relationship but that it runs the other way. Children who, for whatever reason, are altruistic, elicit more love and affection from their parents.

There is no need to view the above list of possibilities as exhaustive. Nor is it necessary to assume that only one of the above mechanisms is implicated. They all may be operative. In regard to future research considerations, however, it is interesting to attempt to disentangle the causal effects. One problem with all the correlational studies discussed in this chapter is the lack of clear control in them. Researchers take relatively global assessments of parental disciplinary styles, for example, parental nurturance, use of inductive reasoning, and use of reactive power assertion, and then correlate these with specific indices of child behavior. The problem is that we do not know what the intercorrelations themselves are among these indices, and further, what the active ingredients of these procedures are. If, for example, we found that the more "authoritative" parents were those who were also the most loving toward their children when the children were good, the most punitive toward their children when the children were bad, the highest in the use of verbal reasoning techniques and the ones who most exemplified self-regulatory morality in their behavior, how would we know which of these parental attributes were the important ones?

Perhaps modeling alone is quite sufficient. It would seem that the only way to answer these questions is to do experiments in laboratory settings so that the various permutations and combinations of disciplinary techniques can be re-created. If such laboratory studies are conducted with sufficient concern for demand characteristics, the artificiality of the situation, and assessment of longer term and generalization effects, there seems no reason why they cannot continue to be the extremely useful tools they have been in the past. Ideally, of course, both laboratory and naturalistic studies will continue to be used to complement each other.

Our conclusion then must be that parents are vitally important agents of socialization for their children. The family system acts as a primary socializer of children's behavior, the effects of which have been found to show up even years later when the children are adults in their own right (London 1970; Rosenhan 1970).

THE BREAKUP
OF THE TRADITIONAL FAMILY

This chapter started with the statement that the family system was society's traditional building block and that one of its key roles was to socialize the young. This undoubtedly has been true for at least the last ten thousand years of human history. It is evident, however, that during the last three or four hundred years the family system has been undergoing drastic change. With the advent of industrialization came the breakup of the traditional extended family system. This occurred first in Western Europe and North America but has, during the last few years, also occurred wherever heavy industrialization has taken place—Eastern Europe, Japan, and, even more recently, in certain parts of West Africa. With the necessity for rapid geographical mobility by the labor force (particularly managerial), even contacts with the other members of the family have become fewer. What are the consequences of these effects for child socialization? I shall make the strong claim that *the family is increasingly a less effective socializer of children in North American society and that unless we soon take active steps to find alternatives, we are in danger of producing a generation of undersocialized children.*

Perhaps the strongest evidence for this assertion comes from the extremely well documented work of Dr. Urie Bronfenbrenner, professor of human development and family studies at Cornell University. In a series of dramatic and relatively self-explanatory graphs, Bronfenbrenner (1975) displayed pictorially this increasing disintegration of the family and its role as a socializer of children. Bronfenbrenner (1975) collated the statistics from such U.S. government publications as *Current Population Reports* and *Special Labor Force Reports* over a twenty-five-year period to illuminate the dramatic trends taking place.

First, Bronfenbrenner (1975) pointed out the rapid increase in the number of working mothers over the last thirty years. The trends shown in Figure 6.1 are applicable only to intact families in which the husband was present. The proportions in the labor force of single parents is even higher, as we soon shall see. From Figure 6.1 we can see that in 1948, 26 percent of married women with children from six to seventeen were engaged in seeking work; in 1974 the figure was up to 51 percent.

Not only have more mothers been going out to work, but in addition there has been a rapidly decreasing number of (nonparental) adults in the home who could care for the children (e.g., grandparents, maiden aunts, etc.). Figure 6.2 graphs this decrease.

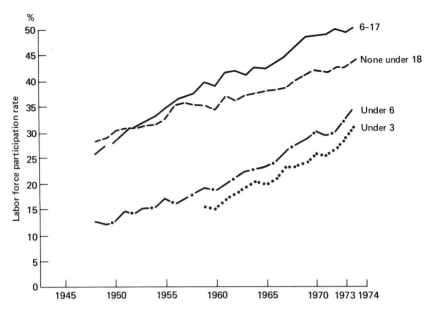

Figure 6-1 Labour Force Participation Rates for Married Women by Presence and Age of Children. 1948-1973. (Source for Figures 6-1 through 6-8: Bronfenbrenner, "Reality and Research in the Ecology of Human Development," *Proceedings of the American Philosophical Society,* 1975, *119,* 439-69.

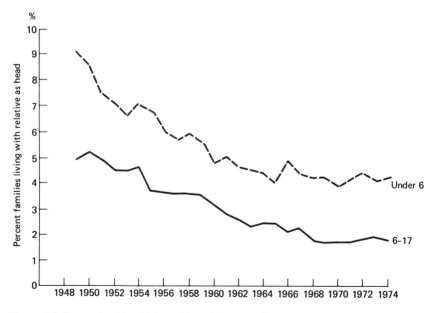

Figure 6-2 Parent Families Living with a Relative as Family Head as a Percentage of all Families with children under 6 and 6 through 17 Years of Age.

Even more striking is the fact that, as Bronfenbrenner noted: *"The adult relatives who have been disappearing from families include the parents themselves"* (1975, p. 441, italics added). Figure 6.3 demonstrates the marked rise in the proportion of families with only one parent present. At the time of writing, *one out of every six children under eighteen years of age is living in a single-parent family.* Furthermore, 90 percent of the children live with their single parent alone; that is, there are no other adults in the home. In addition, the majority of such parents with school age children also are at work (67 percent). Even among single-parent mothers with children under three years of age, 45 percent are in the labor force. The divorce rate is undoubtedly one of the factors leading to the increase in single-parent families, and for Americans it is now estimated that one in three marriages will end in divorce. Bronfenbrenner's figures also show that the remarriage rate, especially for single women with children, lags considerably behind the divorce rate. Of perhaps even more concern is the increase in illegitimacy, particularly the illegitimacy ratio (illegitimate births per one thousand live births). These rates appear in Figure 6.4.

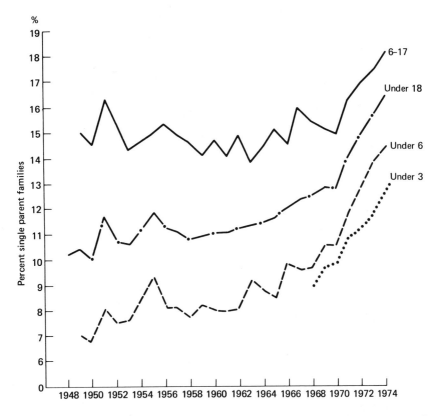

Figure 6-3 Single Parent Families as a Percentage of all Families with Children under 18, under 6, and 6 through 17 Years of Age.

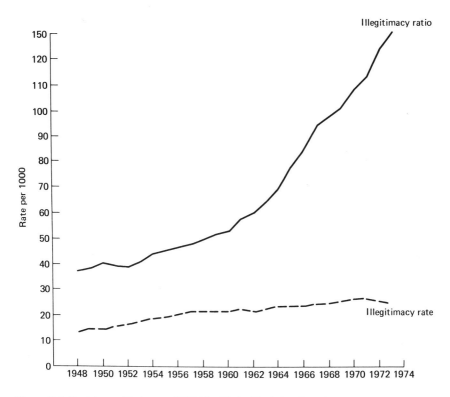

Figure 6-4 Illegitimate Births per 1000 Live Births (Ratio) and per 1000 Unmarried Women (Rate). 1948-1973.

Bronfenbrenner went further than providing indices of what he called the "progressive fragmentation of the American family" (1975, p. 442). He also indicated that the consequences for children are enormous and linked the lack of family members who care for the children to a variety of social ills, such as the drop in academic abilities (see Figure 6.5) and the increases in child suicide rates (Figure 6.6), adolescent suicide rates (Figure 6.7), and juvenile delinquency (Figure 6.8).

After completing his study, Bronfenbrenner called for radical changes:

> How are we to reverse these debilitating trends? If our analysis is correct, what is called for is nothing less than a change in our way of life and our institutions, both public and private, so as to give new opportunity and status for parenthood, and to bring children and adults back into each other's lives. Specifically, we need to develop a variety of *support systems* for families, and for others engaged in the care of the nation's children. (1975, p. 460).

If the thesis advanced here is correct and if these trends increase rather than decrease, as seems most likely, what will happen to the socialization proces-

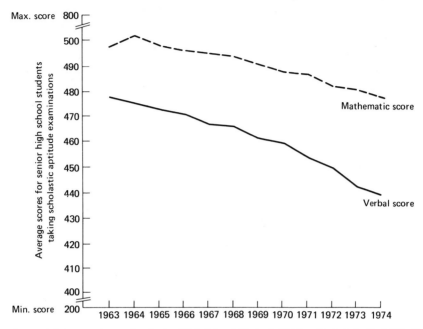

Figure 6-5 Average Scores for Senior High School Students Taking the Scholastic Aptitude Examinations. 1963-1974.

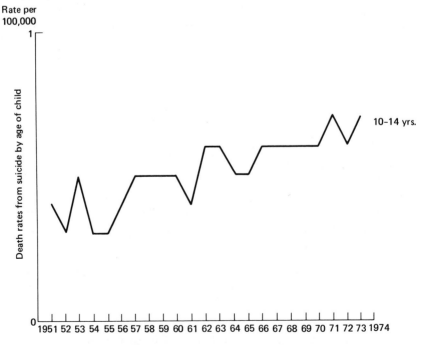

Figure 6-6 Death Rates from Suicide by Age of Child. 1951-1973.

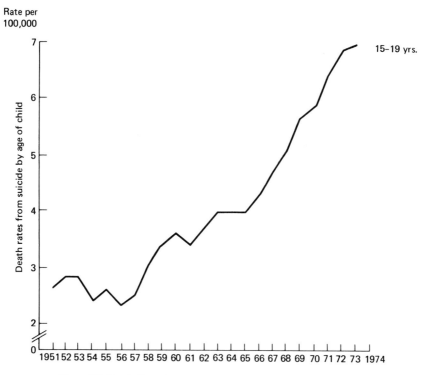

Figure 6-7 Death Rates from Suicide by Age of Child. 1951-1973.

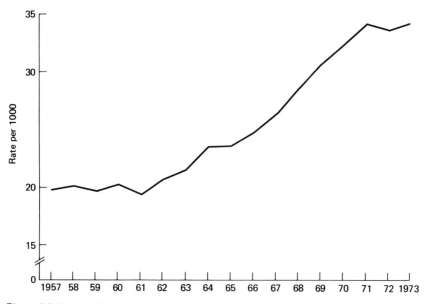

Figure 6-8 Rate of Delinquency Cases Disposed of by Juvenile Courts Involving Children 10 through 17 Years of Age. 1957-1973.

131

ses outlined earlier in the chapter? It will take very little stretch of the imagination to see that parents will cease to be effective socializers of their children. Instead, that role will be taken over by the child's peer group and by the other institutions of society. Before returning to the problem of "What is to be done?", two other major societal institutions that socialize children—the mass media and the educational system—must be considered.

SUMMARY

Traditionally, the family is the primary socializer of children. Certainly many of the processes of social learning, explicated in the last chapter, are to be found taking place there. Two categories of studies have been carried out into the natural socialization of children in the family. The first is that in which the investigator gains his or her information about parental practices from the parents, and information about the children's altruism from the children. The second type of investigation obtains both sets of data from the same source—the child himself or herself. The conclusion from both sets of studies is that parents are vitally important agents of socialization for their children. Children learn appropriate rules of behavior in their early years which even show up years later when the children are adults.

With the advent of industrialization, however, has come the breakup of the traditional extended family. During very recent years even the nuclear family is in a process of disintegration and today one in six children in the United States is being raised in a single-parent home. Furthermore, the majority of these single parents are at work during the day. Even among single parents with children under three years of age, 45 percent are in the labor force. Given that fewer adults are in the home to socialize the children, I shall make the strong claim that *the family is increasingly a less effective socializer of children in North American society and that unless we soon take active steps to find alternatives, we are in danger of producing a generation of undersocialized children.*

chapter 7

THE MASS MEDIA

In chapter 5 we examined how one of the primary ways in which human beings internalize the norms and emotional responses that they have with regard to others is through observational learning. One of the most important implications of this pertains to television. If one of the main ways in which people learn is by observing others, then it follows that people should learn a great deal from viewing others on television. Television provides people with access to a very wide range of observational learning experiences. By simply sitting in front of their television sets in their own living rooms, individuals can observe a vast array of other persons behaving in response to a variety of situations that may be either novel or familiar to the observers and thereby can learn about things well beyond their own direct experience. In this way television can have quite diverse effects. It is capable of promoting valued cognitive and social development. Because of the prevalence of aggressive modeling, however, it also can be an important disinhibitor and teacher of antisocial styles of behavior. This becomes a matter of social concern when we realize how most of the characters on television behave.

Many surveys have demonstrated that the overwhelming majority of North American television programs portray characters who use violence in order to solve their difficulties. Gerbner and Gross (1976) in their survey, for example, showed that eight out of ten programs contain violence (and nine out of ten weekend children's-hour programs) and that six or seven out of every ten leading characters are involved in that violence. It has been estimated that between the ages of five and fifteen, the average person (including children) would see the violent destruction of more than 13,400 characters on television, as well as several hundred violent rapes and assaults. Williams, Zabrack, and Joy (1977) discovered that even many situational comedies contain a large aggressive component. Forty percent depicted psychological aggression in the form of verbal abuse and sarcasm.

Furthermore, this violence is watched. The results of various investigations show (a) that almost every family has at least one television set; (b) that the television is turned on for almost six hours per day in the average household; (c) that both children and adults see, on the average, over three hours of television daily; (d) that about 40 percent of all leisure time is spent with television; and (e) that television ranks third (behind sleep and work) as a consumer of time (*Ontario* 1977). Of concern too are the figures relating to children. Children begin watching television on a regular basis three or four years before entering first grade, and most children watch television every day. It has been estimated that by the time the average person is sixteen years of age he or she will have spent more time with television than ever will be spent in any kind of classroom. Another comparison might also demonstrate perspective: By the time a child is five and reaches kindergarten, he or she has spent more time watching television than a liberal arts student spends in the classroom throughout his or her four years in university! It follows from all the above that television may well be inadvertently teaching viewers to solve *their* problems and to engage in *their* interpersonal relationships with more physical and psychological violence than they otherwise might do.

Research on the effects of television has been quite extensive ever since this medium made its first appearance (e.g., Himmelweit, Oppenheim, & Vince 1958). As television grew to international prominence, with communication satellites allowing the simultaneous reception of the same event in homes around the world, research also has become increasingly extensive. Many nations have had major government inquiries into television's effects, and researchers have attempted to look at these effects in both national and international contexts (e.g., Murray & Kippax 1979). This chapter will examine the research on the effects of showing both aggressive and prosocial television content to viewers.

THE EFFECT OF PORTRAYING
ANTISOCIAL BEHAVIOR

Case studies.

One case involved a seven year old in Los Angeles who was caught putting ground glass into the family meal. He had seen it on television and now was trying it for himself (Goranson 1977, p. 4). Many examples of similar, direct imitations were collected by Stanley and Riera (1977). One is the film *Fuzz*, shown on television in Boston. The film starred Burt Reynolds as a city detective trying to catch a gang of youths who had been pouring gasoline over old men, described as "winos," and setting them afire. Their motive was described as "to get kicks." Two days after the film was shown, a young woman whose automobile had run out of gasoline was returning from a filling station with a can of gasoline when she was confronted by six youths. After dousing her with gasoline from the can, one of the youths set her afire. The young woman died some four hours later. In Miami, some three weeks later, a wino was sleeping on a bench when four youths poured gaoline over him and set him afire. He died as a result of his burns. The youths, when arrested, admitted to having seen the film, although they denied that was the reason for the attack. These two attacks were of a type previously unknown in the United States. The simultaneous occurrence of the film and the attacks seems unlikely to have been entirely coincidental.

Another case study from Stanley and Riera (1977) concerned incidents in Los Angeles in which individuals robbed banks by attaching bombs to themselves and threatening to detonate them if not given money. A few days before five or six incidents such as these had occurred, three different television programs aired at approximately the same time, had depicted similar events. The television programs were *The Rookies, Ironside,* and *Hawaii Five-O.* No crimes of this type had occurred in Los Angeles before the showing of these films.

The examples are numerous and horrific. In November 1976, an episode of *Kojak* presented the story of a child molestor. The following morning a seventeen-year-old Miami youth raped one seven-year-old and nearly assaulted a second. Members of the Miami police department were struck by the similarity between this crime and that depicted during the previous night's program. They later arrested the youth and in questioning him learned that he was a *Kojak* fan and had seen the previous night's episode.

In the summer of 1966 a student, Charles Whitman, climbed to the top of the observation tower of the Austin campus of the University of Texas. Using a high-powered rifle, he shot and killed fourteen people and wounded thirty-one others before being shot himself by the police. A film was made of this incident and shown on television in Toronto, Canada, ten years later. Approximately two weeks after this film was shown, a psychiatric patient bought a rifle, went to the top of a twenty-four-story apartment building in downtown Toronto, and fired into the street below, injuring five pedestrians. He then turned the rifle on himself and committed suicide. It is known that the institution at which he stayed had shown that particular television program.

A particularly illuminating case concerned a 1966 television film, *Doomsday Flight*. The film concerned a man's attempts to extort money from an airline by means of an altitude-sensitive bomb hidden aboard the plane. The bomb had been set so that it would be primed as the plane passed through a certain altitude and would detonate as the plane descended again through that same altitude. The extortionist telephoned the airline and demanded money in exchange for disclosing the precise whereabouts of the bomb aboard the plane. This film was shown over protests from the Airline Pilots' Association, who strongly objected to its showing on the grounds that it was a blueprint for sabotage. They were quite right. Within one week of the film's release on television, airlines in the United States had received a flood of telephone calls demanding money in the manner depicted in the film. Four years later, in 1970, the film was shown on television in Canada and resulted in a similar incident involving British Airways. In the following year, the same film was shown on Australian television. Its showing was followed within days by a phone call to Quantas Airlines making similar demands (the extortionist received some $560,000; there was, however, no bomb). Incredibly, the film was later shown in Europe, and a Frenchman attempted a similar extortion. (He was arrested.)

During a rerun of the film in the United States, there was another flood of extortion attempts. Such attempts rose from a base line of approximately two per month to an average of sixteen per month for the following two months (Bandura 1973, p. 103). As Bandura indicated, similar frequency data could be collected for preshowing and postshowing rates of other dramatic forms of violence.

Examples from many different types of film are numerous. The film *A Clockwork Orange* was particularly successful in getting imitators for its excitingly packaged, exotically enticing scenario of gang rape and violence. The observation of every parent who has seen his or her child hanging from windows attempting to be *Batman* or *Spiderman* or trying out *Kung Fu* karate blows, is tame by comparison. They too, however, demonstrate the pervasive ubiquity of observational learning from television.

Experimental laboratory studies.

Some people are not persauded by case studies such as those cited above. Some suggest that such imitators were probably criminal or insane to begin with and that "normal" people are not disposed to learn from observation quite so readily. Research has now clearly established, however, that very normal people, including children, adolescents, and adults, learn under quite ordinary circumstances.

A dramatic series of experiments by Bandura and his co-workers has demonstrated how quickly and completely children can learn new forms of aggression. In a typical study, Bandura, Ross, and Ross (1963) showed to one group of nursery school children a film of an adult playing in a very aggressive way. They watched as she hit a large rubber Bobo doll in the head with a hammer, punched it in the face, kicked it about the room, and threw things at it, at the same time saying "Pow, right in the nose" or "Bang" every time the doll was hit. A second group of children did not watch the aggressive adult on the film. After watching the film the children were allowed to play with similar sorts of toys in a playroom. The children were clearly influenced by what they had seen. If the children had seen an adult play aggressively then they too were more likely to beat up and kick the Bobo doll. The children who had not seen an adult play aggressively showed very little inclination to beat up and kick the same Bobo doll. It was very evident that most of the aggression shown by the children in this situation had been learned simply by watching what the adult had done (see Figure 7.1). These results have been replicated in many similar experiments (see Bandura 1973 for a review of these).

Children may learn new techniques of aggression from television, but can they remember these for any appreciable length of time? The results of several studies show that they can. Children in these experiments were shown films of adult or peer aggressors, and their imitative behavior was measured immediately after exposure and again six months later. Immediately after exposure children were able to reproduce more than 70 percent of the modeled aggressive responses. Even more striking was that when the children were tested again after a delay of *six months* without any further exposure to the film, they still produced about 40 percent of the aggressive acts they had seen (Hicks 1965, 1968b).

Viewing at one time does not necessarily lead to immediate enactment of what was learned. Given appropriate incentive, as was shown by Bandura (1965), children may well act on what they have learned on future occasions. Neither are film-violence effects limited to the *acquisition* of novel patterns of aggressive behavior. They also lead people to act on what they previously have learned either by disinhibiting behavior that usually is kept inhibited or by socially facilitating noninhibited behavior. These latter effects were demonstrated by Berkowitz and his colleagues.

In a typical study, Berkowitz and Rawlings (1963) showed university students violent film clips from commercial movies and then allowed them to express anger in another setting (e.g., administering electric shocks to a recalcitrant "learner" peer during an "experiment on learning words under conditions of punishment"). Those students who had watched the violent film sequence expressed far more aggression by giving larger doses of electric shock to their

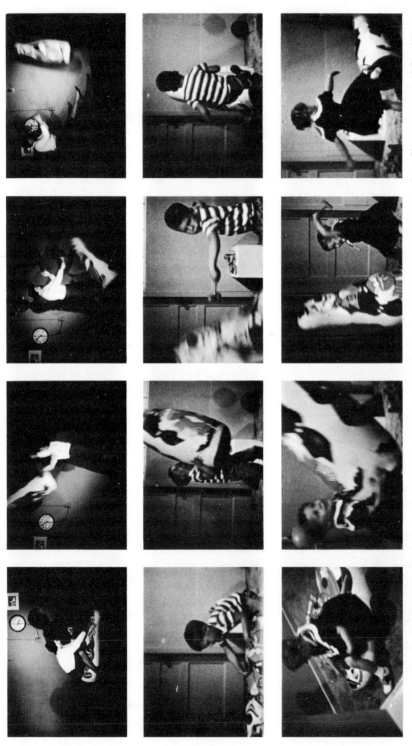

Figure 7-1 Photographs of children imitating the aggressive behavior of the female model they had observed on film. Photo courtesy of Dr. Albert Bandura. (Source: Bandura, A., Ross, D., and Ross, S. A. Imitation of film-mediated aggressive models. *Journal of Abnormal and Social Psychology,* 1963, *66,* p. 8.

peer than those who had not seen the violent film. These results, too, have been well replicated in numerous studies (see Goranson 1970 for a review).

Later studies also produced these latter findings using typical television programming (rather than commercial films) and more typical, "real-life" measures of interpersonal aggression (rather than "laboratory" measures).

Liebert and Baron (1972), for example, showed children standard television fare. The aggressive program consisted of segments drawn from *The Untouchables,* and a neutral program featured a track race. After viewing, the children were placed in a setting in which they could either help or hurt another child by pressing control buttons that would either facilitate or hinder the task behavior of another person in an adjoining room. Children who had viewed the aggressive program demonstrated a greater willingness to hurt another child. Moreover, when the children later were observed during the free-play period, those who had viewed *The Untouchables* exhibited a greater preference for playing with weapons and aggressive toys than did the children who had watched the neutral programming. The problem of better measures of aggressive behavior was addressed by Drabman and Thomas (1974). These researchers assessed children's willingness to intervene in the ongoing disruptive and belligerent behavior of younger children. Children who had witnessed aggressive programs were much slower to intervene than children who had not witnessed the aggressive content. Children who had watched aggressive programs waited until the disruptive behavior had actually escalated into ostensibly serious physical assault before initiating intervention.

No matter how well controlled the experiments, how face-valid the behaviors were or how long the results lasted, some critics will refuse to accept any findings from laboratory studies. Such persons suggest that ubiquitous "demand characteristics" and "experimenter effects" operate to generate artifactual findings not generalizable to the "real world." Such critics suggest that laboratory experiments lack "ecological validity." Thus Silverman (1977), in a wide ranging critique, indicated that ultimately all laboratory findings are suspect because laboratories "are the habitat, in a phenomenological sense, of the experimenter and not the subject" (p. 1).

These criticisms, because they are raised so often, might profitably be addressed here. First, as Barber and Rushton (1975) pointed out, it is simple for an investigator to attribute any phenomenon he or she finds objectionable to the operation of experimenter effects, demand characteristics, and to a lack of ecological validity. But for such assertions to be taken seriously, it is necessary to supply direct evidence that these sources of artifact are present and can account for the findings. This has seldom, if ever, been done. Indeed, the empirical generality of so-called experimenter-effects has itself been seriously questioned by several writers (e.g., Barber & Silver 1968; Stewart 1971). Such critics emphasized the inconsistency of the phenomena, the methodologically poor nature of the experiments, and the extremely limited range of experimental tasks and situations that have been studied. It is remarkable, for example, that the work on experimenter effects rarely touches issues of any substance. There is much psychologically and theoretically impoverished evidence (e.g., person-perception studies with no theoretical content) and no evidence that these criticisms apply to laboratory studies of social learning. In regard to the idea of ecological validity, as Bandura (1978a) noted, the criteria by which one can decide whether a particular procedure or measure is or is not ecologically valid never have been specified, nor is it ever likely that they could be. It seems that the terms ecological validity, demand characteristics, and experimenter effects have, in this context, become negative labels, handy polemical devices, for invalidating laboratory experimentation.

In any case, the criticisms miss the point of experimental laboratory research. Laboratory investigations are not analogues of reality. They are controlled situations for clarifying essential determinants and processes of phenomena. The advantages of conducting experiments in laboratories are threefold. One, it allows for experimental control over all the variables of interest, including extraneous ones. Two, it allows for the systematic exploration of the parameters in which the researcher is interested. Three, it allows for relatively unambiguous inferences about causality to be made. Once principles are discovered in the laboratory they then can be applied to the real world. These ideas recently were particularly clearly reiterated by Bandura:

> This view of experimentation is taken for granted in all other branches of science. Airliners are built on aerodynamic principles developed largely in artificial wind tunnels; bridges and skyscrapers are erected on structural principles derived from experiments that bear little resemblance to the actual constructions; and knowledge about physiological functioning is principally gained from artificially induced changes, often in animals. Indeed, preoccupation with mimicking things as they occur naturally can retard advancement of knowledge—witness the demise of venturesome fliers who tried to remain airborne by flapping wings strapped to their arms in the likeness of soaring birds.
>
> In the final analysis, experiments are judged not on artificiality criteria, but in terms of *the explanatory and predictive power of the principles they yield*. (Bandura 1978a, p. 89, italics added).

Significant progress in understanding how televised influences affect viewers requires basic research into the determinants and processes of observational learning. These have been carried out in laboratory contexts and would seem to have direct relevance to the issue of television effects. Other types of studies also are needed. Field studies, for example, represent a complementary and valuable line of research. A complete understanding requires both types of experimentation. The findings from the field studies strongly support the previously mentioned laboratory findings.

Experimental field studies.

Steuer, Applefield, and Smith (1971) matched five pairs of preschool children on the basis of the amount of home television viewing. Each child was observed in a free-play peer interaction for a base-line period of ten sessions. Following the base-line period, one child in the matched pair viewed a series of aggressive cartoons while the other child viewed a series of nonaggressive programs. The daily viewing period lasted for eleven days. During both the base-line and the viewing periods, the frequency of aggressive interactions was recorded for each child. These measures consisted of actual serious aggression such as punching, kicking, and throwing objects at another child. By the end of eleven days of viewing, the children who had viewed the aggressive programs were displaying more aggressive behavior on these measures than did their matched controls who had viewed the nonaggressive programs.

Parke, Berkowitz, Leyens, West, and Sebastian (1977) carried out a series of field experiments with delinquents from both Belgium and the United States. Unedited commercial films, of either aggressive or nonaggressive content, were shown to groups of adolescent males who were living in small-group cottages in minimum security institutions. The boys' natural aggressive behavior was coded into such categories as physical threats (e.g., fist waving), verbal aggression (e.g., taunting, cursing), and physical attack (e.g., hitting, choking, kicking), as well as a variety of noninterpersonal physical and verbal aggression (e.g., destroying an object, cursing without a social target) and self-directed physical and verbal aggression. In the first study of the series, a three-week base-line rate was established for each boy in the study. Then the boys in one cottage were exposed to a diet of five aggressive films over a one-week period, and boys in a second cottage were exposed to a diet of five neutral films. The results indicated that the boys who had viewed the aggressive movies showed significant increments in aggressive behavior, over base-line, on most of the categories of aggression, compared to the boys who had viewed the neutral films. In addition, there was a tendency for the greatest increase in aggression to be associated with those boys who initially were somewhat more aggressive. In a second study these initial results were replicated. In a third study the results were replicated still again using the Belgian sample. In this case the results were obtained only for those boys who already had high base-lines of aggression.

Correlational studies.

The great advantage of the experimental studies discussed so far is that they strongly imply causality. Some researchers have examined correlational studies which, although not allowing for causal statements, did allow for broad generalization of the experimental findings to natural settings. If it is true, as the experimental studies suggest that it is, that the average person who views a great deal of television violence will be more aggressive in his or her interpersonal behavior than will the average person who views less violence, then there should be a direct, positive correlation between these two events in the real world. Many correlational studies were conducted to examine this question, and most of these found that this was the case. Those individuals who engage in the most aggressive or antisocial behavior are the ones who have watched the largest amount of television. Chaffee (1972) reviewed a dozen or more such studies of literally hundreds of youngsters from a variety of backgrounds and ages and concluded that there was a very definite relationship between watching aggressive television and engaging in aggressive or antisocial behavior. Two recent studies replicated and extended these findings.

Huesmann, Eron, Lefkowitz, and Walder (1973) obtained peer ratings of aggressiveness in a large number of eight-year-old children, as well as preferences for various kinds of television, radio, and comic books. Ten years later, when these youngsters had become young adults of eighteen, the investigators again obtained measures of aggressive behavior and television program preferences. Earlier, when the children were eight years old, a weak but significantly positive ($r = +.21$) relationship was found between the children's preference for violent media and their aggressive behavior (Eron 1963). The question now became: Could aggressive behavior at age eighteen be predicted from knowledge of the individual television viewing habits in early childhood? The answer was yes. There was a significant positive correlation of $r = +.31$ between preference for violent television programs at age eight and aggression at age eighteen. Furthermore, the positive correlation remained significant when the level of childhood aggression was partialled out, thus removing the possibility that initial aggressiveness determined both child-viewing preferences and adult conduct. Other partial correlations were computed to control for a range of background and family characteristics such as socioeconomic status and IQ. In all cases the significant positive correlation between viewing at age eight and being aggressive at age eighteen remained.

Another major correlational study into this question was carried out by Belson (1978) in London, England, using an in-depth interview technique with a representative sample of over fifteen hundred male adolescents, thirteen to sixteen years old. Belson (1978) discovered that the level of violent behavior that his informants admitted to engaging in over the preceding six-month period (including rape, torture, and violent physical assault), was related positively to the type of television program they could recall having seen several years earlier. The level and type of violence in the television programs had been rated previously by members of the British Broadcasting Corporation's viewing panel. The overall finding of Belson's study: The more violence watched on television some years earlier, the more the boys engaged in violent behavior.

Overview of television violence effects.

The combined findings from case studies, laboratory experiments, controlled field studies, and correlational investigations offer substantial testimony that viewing violence on television tends to foster aggressiveness. Only a handful of the major studies have been reviewed here. There is voluminous literature now that demonstrates this apparently causal link between the amount of violence portrayed on television and the amount of violence shown in the social behavior of viewers. For detailed reviews and discussions of this literature, the reader is referred to, among others, Bandura (1973); Bryan and Schwartz (1971); Comstock, Chaffee, Katzman, McCombs, & Roberts (1978); Goranson (1970, 1975); Liebert, Neale, and Davidson (1973); Liebert and Schwartzberg (1977); Murray (1973); Murray and Kippax (1979); Parke, Berkowitz, Leyens, West, and Sebastian (1977); Stein and Friedrich (1975); the five volumes of technical reports to the U.S. surgeon general (*United States* 1972); and the seven volumes of the Report of the Province of Ontario (Canada) Royal Commission on Violence in the Communications Industry (*Ontario* 1977). Although there are dissenters (e.g., Kaplan & Singer 1976; Halloran 1978), the weight of this evidence points directly to the view that television violence has very definite short-term effects and very probably long-term ones too. This conclusion perhaps can be made most explicit by quoting from the conclusions of the recent Canadian Royal Commission inquiry into this problem:

> The Commission was to determine if there is any connection or a cause-and-effect relationship between this phenomenon (the increasing exhibition of violence in the communications industry) and the incidence of violent crime in society. The short answer is yes. (*Ontario,* vol. 1, 1977, p. 50)

> If the amount of depicted violence that exists in the North American intellectual environment could be expressed in terms of a potentially dangerous food or drink additive . . . there is little doubt that society long since would have demanded a stop to it. . . . (*Ontario,* vol. 1, 1977, p. 51)

As Goranson (1977) recently concluded after his review of television violence, we "must recognize the likelihood that real people are being hurt everyday because of it" (p. 22).

There are still dissenters to the above conclusions. One set of dissenters is, of course, the television networks. They have a vested interest in keeping things the way they are, and we need not unduly concern ourselves with them at this point. Others are concerned more from a scientific point of view, and we shall consider their arguments. Kaplan and Singer (1976) presented perhaps the most detailed discussion. First, they strongly implied that 90 percent of the evidence just reviewed is irrelevant to the question. They argued that the case studies were simply anecdotal and should not be included in a scientific discussion, and that the correlational studies showing a link between violence and watching TV were irrelevant to establishing a *causal* connection. These authors also dismissed, in its entirety, virtually all the laboratory research on the grounds that we already have mentioned, that is, demand characteristics and a lack of ecological validity. Having quite arbitrarily dismissed in this way 90 percent of the research literature, they now have only to deal with the experimental field studies. This they attempted to do by discussing three reports of studies that *failed* to find an effect from television violence. They then argued that if three major studies failed to get an effect then it is by no means a definite conclusion that television violence leads to viewer aggression. The three studies they cited were by Feshbach and Singer (1971), Milgram and Shotland (1973), and Friedrich and Stein (1973). Actually, the first two studies were very seriously flawed and were, therefore, very unlikely to produce significant effects. The third, in fact, found *positive* results from the television diet although with ambiguous interpretation. The first study, by Feshbach and Singer (1971), stands almost alone in the literature finding that exposure to aggression on television actually *lowered* aggression in real life afterwards. These authors found support for the *catharsis* view of television aggression, that is, that by watching violence on television viewers will get their own aggression out of their systems by vicarious identification with the actors. We shall return to this theory. The second study, by Milgram and Shotland (1973) consisted of eight different experiments, each of which supported the null view (i.e., that television had no effects). Even Kaplan and Singer (1976) admitted that these studies had major methodological limitations. The real problem with the line of reasoning used by Kaplan and Singer is that *anybody* can fail to get an effect simply by setting up an insensitive procedure in the experiment. Thus, when there is failure to demonstrate an effect, one seldom can know whether this was because reality is actually organized that way or whether it was because of experimenter insensitivity. Hence science accepts only "positive" findings as evidence—unless there is strong supportive evidence that the null finding could *not* have been caused by experimenter inefficiency. Thus, the arguments presented by dissenters such as Kaplan and Singer are very weak indeed. They themselves seem to recognize this in their rather weak concluding statements:

> This paper should not be interpreted as stating that TV fantasy violence cannot cause aggression; rather we have argued that no such link has been demonstrated to date. Further, we have questioned the applicability of laboratory experimentation for this policy-related issue. By nature, scientific inquiry is conservative. We are not contending that the null hypothesis is true, but that the no-effect view is currently the most plausible one given. (1976, p. 63)

These authors then went on to obfuscate the issue entirely by saying that in any case the major causes of violence in society were economic, social, cultural, and the like, and that the television networks simply had become a scapegoat. This line of argument is, of course, totally fallacious. It may well be that the *major* source of violence in society lies beyond the TV system. That clearly cannot mean, however, that the TV system does not have an effect.

THE CATHARSIS VIEW

The concept of catharsis originally was introduced by Aristotle to explain the apparently paradoxical *decrement* in unhappiness among depressed persons after they had been to see a tragic play. Such people, instead of feeling even more unhappy when they came out, actually felt better. Although during the performance their feelings of sadness may have been intensified even to the point of weeping, after the play was over, these feelings may well have been greatly reduced. Aristotle suggested that the spectator's own feelings of unhappiness became, in some way, "drained off" as a result of watching even greater tragic events occur to another. Aristotle's ideas were taken over and elaborated on by both Sigmund Freud and some modern ethologists, and the general idea of "getting it out of your system" by watching others has spread into fairly common acceptance. In Canada, for example, there is currently a debate about hockey violence. In ice hockey, players frequently charge into one another on the ice. When this gets them suitably incensed, they throw down their gloves and sticks and start punching each other. For their sins they get two minutes in the penalty box (rather than being thrown out of the game by the referee and charged with assault by the police). Thus violence is institutionalized within the game. Apologists for this (e.g., team managers and owners who make large profits from attracting large audiences to see the violence) argue that the fans can "let off steam" in this way, with the implication that if they are not allowed to get release, their dammed up desires for violence will ultimately drive them to commit major violence elsewhere. This particular view has been popularized in some of the sillier writings of modern ethologists. Even Nobel Laureate Konrad Lorenz (1966), for example, suggested that in order to get rid of wars between nations, human aggressive instincts would have to be channeled away by providing larger, gorier, and more frequent spectator events such as the Olympics. In short, the wide-spread catharsis view is that humans can "vicariously" get rid of aggressive "drives" by watching others behave aggressively. In this, however, Aristotle, Freud, ethologists like Lorenz, and hockey club owners, are all dangerously wrong. There is no such thing as vicarious catharsis!

How then are we to explain Aristotle's observations that depressed persons feel better after watching a tragic play? The answer is that the spectators were temporarily *distracted* from their own feelings. No feelings were drained off. The same decrement in unhappiness would have occurred if the same ancient

Greek spectators had seen a nontragic, action-packed, adventure. Distraction, as any parent knows, is the best way of changing undesirable feelings in a youngster, and distraction is one explanation for Aristotle's observations. As for other kinds of catharsis notions, as applied, for example, to aggression, the evidence points in the *opposite* direction. Viewing violence does not drain off such feelings. Rather they *increase* the probability of the spectator himself or herself engaging in violence. Apart from the research evidence, this also is common sense, as perhaps the following examples will illustrate. Imagine people who have feelings of hunger. Will showing them scenes of other people enjoyably engaged in eating delicious food *decrease* their own hunger feelings? Of course not! It is far more likely to *increase* such feelings. Now imagine the example of people who are feeling sexually aroused. Will showing them erotic scenes of others engaged in sexual abandon *decrease* their own feelings of sexuality? Again, of course not. Sexual feelings are *increased* by watching attractive sexuality in others. Finally let us consider altruism. Will watching others engage in helpful behavior *decrease* our own tendencies to behave altruistically by draining off these urges within us? As we shall see very shortly, quite the contrary.

The notion of catharsis in general and in particular when applied to the viewing of aggression, has been a persistent and pernicious myth. As noted in many other recent reviews, it is time to discard it.

THE EFFECTS OF PORTRAYING
PROSOCIAL BEHAVIOR

Although there long has been research interest in the possible harmful effects of media violence, the other side of the coin, the potential for benefits from prosocial television, has been investigated only recently. Despite its recency, this research literature has now burgeoned to well over thirty different studies. These have been reviewed in some detail elsewhere (e.g., Rushton 1977, 1979). The next section of this chapter will consider a sampling of these studies in order to demonstrate the potential force for good that television could become. As in the previous reviews the term "prosocial" is used in its widest possible sense of that which is socially desirable and which in some way benefits another person or society at large. Four categories of prosocial behavior will be considered. The first is altruistic behavior such as generosity, helping, and cooperation. The second is friendly behavior. The third category is self-control behavior such as delaying gratification and resisting temptation. Finally, the ability of film material to diminish fears will be considered. Within each category, the laboratory studies will be reviewed separately from the field studies.

Television's effect on altruistic behavior.

(a) Laboratory studies. In a series of experiments, Bryan (Bryan 1971; Bryan & Walbek 1970a, 1970b) showed several hundred six- to nine-year-old

children, of both sexes, a specially constructed, five-minute videotape film of a model who played a bowling game, won gift certificates, and did or did not donate some of these gift certificates to a charity. Then the child was watched through a one-way mirror to see how much of his or her winnings he or she donated to a similar charity. The results showed that the children were strongly influenced by what they had seen the models doing on TV. Those children who had watched the videotape model behave generously gave more of their certificates to the charity than did those children who had watched the model behave selfishly.

Two other studies using similar procedures replicated Bryan's findings on the effectiveness of a TV model's behavior in influencing viewing children's generosity. These studies also tested for generalization and duration effects. In regard to this, they were less successful. Thus, although Elliot and Vasta (1970) were able to show that five- to seven-year-old children were influenced in both how much candy *and* how much money they shared, they were not able to demonstrate generalization to a third measure of altruism, of letting another child play with the more attractive of two toys. Although Rushton and Owen (1975) found that eight- to ten-year-old British children also could be influenced to donate tokens to a charity by means of watching TV models do so, the effects had worn off by the time the children were retested two weeks later.

These studies demonstrated that children's generosity in laboratory situations could be modified after watching generosity portrayed by others on television. One possible limitation is that the film material used in these studies was not like that produced for commercial purposes. It lasted for only five minutes and showed one model acting a number of times in just one way (e.g., generous) in one specific situation. A second limitation is that the child who watched then was tested in exactly the same situation in which he or she had seen the model act. Furthermore, the test for the program's effects was taken immediately.

Sprafkin, Liebert, and Poulos (1975) went further than the above studies and conceptually replicated their findings with a highly successful commercial television program, *Lassie*. They divided thirty white, middle-class children, aged five, into three groups and showed each group one of three half-hour television films, complete with commercials. A prosocial *Lassie* program involved Jeff, Lassie's master, risking his life by hanging over the edge of a mine shaft to rescue Lassie's pup. A neutral *Lassie* film and a neutral non-*Lassie* film were shown to the two control groups. After watching the programs the children were taken to another room where they could earn points toward a prize by playing a game. While playing the game they had an opportunity to aid puppies in distress by calling for help by pressing a "help" button. Pressing the help button, however, would interfere with earning points toward the prize. The average time spent pressing the help button for children who had watched the prosocial Lassie was ninety-three seconds, whereas in the two neutral conditions it was fifty-two and thirty-eight seconds, respectively.

Collins and Getz (1976) also carried out a laboratory investigation using a regular commercial program complete with commercials. They edited a commercial television action-adventure drama made for adults so that in one version a model responded constructively to an interpersonal conflict, and in another he responded aggressively. Fourth, seventh, and tenth graders saw one of these versions or a wildlife documentary control. They then were given an opportunity either to help or hurt a fictitious peer who was apparently completing a task by either pressing a "help" button that shut off a distracting noise or a "hurt" button that increased it. Children who had seen models of constructive coping showed greater prosocial responding than subjects in the other two conditions; that is, they gave more help responses than children who viewed either the aggression or the control programs.

(b) Naturalistic Studies. A pioneering study of prosocial media effects was made by Stein and Friedrich (1972) (see also Friedrich & Stein 1973). They studied ninety-seven children aged three to five years old attending a nine-week summer nursery school program at Pennsylvania State University. For the first three weeks all the children's naturally occurring free-play behavior in the classroom was coded into categories such as "aggressive," "prosocial," and "self-control," and base-lines for each child were established. Aggressive included verbal aggression such as teasing, vigorously commanding, and tattling, as well as physical aggression. Prosocial included such subcategories as cooperating, nurturing, and verbalizing positive feelings. Self-control consisted of adhering to rules, tolerating delay, and perservering at tasks.

Over a three-week period the base-lines were reliably established for each child in each of the categories. The children then were randomly assigned to one of three groups and exposed to four weeks of specially selected television. The first group watched aggressive television films such as *Batman* and *Superman* cartoons. A second group watched neutral films such as children working on a farm. A third group watched *Mister Rogers' Neighborhood*, a prosocial educational television program that stresses cooperation, sharing, sympathy, affection and friendship, understanding the feelings of others, delay of gratification, perserverence, and learning to accept rules. Over the next four weeks, twelve one-hour television programs were shown to each group at the rate of about one film every other day.

During this four-week exposure to one of the three television diets, the children's free-play behavior was recorded by observers who did not know their experimental condition. During the last five days of the following (and final) two weeks, the children's behavior was likewise recorded to evaluate the extended effects of TV viewing.

The results of this experiment demonstrated that the programs did affect the children's subsequent aggressive or prosocial behavior. The aggressive television content led to increased interpersonal aggresssion for those children who were above average in such aggression at base line. However, the effects did not generalize to the two-week retest. Exposure to the prosocial television content led to increased prosocial behavior although only in the children from the lower half of the socioeconomic status distribution. Here, too, the results failed to extend to the two-week retest. Both the aggressive and prosocial films had stronger effects on the measures of self-control as will be discussed later in the section on self-control.

A particularly ambitious and realistic study was conducted by Moriarty and McCabe (1977) with 259 children and youth engaged in organized team sports. Participants in Little League baseball, lacrosse, and ice hockey were included. Measures were obtained for the home viewing habits and preferences of the players and the antisocial and prosocial behavior of the players on the field, before, during, and after experimental treatment. The experimental treatment consisted of providing antisocial, prosocial, and control video presentations of the relevant sport to the teams assigned to these respective treatment groups. The prosocial material consisted of (a) altruism—helping, encouraging, and team work; (b) courtesy—displays of respect; (c) reparation—correcting a wrong or apologizing; and (d) affection—any overt expression of positive feelings toward another. The results indicated that exposure to such prosocial material increased the level of prosocial behavior of the hockey and lacrosse players, although not for baseball players. In addition, the survey data indicated that there was a tendency for those who played in the most prosocial manner (averaged over the experimental conditions) to prefer watching prosocial television at home.

Television's effect on friendliness

(a) Laboratory studies. Fryrear and Thelen (1969) assigned boys and girls of nursery school age to one of three television-viewing groups: a group that observed an adult male demonstrating "affectionate" behavior toward a small stuffed clown, a group that observed an adult female demonstrating the same behavior, and a control group. Children then were given an opportunity to play with a group of toys which included the small clown. An observer sat in the back of the room and watched to see whether the child imitated the affectionate behavior toward the toy. Children who watched television films of affectionate behavior were more likely to express similar affection than were children who had not seen such behavior on television.

(b) Naturalistic studies. O'Connor (1969) conducted a dramatic and potentially important study to see if television programs could be used to enhance social interaction among those nursery school children who tended to isolate themselves from their peers. Thirteen severely isolated children were chosen for the study. These children were interacting on fewer than five of thirty-two possible interactions reliably observed over an eight-day period. One group of these isolated children was shown a specially prepared, sound-color film on a television console. This film portrayed a graduated sequence of eleven scenes in which children interacted in a nursery school setting followed by reinforcing consequences. All the scenes were accompanied by a female narrator

describing the actions of the model and the responses of the other children. For comparison purposes, a second group of the isolated children were shown a film of dolphins engaging in acrobatic feats.

The results were quite dramatic. The children who had watched the specially made film about others engaging in social interaction increased from their base-line scores. Furthermore, a follow-up at the end of the school year showed that the changes had endured over time.

In a subsequent study, O'Connor (1972) selected thirty-three children from four nursery school populations classified as "social isolates" by both teachers' ratings and behavioral samples obtained by trained observers. Half the children viewed a specially constructed, twenty-three-minute modeling film depicting appropriate social behavior, and the other half viewed a control film. Half of the children in each film condition then received social reinforcement contingent upon the performance of peer interaction behaviors. Modeling was shown to be a more rapid modification procedure than was shaping and resulted in more stable social interaction patterns over time, with or without the attendant social reinforcement. In the follow-up assessments, modeling children remained at the original base-line level of *non*isolates, and social reinforcement and control children returned to isolate base-line level.

In another, similar study, Keller and Carlson (1974) showed nineteen socially isolated preschoolers either four videotapes, five minutes long, in which social skills (e.g., how to reinforce peers socially) were modeled (treatment) or four sequences of a nature film (control). The frequency with which children dispensed and received social reinforcement and the frequency of social interaction were rated by observers before and after treatment and at the follow-up. Results indicated that treatment produced increases for the treatment group on all three measures of prosocial interaction.

Coates, Pusser, and Goodman (1976) assessed the effects of both *Sesame Street* and *Mister Rogers' Neighborhood* on thirty-two preschool children. The frequency of these children's behaviors were recorded in one of three main categories: (1) *Positive reinforcement*, consisting of giving positive attention such as praise and approval; (2) *Punishment*, consisting of giving verbal criticism and rejection; and (3) *Social contact*, consisting of any physical or verbal contact with another child or adult.

Following these base-line measures children watched either fifteen minutes of *Sesame Street* or fifteen minutes of *Mister Rogers' Neighborhood* on each of four days. These programs originally had been shown on the U.S. Public Broadcasting System and had been scored on the basis of a content analysis (Coates & Pusser 1975) for the frequency of occurrence of positive reinforcement and punishment.

The results showed that the programs did affect significantly the children's social behavior. For all children *Mister Rogers' Neighborhood* significantly increased giving positive reinforcement to and having social contacts with both other children and adults. For *Sesame Street*, the effects were found only for children who had low base-line scores. For these children, watching *Sesame Street* significantly increased giving both positive reinforcement and *punishment* to and having social contacts with other children and adults in the preschool. For children whose base-line scores were high, *Sesame Street* had no significant effect on behavior. Furthermore, the authors felt that the pattern of results generally were consistent with their earlier content analysis of the two programs.

Television's effect on behavior involving self-control

(a) Laboratory studies. In an early study Walters, Leat, and Mezei (1963) first forbade five-year-old male kindergarten children from playing with some rather attractive toys. Then the children were divided into three groups. Two groups of children observed a film in which a child model, a boy of the same age as themselves, played with the toys that the subjects previously had been forbidden to touch. One group observed a film in which the boy model was "rewarded" by his mother for playing with the toys; one group observed the model "punished" for playing with the toys. The remaining group was a control which saw no film. All the children then were left alone in the experimental room with the forbidden toys for fifteen minutes, and their behavior was observed. Both in the length of time before children gave in to the temptation to touch the forbidden toys and in the total number of times the child touched the toys, there was a clear effect of the experimental treatment: Having seen the model-rewarded film made it harder for the children to resist the temptation, but having seen the model-punished film made it easier for them to resist.

Stein and Bryan (1972), in a laboratory experiment, explained to eighty girls, aged eight and nine, the rules by which they could win money by playing an electronic bowling game. Before playing the game the children watched a television program in which they saw a same-sex peer model playing the same game. This peer model either behaved in violation of these rules or in accordance with them. Children who observed the transgressive modeling were more than twice as generous in rewarding themselves incorrectly as those who observed a model who adhered to the rules. This it was shown that following or breaking rules and, in effect, stealing, could be affected by brief television programs.

Other studies, too, have been made to see whether television programming could influence children's self-control in "resistant to temptation" situations. In an experiment by Wolf and Cheyne (1972), seven- to eight-year-old boys were taken to a games room and allowed to play with some toys. They were forbidden, however, to touch or play with one particularly attractive toy. The investigators reported that an average of four minutes and forty seconds elapsed before an average boy in this situation would touch the toy. But if the boy had watched a TV program of another same-age boy playing with similar toys and this TV child had *not* touched the toy, then the average boy would wait nearly eight minutes before transgressing. If, on the other hand, the TV program had shown another boy violating the rule and touching the forbidden toy, then the subject would be likely to touch the toy in less than three minutes. Very similar results were found when the measure of the child's resistance to temptation was based on the *length* of time he played with the toy. The average boy would play with the forbidden toy for about one minute out of the ten that he was observed. If he watched a TV program depicting violation of the rules, then he would play with the forbidden toy for nearly four out of ten minutes. If, however, he watched a TV program showing adherence to the rules, then he would touch the forbidden toy for only about seven seconds. Wolf and Cheyne (1972) brought the boys back one month later and put them into the same situation. The results still showed an effect from the television program. Whereas children who had seen no television film one month earlier managed to resist the temptation for nearly six minutes, boys who had seen a model giving in to the temptation resisted for only four minutes. In this four-week retest no effect was found for the "self-controlled" model; that is, although the deviant model had an effect on increasing deviancy, the self-controlled model did not increase self-control in observers. In a subsequent study, Wolf (1973) again showed that televised models who obey rules influence children to obey, whereas televised models who deviate from rules influence children to deviate. Interestingly, television had more effect as a bad example than as a good one.

Another form of self-control is the ability to delay gratification to a later time. Yates (1974) carried out a study with seventy-two New Zealand children, aged eight. Base-lines were established by asking children if they would prefer a smaller reward such as money immediately or a larger one seven days hence. Some time later, some of the children watched television programs of an adult female model exemplifying high-delay behavior and/or verbalizing reasons for delaying gratification. Other children did not watch such programs. Compared to the controls, children who had watched the television programs showing delay of gratification were more likely themselves to choose to delay their gratification for a larger reward later. When the children were retested four weeks later their behavior still showed the effects of the exposure to the television film.

(b) Naturalistic studies.   In a study described previously in the section on altruistic behavior (Friedrich & Stein 1973), the prosocial television program *Mister Rogers' Neighborhood*, the aggressive television programs of *Superman* and *Batman*, or neutral fare was shown to ninety-three nursery school children aged four for a four-week period. During this time their naturally occurring free-play behavior was observed. Besides the prosocial and aggressive categories already described in the section on altruism, three categories of self-control behavior were recorded. These were: obedience to rules, tolerance of delay, and perserverence at tasks. In the obedience to rules category, the aggressive

films decreased this behavior in relation to neutral films, but the prosocial films increased it, producing an overall difference. No effects were found on the retest two weeks later. In tolerating delay, the aggressive films significantly decreased such behaviors over both the neutral and prosocial conditions, which did not differ from one another. These effects were maintained across the two-week retest. Finally, the prosocial television content increased perserverence in tasks over the neutral and aggressive films on both the immediate and later observation periods.

Television's effect on diminishing fears

(a) Laboratory studies. The first study to be reported was on young children who were inappropriately afraid of dogs (a common fear in young children). Bandura and Menlove (1968) first measured three- to five-year-old children's willingness to approach and play with a cocker spaniel on a number of occasions, to determine which children were afraid of dogs. Some children then were shown eight specially prepared, three-minute film programs over an eight-day period in which they saw other children playing with dogs. Another group of fearful children instead were shown movies of Disneyland. After watching these films, the children were given opportunities to approach live dogs. Previously fearful children who had watched other children showing courage were now much more likely to approach and play with the dogs than the children in the control group were. This reduction in fear generalized to dogs quite different from those seen in the film and was maintained over a four-week retest period. A similar study by Hill, Liebert, and Mott (1968) revealed similar results with similar-age children using a large German Shepherd as the film stimulus. Eight of the nine boys in a film group subsequently were willing to approach, pet, and feed the live German Shepherd, but only three of nine boys in the control group were, despite high levels of fear in each group prior to testing.

A study by Bandura, Blanchard, and Ritter (1971) investigated whether film programming could help adolescents and adults reduce their fear of snakes. Only those who reported having a severe fear of snakes were used. For example, their dread of snakes had to be so severe as to interfere with their ability to do gardening or to go camping. These subjects then were shown films of young children, adolescents, and adults engaging in progressively threatening inter-actions with a large king snake for thirty-five minutes. Behavioral measures were made in the presence of live snakes. The findings were clear. People who had watched the film significantly reduced their fears. It might be mentioned that the behavioral measures were quite stringent and included actually holding the snake in the hands. The ultimate test (which 33 percent of the subjects performed) included allowing the snake to lie in their laps while they held their hands passively at their sides! Bandura and Barab (1973) later replicated these findings.

Weissbrod and Bryan (1973) attempted to see whether similar techniques would succeed with eight- to nine-year-old children who had indicated an extreme fear of snakes on a fear inventory and also had refused to pet a snake during a pretest. These children watched a two-and-a-half-minute videotaped sequence with a model either approaching a live, 4-ft. boa constrictor (the experimental group) or a stuffed, 5-ft. toy snake (the comparison condition). All children watched both these films twice and then, two days later, watched them twice again. Following this second showing, the children were taken to an aquarium that housed a 4-ft. boa constrictor and were asked to touch, then pet, and finally hold the snake. The experimental group was able to go further into the sequence than the control comparison group was and, furthermore, maintained its superiority on another test taken two weeks later. For example, although none of the ten children in the control condition was able to handle the snake two weeks after watching a neutral film, eleven out of the forty children in the experimental condition could.

(b) Naturalistic studies.   Melamed and Siegel (1975) showed sixty children aged four to twelve who were about to undergo elective surgery for hernias, tonsils, or urinary-genital tract difficulties, either a relevant, peer-modeling film of a child being hospitalized and undergoing surgery or an unrelated control film. The experimental film was sixteen minutes in length and consisted of fifteen scenes of various events encountered by most children hospitalized for elective surgery. Both groups received extensive preparation by the hospital staff. State measures of anxiety, including self-report, behavioral observation, and the Palmar Sweat Index, revealed a significant reduction of preoperative (night before) and postoperative (postsurgery examination three or four weeks later) fear arousal in the experimental as compared to the control film group. Parents also reported more problem behavior in the children who had not seen the modeling film.

Effects from the therapeutic value of film modeling have been demonstrated in a number of other studies. Jaffe and Carlson (1972) and Mann (1972) treated test-anxious university and high school students with videotaped modeling procedures and found significant improvement in performance measures. Shaw and Thoresen (1974) demonstrated that specially constructed films can effectively reduce adults' fears of dental treatment. These authors used actual visits to the dentist for treatment as their measure of success. Melamed and her colleagues discovered that films can be used to overcome similar fears in children (Melamed, Hawes, Heiby, & Glick 1975; Melamed, Weinstein, Hawes, & Katin-Borland 1975). Video desensitization has also been applied successfully to the treatment of sexual dysfunction among women (Wincze & Caird 1976). It would seem, as Rosenthal's and Bandura's (1978) review of this literature indicated, that modeling films have great therapeutic potential.

Over thirty different experimental studies were reviewed from both laboratory and naturalistic settings. These demonstrated that television and film programs can modify viewers' social behavior in a prosocial direction. Generosity, helping, cooperation, friendliness, adherence to rules, delaying gratification, and absence of fear all can be increased by television material. This general statement agrees with the partial reviews of this same literature made previously (Bryan & Schwartz 1971; Liebert, Neale, & Davidson 1973; Rushton 1979; Stein & Friedrich 1975). On the basis of the studies reviewed here, therefore, it must be concluded that television *does* have the power to affect the social behavior of viewers in a positive, prosocial direction. This conclusion is a mirror image of the even larger body of research implying a relationship between television and antisocial behavior.

OTHER TELEVISION EFFECTS: CREATING EXPECTATIONS OF OCCUPATIONAL, ETHNIC GROUP, AND SEX ROLES

To what extent are our conceptions about the roles of various occupations, ethnic groups, and sex roles influenced by how we see them portrayed on television? Given the power of television to alter viewers' aggressive and prosocial behavior, it might well be that such expectations *would* be readily influenced. Strangely enough, far less research has been aimed at this particular question. Although researchers have made several content analyses of the social roles portrayed on television they generally have not, unfortunately, done research to see whether these particular portrayals are subsequently mirrored in viewers' perceptions. Let us examine the content analyses.

In regard to occupational roles, Smythe (1954) in an early study, found that teachers were portrayed as the kindest and fairest, journalists the most honest, and scientists the least kind, the most unfair, and the least honest of all the occupations he examined. DeFleur (1964) found that television portrayed the police as generally hardened and often brutal, private investigators as resourceful and more capable than the police, salespersons as glib, and truck drivers as aggressive. In a more recent study, Williams, Zabrack, and Joy (1977) found that the police were portrayed as powerful, interesting, satisfied with their lives, and overwhelmingly emotionally stable.

In regard to ethnic groups, the characters portrayed on North American television are overwhelmingly young, white, middle class, and American (Williams and others 1977). Most ethnic minorities and citizens of foreign countries are ignored. When they are presented they often are made to look either ridiculous or villainous, and this has been a source of hurt and irritation to groups as disparate as Chinese, Italians, Mexicans, and perhaps particularly, native peoples. Even Canadians have sometimes been irritated at the way in which they have been portrayed, particularly in Hollywood movies (Berton 1975). In response to black American protest, portrayals of black Americans seem to have shifted somewhat in recent years, so that they now are presented both more frequently and in higher status positions. In a recent content analysis, Donagher, Poulos, Liebert, and Davidson (1975) found that black males, for example, were usually portrayed as nonaggressive, persistent, altruistic, and more likely to make reparation for injury than any other group. Black women expressed a high ability to explain feelings in order to increase understanding, resolve strife, and reassure others. Unfortunately, as mentioned, no studies have been carried out to see whether these particular portrayals actually are mirrored in viewers' perceptions. On the other hand, one very early British study did find that television could increase children's knowledge of foreigners (Himmelweit, Oppenheim, & Vince 1958). A recent Canadian study found that children's verbalized play preferences could be made more favorable to minority groups after viewing specially prepared inserts on *Sesame Street* (Gorn, Goldberg, & Kanungo 1976).

In regard to the portrayal of sex roles, some concern has been expressed about how females have been represented. A study by Sternglanz and Serbin (1974) supported this concern. These authors content analyzed a number of children's programs that had high Nielsen ratings. They found, first, that males were shown nearly twice as often as females were. There also were major differences between the sexes in the types of behavior portrayed. Males, for instance, were more often portrayed as aggressive and constructive (e.g., building, planning) but females were more likely to be shown as deferential and passive. In addition, the consequences for males and females for displaying behavior were different, with males more often being rewarded and females more often receiving no consequence. An exception to this was that females were more often punished for high levels of activity than were males. On the other hand, at least when women were portrayed, they were presented as "interesting" and "emotionally stable" (Williams and others, 1977). Thus it appeared that commercially produced television programs were carrying quite different messages about the appropriate behavior for males and females. Given the general evidence of the effectiveness of modeling on television as a means of teaching behavior, television may well be an important source in the learning of stereotyped sex roles.

GENERAL OVERVIEW
OF TELEVISION EFFECTS

There is considerable evidence that television has the power to influence the social behavior of viewers in whatever direction the content of the programs dictate. If, on the one hand, prosocial helping and kindness make up the content of television programming, then this is what is learned by viewers as appropriate, normative behavior. If, on the other hand, antisocial behaviors and uncontrolled aggression are shown, then these are what viewers will learn to be the norm. This view is supported by the fact that billions of dollars are spent annually by advertisers on North American television. Advertisers believe, correctly, that- brief, 30 second exposures of their product, repeated over and over, will significantly modify the viewing public's behavior toward those products. In this regard it is interesting to note that while television companies encourage advertisers to believe that this is the case, they are not so eager to agree that their drama sequences can have equally powerful effects. It does not seem altogether reasonable that television companies can have it both ways. The message therefore is quite clear: People learn from watching television and what they learn will depend on what they watch.

One of the clear implications of this conclusion is that we ought to alter our conceptualization of what the nature of television is. As has also been suggested elsewhere (e.g., Liebert, Neale, and Davidson 1973; Leifer, Gordon, and Graves 1974; *Ontario* 1977), television is much more than mere entertainment. It is also a source of observational learning experiences, a setter of norms. It helps to determine what people will judge to be appropriate behavior in a variety of situations. Indeed, television has become one of the major agencies of socialization that our society possesses. There has been some reluctance to adopt this view of television and, as mentioned earlier, probably for the very good reason that television was never intended to be an agent of socialization. Once we accept that television *is* an agency of socialization (however unintentionally), then issues of power and control become more apparent. Although there is some evidence that adults' evaluative comments about the behavior being portrayed on a television screen does affect its impact on young viewers (Grusec 1973; Hicks 1968a; Horton and Santogrossi 1978), it is questionable whether adults can possibly continually monitor their children's TV watching behavior. Perhaps some greater measure of public control will have to be exerted over the content of television before it comes on the air. This problem will be considered in the final chapter.

THE EFFECTS OF OTHER MEDIA

In this review of the socializing effects of the mass media, the emphasis has been on television. This is partly because most of the research to date has been concerned with this particular medium, and partly because television, by providing direct access to the detailed behavioral sequences engaged in by conspicuous and prestigious models would be expected to be a particularly powerful socializing influence. This does not mean that the other media are unimportant. Unfortunately, content analyses of other media show the pervasiveness of violence there, too. Analyses of literature, both adult's (Fulford 1977) and children's (England 1977), and in magazines (Beattie 1977) and in popular music (Goddard 1977) show an overwhelming amount of violence and antisocial behavior. (Jowett, Reath, and Schouten 1977, is an excellent discussion of the history of the public's response to these media and the problems of censorship). For our purposes let us examine some selected examples from the above reviews to illustrate what lies everywhere in our environment. The reader can judge for himself or herself their probable consequences or meaning. Let us start with nursery rhymes for the very young, move on to comics, then to rock music, and finally to modern literature.

In "Jack the Giant-Killer" the rather stupid cannibalistic giants first threaten humans in their traditional manner:

> Fee Fi Fau Fum
> I smell the blood of an Englishman!
> Be he alive or be he dead
> I'll grind his bones
> To make my bread.

Not to worry. Jack dispatches them quite readily with pick-axe, knife, and magic sword.

Stepmothers too, evil beings, often have as unhappy endings as people-eating giants. The one in "Snow White," in some versions, chokes to death on her own thwarted rage; in other versions, less concerned with a literary nemesis and more concerned with a vengeful justice, she is forced at the wedding feast to dance in slippers of red-hot iron until she drops dead (England 1977).

As the younger child sits at his or her parent's knee listening to the above, its older sibling is engrossed in a comic book. An example from one:

A woman kills her husband with a kitchen knife. Picture shows blood on the knife but no injury on the husband's body. (words) "The rapier sharp blade sliced him directly between the shoulder blades . . ." Then the woman dragged him to a pen where a crazed bull was kept. Caption: "Even a stomach as strong as Hazel's couldn't stand the sight of the bull's attack on Ezra's corpse. Gagging she turned and fled back to the house." (Jowett and others 1977, p. 68)

Meanwhile, these younger children's teenage sibling is upstairs listening to one of the crazes in pop music, "punk rock." Punk groups, such as the Sex Pistols, were made up of individuals calling themselves by names like Johnny Rotten and Side Vicious. They produced songs with title like *Anarchy in the U.K.* and lyrics like "God save the Queen/God save the Fascist regime/It made you morons into human H-bombs." With the music has come punk-clothing styles where jewelery consists of safety pins, bondage chains, and Nazi insignia. This movement, of course, is heavily supported by the music and pop industry (a several billion-dollar-a-year industry). The day after the Sex Pistols said "fuck" on a BBC television show, sales of the band's single, *Anarchy in the U.K.* skyrocketed, and the group became internationally known. Rock music ever since Elvis Presley, has always had overtones of pugnaciousness. The Who's song, My Generation from the 1960s:

> People try to put us down
> Just because we get around
> Things they do look awful cold
> Hope I die before I get old.
> This is my generation, baby.
> Why don't you all f-f-f- fade away?
> Don't try and dig what we all say . . .*

Then there are the rock shows themselves. The Who simply used to smash up their instruments on the stage in the 1960s. In the early 1970s, Alice Cooper simulated hanging and decapitation along with a bizarre and gruesome entourage of grotesques including dancers dressed as spiders and a Cyclops-like monster. "But it's just fantasy," Cooper claimed. "It's just fun" (Goddard 1977, p. 229). In the mid-1970s, Cooper's grotesqueries paled in comparison with those of the rock band, Kiss. A typical Kiss show included the four band members strutting around the stage in tight black leather suits, each draped in chains and wearing jackboots. Their faces were smeared with white paste make-up which gave them a skull like mask quality. On stage they engaged in lascivious sadomasochistic activities which some called "Nazi rock." Said Gene Simmons, bassist, "We're just trying to put on the best show they've ever seen" (Goddard 1977, p. 230).

Meanwhile, in the living room, the father is reading modern literature. Here is Norman Mailer's hero, Steve Rojack, murdering his wife in *An American Dream:*

> "I struck her a blow on the back of the neck, a dead cold chop which dropped her to a knee, and then hooked an arm about her head and put a pressure on her throat . . . For a moment I did not know if I could hold her down . . . For ten or 20 seconds she strained in balance, and then her strength began to pass, it passed over to me, and I felt my arm tightening about her neck. My eyes were closed. I had the mental image I was pushing with my shoulder against an enormous door which would give inch by inch to the effort.
> One of her hands fluttered up to my shoulder and tapped it gently. Like a

---

*My Generation words & Music by Peter Townshend © Copyright 1965 Fabulous Music, Ltd., London England, TRO-DEVON MUSIC, INC., New York, controls all publication rights for the U.S.A. and Canada. Used by permission.

gladiator admitting defeat, I released the pressure on her throat, and the door I had been opening began to close. But I had had a view of what was on the other side of the door, and heaven was there, some quiver of jewelled cities shining in the glow of a tropic dust, and I thrust against the door once more and hardly felt her hand leave my shoulder, I was driving now with force against that door: spasms began to open in me, and my mind cried out then, 'Hold back! You're going too far, hold back!' I could feel a series of orders whip like tracers of light from my head to arm, I was ready to obey, I was trying to stop, but pulse packed behind pulse in a pressure up to thunderhead:some black-billed lust, some desire to go ahead not unlike the instant one comes in a woman against her cry that she is without protection came bursting with rage out of me and my mind exploded in a fireworks of rockets, stars, and hurtling embers, the arm about her neck leaped against the whisper I could still feel murmuring in her throat, and crack I choked her harder, and crack I choked her again and crack I gave her payment—never halt now—and crack the door flew open and the wire tore in her throat, and I was through the door, hatred passing from me in wave after wave, illness as well, rot and pestilence, nausea—I was floating—I was weary with a most honorable fatigue and my flesh seemed new. I had not felt so nice since I was twelve. . . ." (1965, pp. 30-32)*

Fantasy is bad enough, and we have reviewed it in this chapter from television, film, nursery tale, comic strip, popular music, and literature. Let us not forget that it is based on fact. In *Night*, Elie Wiesel wrote about life in Auschwitz, where he spent his boyhood. At one point he related how three prisoners, two men and a boy, were accused by the camp guards of sabotage. They were hanged before thousands of inmates. Then the prisoners were forced to march past the dangling bodies:

> The two adults were no longer alive. Their tongues hung swollen, blue-tinged. But the third rope was still moving; being so light, the child was still alive . . .
> For more than half an hour he stayed there, struggling between life and death, dying in slow agony under our eyes. And we had to look him full in the face. He was still alive when I passed in front of him. His tongue was still red, his eyes were not yet glazed.
> Behind me, I heard a man asking:
> 'Where is God now?'
> And I heard a voice within me answer him:
> 'Where is He? Here He is—he is hanging here on this gallows . . .'
> That night the soup tasted of corpses. (1960, p. 71)

Violence is real . . . in some cultures. In those cultures that do not provide aggressive models and that devalue injurious conduct, people live peaceably.

*Excerpted from the book AN AMERICAN DREAM by Norman Mailer, Copyright © 1965 by Normal Mailer. Reprinted by permission of THE DIAL PRESS.

SUMMARY

Concern about the effects of television and the mass media has been apparent from the earliest studies in the 1950s. This concern has now grown to become one of vital importance due to the large number of studies that clearly demonstrates a causal connection between television violence and the amount of violence shown in the social behavior of viewers. The evidence for this conclusion comes from a variety of different types of investigation: case studies, laboratory experiments, field experiments, and correlational studies. All demonstrate the pervasive power that television has to alter the norms of appropriate behavior.

Television not only has the ability to produce harmful effects by depicting violence and antisocial behavior. Television also has the potential of being a force for good. Over thirty different studies have now demonstrated, through experiments carried out in both laboratory and naturalistic settings, that if prosocial content is shown the viewers' social behavior is modified in a prosocial direction. Generosity, helping, cooperation, friendliness, adherence to rules, delaying gratification, and absence of fear can all be increased by television material. This conclusion is a mirror image of the even larger body of research that implys a relationship between television and antisocial behavior. There is also evidence that television has the ability to affect our expectations of occupational, ethnic group, and sec roles; consumer products; politicians; and expectations from life. The message therefore is quite clear: People learn from watching television and what they learn depends on what they watch.

Other media are important also. Unfortunately, content analyses of other media show the pervasiveness of violence there, too. Analyses of literature, both adult's and children's, and of magazines and popular music, show an overwhelming amount of violence and antisocial behavior.

One conclusion from this chapter is that we ought to alter our conceptualization of what the nature of the mass media is. It is much more than mere entertainment. It is also a source of observational learning experience, a setter of norms.

chapter 8

THE EDUCATIONAL SYSTEM

Education is one of humankind's most ancient concerns. Even in the simple palaeolithic and neolithic societies of hunters, food gatherers, hoe cultivators, and the like, long before the invention of writing, care must have been taken to teach the young the skills and knowledge necessary for the community to survive. Education thus is the intentional imparting of knowledge. Its explicit function is to impart "knowledge." This includes cognitive competencies as well as behavior and outlook. Education is not really very different from other terms such as "training," "socialization," and "learning." The *processes* are probably the same. The differences between education and the others are that education is associated (a) with being carried out by a special person, a teacher, and (b) with having an explicit agenda.

The teacher and the school as agents for socialization have, relatively speaking, been ignored by those looking at the development of children's social attitudes, values, and behavior. As Himmelweit and Swift (1969) and Zigler and Seitz (1978) pointed out, most of the literature on socialization research has been on processes in the family. It has tended to neglect such important societal institutions as the mass media and the educational system. The educational system's function as an agency for socialization can hardly be doubted. This chapter will document the influence of education in the socialization process in the world's historical past and will raise questions of its possible influence in Western society in the future.

EDUCATION IN HISTORICAL PERSPECTIVE

In the conceptually most simple types of society we might imagine that the child would, by watching, listening, and imitating, acquire the particular language used by his or her group. Again through observation, he or she would develop attitudes of liking and disliking toward objects, people, and ways of behaving appropriate to his or her group. In addition, he or she would learn how to gather food, kindle a fire, build boats and shelters, and make spears, boomerangs, and pots. Amid all this relatively informal acquisition of knowledge, there also must have been some deliberate instruction. We probably can safely assume that in most cultures a mother would instruct her daughter how to care for the young and that a father would instruct his son how to hunt, fish, or otherwise gather food. Even here the learning process may have been spontaneous, with parent and child largely unaware that it was happening.

Soon it would become apparent that certain individuals were better at certain skills than others; they became artisans, making copper pots, weaving baskets, or making wheels. Young men would come to watch and to learn. They became apprentices, helping and learning at the same time. Such learning would continue until the youth passed through his apprenticeship and became recognized as a skilled and proper member of his society. The apprenticeship or training required would, of course, depend heavily on the social and economic needs of the particular society.

An example of such a type of education might be found in the history of the native peoples of America. Jenness (1977) in writing about the Indians of Canada before the advent of Europeans, described two broad curricula recognized by most tribes. The first was a secular course and consisted of what we might call manual training. Children were taught to hunt and shoot small game such as rabbits and squirrels. Later they were to accompany the hunters on their expeditions, so as to become inured to the hardships of the chase. To harden the boys physically and mentally, the Iroquois, for example, taught them to endure torture, and the Pacific Coast tribes made them bathe in cold water daily and whipped them with cedar boughs when they emerged. Among the Plains Indians, the *elderly men who supervised their training* kept a bathing hole open for them all winter or made them roll naked in the snow. The second curriculum was an ethical or religious course. This usually took place around the campfire at night and consisted of listening to a story teller, usually an older man, who would narrate some tradition or folk tale of the distant past and would make clear the moral of the story by referring to the conduct of the children during the preceding hours. *These beginnings of formal education thus were concerned with acquiring a moral character as well as learning specific skills.* In native tribes further south, as among the Aztecs of what is now Mexico, this latter concern was made quite explicit. Aztec boys attended schools where many were expected to learn to read and write and to learn the history of their people from books. Much of this history was moral, political, and religious in nature, with strong emphasis on what had been correct and incorrect behavior in the past. In addition to such ethical education, the future leaders of Aztec society also were taught how to read the stars, the Aztec calendar, and foretell the future. The education of these people followed the requirements of their society.

The relationship between the ecology of a society and the education of the young becomes clearer with a few cross-cultural comparisons. One particularly illuminating example is the Greek city-state of Sparta which existed from the eighth to the fourth century B.C. Sparta had managed, with a very small population, to dominate militarily its more numerous neighbors. It had done so by directing all the energies of its people to military life. All unnecessary goods were stripped from Spartan life, and all unnecessary speech was discouraged. The aristocratic Spartans made a virtue out of the austerity that circumstances had forced upon them, rejecting luxury or softness, ignoring the arts, idealizing military prowess, and enduring hardships.

In order to maintain Spartan ascendancy over the Helots, the conquered serfs who outnumbered them ten to one, strict attention was given to the education of the young. From the moment of birth, the society as a whole took responsibility for the training of the young. All babies were inspected by a committee, and those deemed puny were tested by being left overnight either to die of exposure or to survive and join their fellows. At the age of seven, boys began to attend classes for games and physical training. At twelve they left home and began their military careers. They lived in communal barracks and were given very little in the way of clothes or food so that they had to learn how to steal the extras they needed. This, it was felt, would teach them stealth and initiative. They also were taught to fight and were encouraged to do so with each other so that beatings could be taken without flinching. Courage and bravery were seen as the highest moral virtues, as well as immediate obedience to orders, no matter what they were. Between eighteen and twenty, young men were taught to spy on the conquered serfs and kill without mercy those who showed signs of diminishing subservience. Girls too, though they stayed at home, lived vigorous outdoor lives and were trained in running, wrestling, and discus throwing. Here the primary concern was to develop healthy bodies so that they could produce healthy offspring. By this strong focus on a particular type of educational process, Sparta was able to survive and long remain the most powerful city-state, militarily and diplomatically, of the entire Greek world and indeed, eventually to triumph over its rival Athens after the long struggle of the Peloponnesian War (431 – 404 B.C.). Interestingly, this educational system continued to exist long after it had ceased to serve its original purpose. Over the centuries, the rigor and ferocity were increased even as the behaviors being inculcated became anachronistic and without real use. Rites of initiation were transformed into barbarous tests of endurance, the boys undergoing flagellation and competing in enduring it, sometimes to the death, under the eyes of tourists attracted by the sadistic spectacle. This occurred even in times of complete peace as when, for example, under the Roman Empire, Sparta was nothing but a provincial city with neither independence nor army.

A contrast often made with Sparta is that of the Greek city-state of Athens. The evolution of Athenian education also reflected that of the city itself, which was oriented toward increasing democratization–though, it must be remembered, the society as a whole was based on a large slave population which certainly was not included in the educational process to be described. The slaves had their own, quite different training. In the Athens of the sixth and fifth century B.C., only boys attended schools. At the age of seven they learned athletics, music, and poetry. Later they learned to read, write, and count. But the moral aspect of education was not neglected. The teachers were as much preoccupied with overseeing the child's good conduct and the formation of his character as with directing his progress in the various subjects taught him. In Athens, education was concerned with a far broader range of knowledge and behavior than in Sparta. This was largely the result of having an aristocracy and a wealthy middle class with enough leisure time for such pursuits. Partly too, it was due to the type of democratic political system that had evolved with the maritime trading on which the economy was based. This latter economic factor had a more apparent effect on the educational system with the appearance of the Sophists, who were the contemporaries and adversaries of Socrates (c. 470 – 399 B.C.). The Sophists were professional educators who simply wanted to teach persons how to be a success in political life, which meant, above all, being able to win arguments. They taught how to persuade and how to speak well. They were concerned with worldly success. They were much less concerned with morality and truth. It was this that led to Socrates' opposition. He felt that education should be directed to the moral and the virtuous, both of which he saw as resting on the disinterested search for Truth and Wisdom.

Socrates founded no formal institution, nor did he write any books. His ideas have come down to us through his most famous pupil, Plato. Plato's ideas on education stressed the moral aspects as can be seen in his book *The Republic*, which was his view of the ideal society. At the top in this society were the philosopher-kings who would rule justly and seek out goodness. They were to be educated to age fifty before they could acquire their full status. By the judicious study of not only mathematics, science, and philosophy, but also music and gymnastics, Plato felt that an integration of the soul and the discovery of moral excellence in the populace would be brought about through control of the environment. He believed, for example, that the myths and epics ought to be censored and made wholesome for children. He did not believe that morality would occur spontaneously. Plato's ideas, however, were only that; they were never translated into action. They are included here to give the flavor of those times and to show that the link between moral development, however conceived, and education was strong at that time, too.

The relationship between a society's values and its educational system will be evident after a brief consideration of mediaeval Europe where church schools and universities flourished. Here the Christian Bible was considered, in its variety of versions, to be the main source of moral virtue. Although in the monasteries the learning of the Greeks was maintained and, from time to time, added to, and although lay schools were established to teach writing and arithmetic, religion still was all-important and the moral purpose of education was recognized. For boys of high rank, however, there was quite a different type of educational process. These boys served as pages and then as squires in the halls and castles of the nobility where they received prolonged instruction in chivalry. The training was designed to enable the noble youth to become a worthy knight, a just and prudent master, and a sensible manager of an estate. Much of this knowledge was gained from daily experience in the household, but, in addition, the page received direct instruction in reading, writing, courtly pastimes such as chess and playing the lute, and of great importance, the rules and usages of courtesy and the knightly conception of duty. As a squire he practiced more assiduously the knightly exercises of war. Although the morality here was very different from that of the American Indian societies and from that of the Ancient Greeks, there is a common theme running through these cross-cultural examples, that is, society's effort to inculcate the virtues they believe in at the time.

EDUCATION IN THE MODERN WORLD

Although differences can be discerned readily among the various educational systems of the modern world; nonetheless, the commonalities are obvious. In the main, modern education came into being as a result of the needs of the industrial revolution. In all countries affected by the industrial revolution, the training of intelligent workers was a common aim. As science and technology became more and more important to the development of wealth within the country, it became necessary for each nation to educate more and more of its populace to a higher and higher degree. Education became a matter of national priority in the competition among states. This was as true for the rivalries between, say, France and Prussia under Bismark in the late nineteenth century as it is today between the United States and the Soviet Union. It might be remembered, for example, that when the Soviet Union launched its first Sputnik in 1959, one of the American government's responses was to make federal funding available for updating science courses in high schools and universities so as not to lag behind the Soviets in space technology.

Education in developed economies is estimated to consume somewhere between 5 and 10 percent of the gross national product and to involve something like 20 or 25 percent of the population in terms of being employed full time in the educational system, either as teachers or as students. In developing economies the figures are much lower. Even in those countries, however, education consumes between 2 and 3 percent of their gross national products and the demands by the populace for education are enormous and growing. The right to free primary education is not only written into the Universal Declaration of Human Rights but also is often embodied in the basic constitutional documents of developing countries. Many countries devote substantial amounts of their public resources to universal primary education and adult literacy programs. Developing countries are very concerned with using education to foster economic and social development.

The growth of education the world over has been enormous. In North America and Western Europe, it is not uncommon for a child to enter nursery school or kindergarten at the age of four and to emerge from the educational process only after he or she has completed studies for a higher degree, more than twenty years later. Frequently, during the years of his or her working life, he or she also will take refresher courses and other postgraduate courses in order to bring his or her knowledge up to date. Individuals spend as much time in schools and educational institutions as they do with their parents (although as we have seen, not as much as they do with television). All this makes it perhaps surprising that relatively little research attention has been paid to the school system as an agent of socialization. Himmelweit and Swift (1969) conjectured that one of the reasons for this neglect is that the North American school system is not as noticeable a source of differences among groups as it might be elsewhere. This is because the North American education system is comprehensive and unified: The children all proceed from primary school to secondary schools with relatively little separation into different school systems. When attempts are made to account for differentials in student performance and behavior, therefore, attention is focused on factors outside the apparently shared school environment. The one exception to this is in the racially segregated school systems (*de facto* or otherwise).

In many other parts of the world, the school system is extremely conspicuous as an independent socializing force. This is because many countries, not being able to afford to educate all their future citizens to the same high levels as in

North America, are forced to choose those whom they will educate fully and those whom they will educate only partially or not at all. For example, although throughout Europe there is universal primary education, a secondary education that leads to university is the privilege of a much smaller proportion of the population. In the least industrially developed countries, even primary school cannot be available to everyone. In countries such as these, there are great differences in attitudes, values, knowledge, and behavior between those who go to the academically oriented schools and those who do not. It is the absence of such group differences in North America that Himmelweit and Swift (1969) speculated had led to the low salience of the school system as an agency of differential socialization.

In England, until very recently, a two-tiered secondary school system was in operation. (It is now a comprehensive system much like the one in operation throughout North America.) At the age of eleven, on the basis of intelligence and performance tests, some 20 percent were *selected* to fill available grammar school places. The remainder was *placed* into secondary modern schools. The grammar schools led to middle-class occupations and/or university. The secondary modern schools resulted in leaving school at age fifteen and entering relatively working-class occupations. The differential effects of this education was examined by Himmelweit and Swift (1969) in an extensive longitudinal study of six hundred adolescent boys, aged thirteen and fourteen, who were reinterviewed eleven years later at age twenty-five. The results indicated that the school to which the children were allocated influenced their life chances far more than did their initial ability, social background, motivational states, or personality predispositions. Furthermore, allocation to *streams within the grammar school* affected the boys' ultimate performance far more than did their ability or motivation.

Other factors in the British educational system also support the idea that schools are powerful agencies of socialization. Ten percent of British children go to fee-paying private schools. These produce quite definite class differences not only in many social attitudes but also in such social mannerisms as speech style and accent. Perhaps more importantly they also greatly increase the child's probability of success in later life as measured in both university entrance exams and occupational role. It is no accident that the majority of persons on the higher levels of the British civil service, diplomatic corps, and industrial management went to a handful of private schools before university.

In the United States, the role of the educational system as a socializer became particularly noticeable with the Supreme Court decision on the *Brown v. Board of Education* (1954) case. Here it was decided that separate educational facilities for blacks were inherently unequal. Many social scientists at the time argued that integrating blacks into the mainstream school system would have many positive effects, including, particularly, a "better education." As for the ability measures, although the final verdict is far from determined, it seems that improvement in fact, has occurred (Stephan 1978).

Given the central place of the educational system in our lives, we might well ask ourselves what influence, if any, it has in socializing morality in children, as opposed to cognitive knowledge and ability. One type of morality that *is* inculcated by almost all educational systems is national loyalty and solidarity. The extent to which attempts are made to influence the political and social ideas of youth varies considerably from country to country and even from school to school. For example, in the United States, most school curricula provide instruction in the history and practice of parliamentary democracy, and students are encouraged to participate in open decision making, as in debating societies and in the election of student officials.

In the United States the political nature of education sometimes has gone beyond this. For example, textbooks, particularly in the social sciences, have been rejected because of "subversive tendencies." Certainly history and social studies textbooks place great emphasis on the moral justification of all the American wars of liberation and expansion, although, of course, it is obvious that those defeated in such wars have quite different stories to tell. This glorification of national history and veneration of national heroes is a universal phenomenon. It obviously affects the political attitudes of the young.

In the United Kingdom and the other countries that make up the European Economic Community, there has been a move away from history textbooks and the like that stressed the glories of the particular nation-state toward an integrated European-history outlook. This change only reflects the new economic-political situation and does not represent a break from the general idea that educational systems attempt to inculcate a morality of ingroup loyalty. We might begin to ask ourselves, however, whether the world of the late twentieth century can afford to continue to socialize this moral virtue of ingroup loyalty to such a narrow conception as a particular nation-state. Perhaps we ought to attempt to socialize with more of a world view, with the whole history of *Homo sapiens* as the point of attention, rather than focus on the peoples who happen to be living at one time in a particular political entity or geographic locale.

Some readers may object to the idea of considering patriotism or even civic education as moral education. Admittedly, such training is not explicitly labeled as moral training. But it is evident from the cross-cultural comparisons cited earlier in this chapter that the particular civic duties and "good behaviors" required by particular societies depends very much on the needs of the particular society. For ourselves, in a pluralistic, free-enterprise democracy, the "good citizen" requirements are different from those of other societies, and the training in our school system reflects this. Perhaps this will become clearer when contrasted with the moral socialization that occurs, for example, in the Soviet Union.

MORAL EDUCATION
IN THE SOVIET UNION

The aims of the Soviet educational system are, in addition to fostering general and technical education, moral in nature. It has as its aim the propagation of "socialist morality" and the making of the "New Soviet Man." Great stress is put on prosocial behavior, consideration for others, and self-discipline. Bronfenbrenner wrote a detailed, descriptive account of how the Soviet system of education inculcates these values. Based on a number of visits to the Soviet Union, Bronfenbrenner (1970) wrote *Two Worlds of Childhood,* contrasting the different ways of bringing up children in the United States and the Soviet Union. The account of the Soviet approach to moral education that follows is based largely on Bronfenbrenner's (1970) observations.

First, as can be seen in Table 8.1, there is a clear statement by Soviet education authorities of what kinds of behavior are expected from the children at

TABLE 8-1
SUMMARY OF STATED OBJECTIVES OF UPBRINGING FOR YOUNGEST (7-11) AND OLDEST (16-18) AGE GROUPS

Ages 7-11	Ages 16-18
Communist morality	
Sense of good and bad behavior	Collectivism, duty, honor, and conscience
Truthfulness, honesty, kindness	Development of will, patience, perseverance
Atheism: science *vs.* superstition	
Self-discipline	
Diligence in work and care of possessions	A Communist attitude toward work and public property
Friendship with classmates	Socialist humanism
Love of one's own locality and the Motherland	Soviet patriotism and proletarian internationalism
Responsible attitude toward learning	
Interest and striving for knowledge and skill	Understanding of the social significance of education
Industry in study	Perseverance and initiative in learning
Organizing intellectual and physical work	Increasing one's power of intellectual work (learning to plan one's work better, development of good work habits, self-criticism, etc.)
Striving to apply one's knowledge and ability in life and work	

TABLE 8-1 (continued)

Cultured conduct

Care, accuracy, and neatness

Courtesy and cordiality

Proper behavior on the street and
in public places
Cultured speech

Assimilation of norms of socialist
community life
Good manners and standards of
behavior

Bases of esthetic culture

Understanding of the beautiful in
nature, in the conduct of
people, and in creative art
Artistic creativity

Esthetic appreciation of nature,
social life, and works of art

Artistic creativity

Physical culture and sport

Concern for strengthening and
conditioning one's body
Sanitary-hygienic habits

Preparation for sports and athletics

Maximizing the development of
physical skills
Mastering the rules of personal and
social hygiene and sanitation
Training and participation in sports
Mastering hiking and camping skills

*Adapted from N. I. Boldyrev (ed.), *Programma vospitatelnoi raboty shkoly [The Program of the Upbrining Work of the School]* (Moscow: Izdatelstvo Akademii Pedagogicheskikh Nauk RSFSR, 1960), 20-25, 110-118. (Source: from TWO WORLDS OF CHILDHOOD: U.S. and U.S.S.R., by Urie Bronfenbrenner, (C) 1970 by the Russell Sage Foundation, New York.)

different ages. Rules of social conduct are prescribed that require students to behave with much courtesy and respect toward both their teachers and their fellow students. For example, children are expected to greet by name their teachers on arriving in the classroom and also their seatmates. Standing when speaking or being spoken to is considered to be cultured conduct. Students are expected to be class monitors and to help the teacher in a variety of classroom duties ranging from cleaning the blackboards and handing out classroom materials up to, and including, dusting the furniture and polishing the floors. At later ages this collective responsibility for work can include removing snow from the school grounds, gardening, and making simple repairs to the school buildings.

Altruism and concern for others rather than the self, permeates the whole Soviet educational system from kindergarten upwards. From the very beginning, stress is placed on teaching children to share and to engage in joint activity. Frequent reference is made to common ownership. Collective play is emphasized. Even special toys are constructed that require the active cooperation of two or more children to make them work. Even at the nursery school level, children are given training in evaluating and criticizing each other's behavior from the point of view of the group. At all times polite behavior is stressed. For example, children are expected to behave particularly well at the table even in the absence of adults. Good manners are seen as reflecting consideration for others.

Throughout the educational system and starting even in nursery school, children are expected to take on ever-increasing communal responsibilities, such as helping others, serving at table, cleaning up, gardening, and caring for animals. "Collectivism" is a vitally important concept to the Soviets. Individuals are expected to consider themselves members of a series of overlapping and interlocking groups. Thus, collective responsibility for, say, the garden or the appearance of the classroom is emphasized. Rewards and punishments, too, are doled out collectively rather than individually. Allied to the notion of collective responsibility is the idea of "socialist competition" in which different collectives compete against each other. This competition involves all phases of activity and behavior: scholastic activity, moral conduct, and even personal grooming. The competition is between such small collectives as "links" in classes (five to eight children), between different classes in schools, between different schools, and even between cities and republics (states).

Each individual is evaluated weekly by his or her peers, following standards and procedures taught by the upbringers (teachers). Since rewards are given to collectives rather than to individuals, it is in every individual's interest to ensure that the behavior of no one lets down the collective. Any one individual has to subordinate, to some extent, his or her own selfish interests to the interests of the collective. By the same token, if one individual is having difficulties, say with mathematics, then it is necessary for the other members of the collective to help him or her to catch up and to stay caught up.

Collective altruism also occurs on another level. Through a system of "group adoption," each class takes on the responsibility for the upbringing of a group of children on a lower grade level. For example, a fourth grade class "adopts" a first grade class in the same school; the older children escort the younger ones to school, play with them in the school yard, teach them new games, read to them, and help them with their schoolwork. Collective altruism, such as the above, also is evaluated by the school authorities as a regular part of school activity.

What happens in this system if a particular child or two departs from good conduct and behaves in a delinquent manner? Once again, it is the collective that often is called upon to decide an appropriate punishment. Frequently this will take the form of making the guilty parties make up for their antisocial behaviors by doing extra work for the collective. Before being fully accepted back into the group, such individuals may have to apologize publicly for their behavior and acknowledge how they might have caused difficulties for others.

Collectives in the school system interlock with collectives and organizations outside it. For example, there are the Communist Youth Organizations which consist of the Octobrists for the first three grades (ages seven to nine), the Pioneers for the fourth through eighth grades (ages ten to fifteen), and the Komosol Young Communist League in the higher grades. Membership in the Octobrists and Pioneers is virtually universal. (The closest equivalent we in the West have are the Boy Scouts and Girl Scouts.) Organizations in factories and collective farms also overlap with the school system, and students may well spend some of their time in these other locales. Essentially, then, a student's life in the Soviet system is far more organized and, moreover, organized into definite social units of which the student is expected to feel a part. This in itself, and with a quite explicit code of behaviors, is expected to socialize each person into behaving extremely altruistically toward others.

What are the consequences of such an upbringing for the Soviet child? First, as Bronfenbrenner (1970) documented, relations with teachers are marked by courtesy and respect. The start of each school year is seen as a generally joyous occasion, and students individually present flowers to their teachers, who are accorded much respect in Soviet society. What about their moral behavior? It is apparent to most visitors that instances of aggressiveness, violation of rules, and other antisocial behavior are genuinely rare. Moreover, these impressions are strongly supported by empirical data. Bronfenbrenner (1970) presented students with a number of "dilemmas" to which they were to respond. For example:

The Lost Test: You and your friends accidentally find a sheet of paper which the teacher must have lost. On this sheet are the questions and answers for a quiz that you are going to have tomorrow. Some of the kids suggest that you do not say anything to the teacher about it, so that all of you can get better marks. What would you really do? Suppose your friends decide to go ahead. Would you go along with them or refuse? (Gabarino & Bronfenbrenner 1976, p. 81)

Other dilemmas dealt with neglecting homework to join friends, leaving a sick friend to go to a movie with the gang, joining friends in pilfering fruit from an orchard, and running away after accidentally breaking a window while playing ball.

The results indicated that Soviet children were much less willing to engage in antisocial behavior than their agemates in the United States were. In addition, the effect of the peer group was quite different in the Soviet Union and the United States. When told that their classmates would know of their actions, American children were even more inclined to take part in misconduct, whereas the Soviet youngsters showed even more self-control. If the children were asked what they would do if they saw a peer engaging in an antisocial behavior (e.g., taking things belonging to others), the Soviet children were far more inclined to intervene directly and talk to the person than were their Western counterparts. Bronfenbrenner (1970) reported an even sharper discrepancy between the

Soviet and Western students in regard to yet another option in this last dilemma; that is, "Do nothing, since it is none of my business." Whereas 20 percent of the Western sample chose to look the other way, less than 1 percent of Soviet students picked this alternative. Soviet children appear to be better behaved and more socialized than are American children.

MORAL EDUCATION
IN NORTH AMERICAN SCHOOLS

Traditional morality in North America often has consisted of a list of prohibitions. For example, one should not steal, lie, or cheat (or smoke, or drink, or have sex outside of marriage). When positive behavior is stressed, it tends to be as some sort of abstract rule such as the "Golden Rule" or "Do unto others as you would have them do unto you." Formal rules also had to be known in the sense of having the moral knowledge that "freedom of speech" was a good thing. Such moral values would be expected to be inculcated by teachers during the natural course of disciplining the children in the school. Thus, children who cheated or stole would expect to be punished; children who were honest would expect to be praised; and the teacher was expected to be a model of good behavior in his or her private life so as to set a "good example" to the children. It also might be expected that the teacher occasionally would make verbal exhortations to the children to lead exemplary lives. Such traditional approaches to morality in North American schools are of unknown effectiveness. They might well have been quite ineffective.

Major changes in this traditional approach began to occur in the late 1950s and early 1960s. Rather than instituting stronger measures that might have been more effective in producing generalizable moral behavior, there was a reaction against *any* type of moral training. It was not the place of the school, so this argument ran, to inculcate moral values in the child. That was the job of the home and the child's family, and the school should stick to teaching "school subjects." This "hands-off" approach no doubt gained a lot of support from the notion of cultural pluralism, or moral relativism. According to this view, the United States and most Western nations are pluralistic societies. Different cultural groups have different values. What might be right for white Anglo-Saxon Protestants, particularly those of the middle classes, it was argued, might not be right for urban-ghetto blacks, for example, in the efficacy of using violence to solve social problems. The then current philosophy suggested, rather, that individuals were expected to "do their own thing" (and leave others to do theirs). No one had the right, it was argued, to impose his or her values on anybody else. The traditional idea of using the American public school system to socialize the hundreds of ethnic minorities (and millions of individuals) into a common "melting-pot" mold appeared to be gone forever.

More recently again, moral education has emerged in both North America and Western Europe and shows signs of skyrocketing growth now in the early 1980s. A number of different approaches are being used, and these have been catalogued and described by Superka, Ahrens, Hedstrom, Ford, and Johnson (1976). These authors indicated that most of these approaches fall into a five-fold typology: *inculcation, moral development, analysis, clarification,* and *action learning.* These approaches will be discussed below.

Inculcation.

This is perhaps the traditional approach to moral education and the one that led to reaction against, for example, religion being taught in the schools. The purpose of inculcation is to instill or to internalize certain values considered desirable. Naturally, these could be political and religious values, as well as the more social, personal, moral, and, for example, scholarly ones.

Inculcation is often mistakenly associated with a narrow range of values to be instilled. This approach can be used for a variety of value positions, including those generally labeled "humanistic." Perhaps more importantly, they can be used to instill values that are presumably universal to all "value ideologies," and altruism and prosocial behaviors surely would be among these. Values of human dignity and respect and concern for others, can be taught easily in classroom settings. Indeed, the naturally occurring social constraints on people's behavior require it to some extent. For example, two individuals both cannot speak at once, and persons cannot walk in and out of classrooms at will without disrupting others. Thus rules have to be generated to control the social interactions for the benefit of the majority. Individuals must learn self-control and to inhibit their own immediate wishes out of consideration for others.

From the learning processes discussed, particularly from chapter 5, we expect both reinforcement and modeling to be very important to the inculcation of values. Positive reinforcement and punishment, made contingent by the teacher on behavior that is in accord with certain values, would be an example. Indeed, it would be very difficult for a teacher not to respond differentially to students' behavior. Reinforcement also can be applied quite consciously and systematically to shape behaviors, as in behavior modification programs. Manuals such as those by Sarason and Sarason (1974) and White and Smith (1972) have been developed to help teachers to apply these techniques to many classroom behaviors. Tokens or points, for example, can be used to motivate doing difficult math problems, remaining quiet for twenty minutes, or helping another student.

Modeling too is a prime candidate for shaping values. As with reinforcement procedures, differential modeling by the teacher is, in fact, inevitable. The teacher inadvertently *must* model the values according to which he or she behaves. For example, the teacher's attitude toward the subject matter he or she teaches will be observed by the students whether that attitude is positive, neutral, or negative. Similarly, whether the teacher is structured or unstructured, strict or permissive, enthusiastic or bored, fair or biased, or involved or uninvolved in approach, will be recognized by the student. Even if teachers attempt to be objective and to conceal their values, they become models for objectivity and hiding one's values.

Combinations of modeling and reinforcement would be particularly effective. Again, much of this occurs naturally and unwittingly. One example would be a teacher praising a student for doing his or her homework (modeling) while other students look on. Other examples happen contrary to the intentions of the teacher. A student who models humorous wisecracks during class, causing the teacher and other students to laugh, might well cause behaviors such as being a class clown or distractor to become valued.

Differential modeling and reinforcement of values in the classroom is inevitable. Much of it is implicit and unwitting (e.g., the notion that being concerned about schoolwork is a good thing). The suggestion here, however, is that the values being transmitted be made more explicit. Then, having decided which values *ought* to be transmitted, steps can be taken to encourage them. For example, cooperative interdependence might be considered a positive value. If so, then perhaps this ought to be made explicit and modeled and reinforced. For example, much schoolwork at the moment, both in games and in scholastic performance, encourages individual competitiveness. This could be changed by stressing cooperative games rather than competitive ones. In regard to scholastic activities, cooperation also could be encouraged by giving extra points to students who help others or giving points to groups of students who cooperate, rather than to individuals. This, as we have seen, is typical of the Soviet educational system.

Many people will react against the idea of deliberate inculcation, and may assert that teachers have no right to impose their values on children. This is understandable. It is perhaps not appropriate to have teachers preaching certain religious and political beliefs to their students. Certain other social attitudes, such as those of a sexual nature, also might be thought to be inappropriate for inculcation (e.g., "Abortion is a good/bad thing"). The thesis here, however, is that the public should help decide what values are to be promoted in the schools. If altruistic values are chosen, as this book suggests they should be, these ought to be made explicit and then taught by teachers throughout the system. The argument in favor of this is as follows: (1) Altruistic behavior is common to all idea systems. Since it is a cultural universal, no one's values are being violated. (2) Regardless of whether or not we make it intentional, altruistic behavior is being shaped to some point on that continuum from pure egoism to pure altruism; that is, students' egoistic-altruistic behavior is determined in part, unwittingly, by the school system whether or not we like it. Therefore, we ought to make it explicit and by so doing, shape it more effectively. (3) If the schools do not teach these moral behaviors, who will? As we have seen, the mass media are shaping selfish and egoistic behavior more than prosocial behavior, and the family is increasingly a less effective socializer. The educational system is all that we have left. It has great potential to be used much more effectively than it currently is. It is where people first learn to work and create a society together. It is a major influence upon later behavior. Much greater care should be invested in what kind of influence it is. Perhaps we should no longer evade the moral responsibility of determining the values that our school systems inculcate.

Moral Development.

This is the approach particularly of Lawrence Kohlberg at the Center for Moral Education at Harvard University. Kohlberg's work, as has been discussed in previous chapters, extends Piaget's (1932) work in important ways (see Kohlberg 1976). Kohlberg argued that morality is not a property of behavior; behavior, as such, is neither moral nor immoral. Rather, it is the intention behind the action, the *reason* for the behavior that must be judged as moral or immoral. To lie and steal, according to this approach, can be seen as either morally good, morally neutral, or morally bad, depending on the reasons for the behavior (e.g., in order to save a life *versus* not realizing it was wrong *versus* in order to become richer). It follows that the proper study of morality, for Kohlberg, is the study of moral reasoning. Moral education, therefore, becomes improving the way a person reasons morally. Chapters 4 and 5 discussed some aspects of Kohlberg's theory of moral development. Because of the importance of Kohlberg's ideas to modern educational theory, we shall review them here.

Kohlberg (1976) viewed children's moral reasoning as progressing through six developmental stages. These were outlined in Table 4.2. People are seen as progressing naturally through these six stages as a result of their life experiences, particularly those that require taking the role of others. As people progress through the stages, the moral reasons for their behavior alter. Early in life, a child will refuse to steal out of fear of being caught, later because it is against the law, and later still because it would mean violating one's own principles. It is only when the later stages of reasoning are acquired that Kohlberg considers the behaviors to be truly moral.

This approach to morality appeals to educators with various points of view. First, the educators can deny any implication that they are inculcating any one set of values or behaviors. This is because, according to Kohlbergian theory, the stages are free of any particular content, and, furthermore, they are said to be universal. For example, cross-cultural studies made in Taiwan, Mexico, Turkey, and Yucatan show the children there making the same progression through stages of thinking as North American children do (Kohlberg & Kramer 1969). It is argued that there is no imposition of white middle-class values. Rather, people are allowed to develop higher ways of considering whatever values they do hold. Another appeal of this theoretical approach to educators is that it can be readily incorporated into virtually every curriculum. The "moral training" is relatively straightforward. All educators must do is stimulate classroom discussions of a variety of moral dilemmas. These dilemmas can be chosen from events in history, choices facing protagonists in literature, current events, or personal problems that the students themselves are likely to face. It is thought that by requiring student participation in such discussions, particularly when the teacher tries to get everyone to see everyone else's point of view and the different perspectives, it is possible to take up the issue and then to resolve the different points of view according to some moral principle. This, it is suggested will help to accelerate the students to progress to higher stages and to prevent "developmental arrest" or fixation at any stage lower than the highest. (In most cases the theory does not allow for regression.)

There are a number of questions to be raised about this theory. Some of these have been discussed in previous chapters. A problem of concern here is of the nature of the relationship between moral reasoning and moral behavior. It is not altogether clear from Kohlberg's writings just what the relationship between moral judgment and behavior should be. On the one hand, Kohlberg and the cognitive-developmentalists write as though the stages of moral reasoning are "content-free" of behavior. Thus, in solving the moral dilemma of whether Heinz should or should not steal a drug in order to save somebody's life (discussed in chapter 4), the moral reasoning used can support either that Heinz should steal the drug to save the life or that he should not steal the drug. Too, the decisions can be made at each of the six stages (see Kohlberg 1969, Tables 6.5 and 6.6, pp. 379-382). Thus it *would* appear as though moral reasoning is independent of any particular kind of behavior.

If moral reasoning is independent of any specific behavior, then there appear to be two problems. First, it might be asked whether this approach to moral education in the schools is sufficient. After all, most people are concerned with moral behavior as much as they are with the intentions (justifications?) behind an action. Most parents would be dismayed if their children came home from school and lied and stole but were able to justify such actions in terms of very high levels of moral philosophy and reasoning. If it is the intention rather than the behavior that is moral or immoral, then we could be left with a very unsavory moral system. Adolf Eichmann gassed thousands of human beings while acting on the best Nazi intentions of "improving" the human race by ridding it of its "subhuman undesirables." The Holy Wars were conducted on the best of moral intentions. Higher ways of thinking do not necessarily produce considerate behavior. Some of the most heinous social crimes have been perpetrated by moral elitists acting on private principle. Having the right "intentions" and "reasons" is not good enough, and the moral reasoning approach might be thought to be teaching people simply to be glib.

The second problem with Kohlberg's theory is that the empirical literature demonstrates that in fact, there is a moderate relationship between measures of moral reasoning and moral behavior. Studies done by, for example, Anchor and Cross (1974), Eisenberg-Berg (1979), Eisenberg-Berg and Hand (1979), Emler and Rushton (1974), Haan, Smith, and Block (1968), Harris, Mussen, and Rutherford (1976), Krebs and Rosenwald (1977, Rubin and Schneider (1973), Rushton (1975), and Staub (1974) all found that those individuals with the highest levels of moral judgment behaved more morally (helped more, cheated less, etc.) than those with lower levels of moral judgment.

Why should this relationship occur if the type of moral reasoning advocated by Kohlberg is independent of particular behavior? If the nature of the stages of development really are content-free, then, theoretically, a Stage 6 person could engage in as much rape and murder as any Stage 2 psychopath; could engage in as much mass murder as a Stage 1 Eichmann; and could engage in as much hedonism as he or she wished. The reasons for the positive correlations between moral judgment and behavior may well be that the moral behaviors have been socialized by society and that the moral reasoning tends in some way to anchor them or to provide more generalized internalization. If this argument is correct, then the moral judgment approach to moral education as advocated by Kohlberg, while necessary, is certainly not sufficient. For maximum socialization to occur, both the person's behavior *and* his or her moral judgment must be emphasized.

There is a final point. One of the suggested advantages of the moral development approach to moral education is that people are free to choose the values they think best for themselves. This approach is often contrasted, in this respect, with the view of inculcation. Although it seems likely that people may well *feel* freer to choose and that this may have important implications in its own right (see Brehm 1976, for a discussion), the epistemology of Kohlberg's approach and of others is in fact no different. It is, rather, that although the one approach makes its goals behaviorally content-explicit, the other, wrongly, imagines that its goals are behaviorally content-free. Kohlberg's moral education programs rely on modeling and reinforcement of modes of moral reasoning. Too, in attempting to move children to higher stages of moral reasoning, the implementers of Kohlberg's system are imposing their values on children. The *processes* of social learning outlined in chapter 5 and discussed throughout the book apply equally to Kohlbergian theory (as indeed to the approaches yet to be discussed).

Values Analysis.

This is the approach to education advocated by perhaps most of today's social science educators. As Superka and others (1976) outlined it, the purpose of the analysis approach is to use logical thinking and scientific investigation objectively to study ethics and morality. The belief that a rational restructuring of thinking will lead to rational behavior patterns is a superrational approach. At an extreme, it proposes that human beings are rational actors who can attain the highest good by subordinating feelings and passions to logic and scientific methods, thereby resolving value issues according to reason and science.

As for teaching this in the schools, the teacher, usually in a social studies class, has the class analyze a moral problem. For example, what is the morality of providing money (e.g., welfare, pensions, sick benefits) to people who are not working? Or aid to poorer countries? Usually it has to be stressed that the focus ought to be more on the moral as opposed to the political or economic, inasmuch as these can be distinguished. One procedure might be to get those in favor to specify the "good" consequences they see as resulting (e.g., feelings of being cared about, gratitude and belonging on the part of the recipients). In addition, those who were against would specify what they thought would be the "bad" consequences (e.g., increasing dependency, removing the work ethic, etc.). The students then would be divided up into groups to do library searches and even to conduct surveys, to see if they could find out if indeed the conjectured consequences did occur. They would be expected to feed such results back to their original values and change them, if necessary. Other examples of moral issues might be debating abortion, abolition of the death penalty, busing to achieve racial quotas, and so forth.

Although it is easy to generate topics to be researched, Superka and others provide details of student materials from a variety of educational publishing outlets, for example, an educational film entitled *Moral Dilemmas of American Presidents: The Agony of Decision* (1974; Superka 1976, p. 74). Students are expected to research questions about Abraham Lincoln's position on slavery, such as "Would a 'do-nothing' policy have been morally acceptable to you? Why?" "Would a 'giving-in-to-the-Confederacy' position have been morally acceptable to you? Why?" "Is a decision that avoids bloodshed always a good decision?" and "Would you have gone to war to preserve the Union if you were President Lincoln?" Among the generalizations to be tested in this case are: "Abraham Lincoln was indifferent to the continued existence of slavery. His main concern was the preservation of the Union" and "Abraham Lincoln hated slavery and he felt that the Civil War was the only means by which the Union could be scourged of that evil institution." Perhaps fortunately, additional information on each issue is provided for the teacher on how research into these questions can be conducted.

Values clarification.

This approach is in some ways, at least on paper, the most eclectic. The intention essentially is to help students become aware of their own values, whatever they are, and also to see the interrelationships among these values. Many techniques have been proposed to help make students aware of their values. These would include group discussion of both hypothetical and real dilemmas. In addition, many highly personalized exercises are suggested, such as those outlined by Simon, Howe, and Kirschenbaum (1972). One such strategy is for the teacher to ask students to list, as rapidly as possible, twenty things in life that they really love to do. It is stressed that such exercises are optional and that there are no right or wrong, or correct or incorrect answers. When everybody has listed twenty items, the responses are coded. For example, students might be asked to place a $ sign next to any item costing more than three dollars. Or the letter R might be placed by any item entailing some degree of risk. Another code might be to place either the letter P or the letter A before each item. The P is used for items that one prefers doing with people, and the A for items that one prefers doing alone. Again, the number 5 might be placed by any item that probably would not be on the list five years from now. Finally, the student might be asked to place near each item the date when he or she last did it. The author suggested that the discussions that would follow can lead to gaining a perspective of, and an insight into, one's values.

Insight is not quite enough. It is only the first step. There are five others. After gaining insight, the values clarification approach then expects that students will *choose* their values. These choices ideally should (a) be made from alternatives, (b) be made thoughtfully, and (c) be made freely. Having chosen, students ought to be encouraged to be *proud* of their values and indeed make public an affirmation of their choice. Often this will be done by asking the students to *share* their values with the rest of the class. Finally, the values clarification approach requires that students *act* and act repeatedly in accordance with their chosen values. It is perhaps worth repeating that educators who use techniques such as values clarification cannot really evade the broader issue of value inculcation. Which values are to be strengthened? The Nazi youth were proud of their values and, unfortunately, affirmed their choices behaviorally.

Action Learning.

The distinguishing characteristic of the action-learning approach is that it provides specific opportunities for learners to act on their values. As do those who favor values clarification, proponents of action learning see that one must choose prize affirm, and act on their choices. Action-learning advocates extend this to specifying the idea of acting on values by making opportunities available to do so. Thus, if altruism and helping others were seen as values, opportunities would be provided to enable students to act on these values. Voluntary work in a hospital might be an example.

Integration of the Different
Approaches to Moral Education.

These five approaches are those currently most prevalent in school systems in North America and Western Europe. They are not, however, implemented in any major or systematic manner. Rather, individual teachers, for example, in history and social studies, may attempt to implement them. An occasional school board or individual educational psychologist also might attempt to evaluate such a program. But there is nothing in the West remotely approaching that of the Soviet educational system in this regard.

These five approaches are not mutually exclusive. If our educational system ever decides to implement a more thorough moral education curriculum, it would be easy to combine all the approaches. Clearly, that which can be inculcated by rewarding and punishing and modeling allegiance to, is only one part; moral reasoning by itself is not enough either. Rules need to be acted on after being discussed. These five approaches do not include all the aspects of moral education that need to be considered. Neither moral rules nor action is enough for an altruistic society. Human compassion also is needed. Role playing and empathy, for example, need to be highlighted. Moreover, the student's own ego-development and self-esteem needs probably ought to be considered, for it might well be thought that only those who are secure in themselves can be truly concerned about others.

SUMMARY

The education system's function as an agency for socialization goes back to antiquity and is universal. The Indians of Canada for example, before the advent of Europeans, described two broad curricula. The first course was a secular one and consisted of learning to hunt and the acquisition of other skills suitable for their society. The second curriculum was a moral, ethical, and religious one. This two-pronged view of education is found in many other societies of the past, including Spartan and Athenian Greece, and Mediaeval Europe.

Education in the modern world is also divisible into secular and moral parts. Whereas all nations of the world today provide, or aspire to provide, universal secular education, only some provide intensive moral training. The Soviet educational system is particularly involved in moral education. It has as its aim the propagation of "socialist morality" and the making of the "New Soviet Man." Great stress is put on prosocial behavior, consideration for others, and self-discipline. Studies carried out by Bronfenbrenner (1970) demonstrated, over a variety of tasks, that Soviet children were indeed more morally well-behaved than were children in the United States.

Moral education in North American and Western European schools is far less intensive. A five-fold typology of approaches to moral education in the West can be identified: inculcation, moral development, analysis, clarification, and action learning. These are not, however, implemented in any major or systematic manner. There is nothing in the West remotely approaching that of the Soviet educational system in this regard.

chapter 9

ALTRUISM
AND SOCIETY

In chapter 6 it was suggested that because of recent changes in economic development the family, the traditional source of primary socialization, is no longer as effective as it once was in teaching children a prosocial consideration for others. Because of the breakup of the extended family system, the increases in the divorce rate, single-parent families, and working mothers, there are fewer and fewer adults left in the family to socialize children. Thus, it was proposed, there is an increased likelihood that people will grow up undersocialized, caring relatively little about the consequences of their behavior for others. Aggravating this situation, it was indicated in chapter 7, were the new, powerful, alternative means of socialization available. Foremost among these are the mass media, especially television. Although television can promote valued cognitive and social development, it currently serves largely as an important disinhibitor and teacher of antisocial styles of behavior. This is due to the prevalence of aggressive and antisocial modeling by television characters. In chapter 8 the educational system was discussed, and although a variety of approaches to moral education were described, it had to be admitted that, in the main, the educational system had evaded any major responsibility for socializing children's behavior. To summarize the bleak situation: The family is an increasingly ineffective socializer of children; the television system is socializing them in an increasingly antisocial direction; and the educational system is not socializing children at all.

Is there any evidence that this gloomy scenario is actually producing the predicted "undersocialized personality"? Unfortunately there is. As discussed in chapter 6, Bronfenbrenner (1975) catalogued the alarming rise over the last several years in such social pathologies as child and adolescent suicide rates, juvenile delinquency, and illegitimate births. Perhaps most noticeable of all is the amount of violence and aggression that characterizes and distinguishes much of contemporary American society. Many people in the United States know at least one personal instance of an assault or robbery, and some people in large cities are actually afraid to walk out at night for fear of assault. This differs markedly from many other countries where, indeed, visitors from the United States are often struck by how safe it is. This, however, seems to be changing. Delinquency and violence are increasing in European countries as in the U.S., and muggings on the street are becoming more common there, too. It would seem that many other societies are moving in a similar direction—toward undersocialization.

The question still remains as to whether society is becoming increasingly unsocialized. Perhaps the United States always was a particularly violent society. Perhaps Bronfenbrenner's (1975) figures only reflect better statistics gathering now compared with that of twenty years ago. Unfortunately, the evidence from diverse sources is too much in agreement for this to be the case. For example, Southern and Plant (1974) used the self-report *California Personality Inventory* (Gough 1956) to compare the personality profiles of first-year college students in 1970-71 with those who had preceded them in 1958-60. They found that the 1970-71 group scored significantly lower on several measures including self-control and social responsibility. A study by Schubert and Wagner (1975) used the clinically oriented *Minnesota Multiphasic Personality Inventory* (MMPI) to compare 1968 university students with those from 1958. The general profiles of the 1968 students showed significant increases in emotional disturbance and alienation. Persons with the patterns of MMPI validity scores of the 1960s students are interpreted in the *MMPI Handbook* (Dahlstrom, Welsh, & Dahlstrom 1972) as rebellious, not caring about making a good impression, and exaggerating their own problems.

Further indication of growing self-centeredness is suggested by a perusal of the self-help books and therapies offered in the late 1970s. Masses of people are suddenly asking themselves questions that just twenty years ago would have been almost inconceivable—questions like "Who am I?", "What should

I be doing with my life?" and "How can I be happier?" The Human Potentialist Movement grew to fill this very different sort of consumer need. As Weiner commented:

> By and large you don't hear words like "cure" and "adjustment" very much in psychotherapeutic circles these days. What you do hear is a great deal of talk about helping people *grow*, putting them *in better touch with themselves*, making them more *self-actualized, self-directed, self-assertive, self-fulfilled* . . . well, almost certainly, self-something. (1978, p. 3)

Behavior therapy, too, joined the ranks of the self-enhancers with its own variation; assertiveness training. "Why say yes when you want to say no? Why feel guilty? Stand up for your rights!" Originally designed to help chronically shy, passive people, assertiveness training quickly achieved mass popularity in North America. (By contrast, in the United Kingdom, for example, some of the best selling self-help programs are referred to as "social skills training" —a very different orientation indeed to problems of personal adjustment.) All of this led Tom Wolfe (1976) to so accurately tag the 1970s as "The Me Decade." Or as Weiner wrote:

> . . . perhaps no one summed up the mood of the times as well as Robert Ringer in his 1977 blockbuster book, *Looking Out for Number One.* One hardly needs to read beyond the title. Say it loud, I'm selfish and I'm proud! No Human Potentialist himself, Ringer could say explicitly what the Potentialists had only implied: that nothing could be more important than the gratification of the self . . . (1978, p. 5)

All of the above creates the impression of a society moving toward increasing self-centeredness and away from altruistic consideration for others. Numerous other researchers and thinkers have also expressed their concern about this (e.g., Campbell 1975; Harmon 1977; Hogan 1975; Kanfer 1979). For example, Harmon (1977) perceived in Western society: (a) a decreased sense of community; (b) an increased sense of alienation and purposelessness; (c) an increased frequency of personal disorders and mental illness; (d) an increased rate of violent crime; (e) an increased frequency and severity of social destruction; (f) an increased use of police to control behavior; (g) an increased public acceptance of hedonistic behaviors and lax public morality; and (h) an increased interest in noninstitutionalized religious activities. Kanfer (1979) argues that, taken together, disparate evidence suggests an "increased trend toward self-absorption and the denial of individual responsibility for the maintenance of the social environment." The impression of undersocialization is pervasive.

If our society is to reverse the trend toward undersocialization, it is necessary to bring about changes in the process of socialization. But how should we socialize? Should the majority impose its values on the various minorities? In pluralistic societies such as ours in which quite diverse groups co-exist, isn't it a matter of relative value what one chooses to socialize? After all, it might be argued, if the goal of socialization is to prepare people for group living, then socialization must be tailored to the particular group to which the person belongs, since different groups have different values and life-styles. But is this completely true? Don't all groups require their members to show consideration for others? Can groups, let alone complex societies made up of quite diverse groups, even exist without it? *It is the thesis of this book that altruism is the central problem facing society today.*

How can altruism, which by definition reduces self-centered behavior, possibly be fostered? Let us consider some possibilities of how to do this within the three major systems of socialization that have been discussed, that is, the family, the mass media, and education.

THE FAMILY SYSTEM AS A SOCIALIZER IN THE FUTURE

In chapter 6 it was seen that the nuclear family, the traditional primary socializer of children, is increasingly ineffective and may even be disintegrating: One in three marriages ends in divorce, one in six children is brought up in a single-parent home, more and more mothers are working, and fewer and fewer adults remain in the home to socialize the children. Children who are left unattended are not socialized to the same degree as children who spend much time with adults. Even in middle-class suburban homes with intact families, it may be questioned whether parents spend as much time with children as they once did. With increased standards of living and more recreational space, it is not at all uncommon to see children given their own play area (often consisting of a whole recreation room, or at least their own bedroom) in which they are left to themselves and their peers. This "unmaking of the American child," as Bronfenbrenner (1970) characterized it, has resulted in increased numbers of undersocialized adults.

The proposal being presented here is that the greater the amount of adult-child interaction there is, the more opportunities there are for limit-setting and prosocial socialization. The solution to the problem of undersocialization therefore is to increase the frequency of adult-child interactions. One way of doing this would be to help parents to be home when their children return from school. As Bronfenbrenner (1975) found, one growing problem is the increasing number of "latchkey children"—youngsters who come home from school to an empty house. Such children are especially prone to academic difficulties, school absenteeism and dropout, juvenile delinquency, and drug addiction. Perhaps factories and businesses employing large numbers of workers could be encouraged to produce flexible work schedules that would enable parents to be at home when their children return from school.

Other solutions to the problem must include the more conservative ones of trying to keep families intact and decreasing the number of illegitimate births. Some, for example, have suggested that certain social welfare policies may inadvertently reinforce undesirable behavior. June Brown (1978), a concerned black woman writing in the *Detroit News,* pointed out that according to the American National Center for Health Statistics, more than *half* the black children born in the United States during 1976 were born out of wedlock. This figure was double the number of out of wedlock births in 1965. The figures among whites also had increased, from 3.96 percent in 1965 to 7.68 in 1976. As Senator Edward Kennedy said in a speech at a National Association for the Advancement of Colored People (NAACP) dinner, the government must stop its practice of offering a teenage girl the bonus of her own apartment, her own phone, and color TV—provided she has an out of wedlock baby. Clearly, welfare can be used to reinforce inadvertently a variety of selfish behaviors.

Social policy also can be used more positively. There could be greater support systems for nuclear families, particularly in the area of good daycare services. Although group care has been available in other industrialized countries for many years, it is only recently that it has become available to large numbers of young children in the United States. Many daycare centers have been concerned with society's recent effort to reverse the problems found in children from socioeconomically disadvantaged backgrounds. The results for short-term cognitive development have been largely favorable, especially for lower class children, with no adverse effects on emotional development (e.g., Etaugh 1974; Robinson & Robinson 1971). Larger scale, community-based daycare, designed to provide care for young children of working parents is even more recent. The dramatic increase in the number of mothers with young children entering the labor force has increased the demand for such services. The literature suggests that well-run community daycare centers are not at all detrimental to children and indeed can have very good effects on children's social and emotional development (e.g., Rubenstein & Howes 1979). In countries such as China, Israel, and the Soviet Union, mothers are encouraged to work while their children are cared for in state-run institutions. In China, for example, mothers can leave their infants in a nursery at their place of work as soon as the infants are two months old. The mother leaves her job at intervals to nurse the infant. On the collective farms of Israel the children are cared for from early infancy by professional caretakers and are housed in communal nurseries. These children seem as happy and emotionally responsive as children raised solely in their own homes.

A more radical possibility for daycare and one that would help solve the problem of staffing, would be to involve directly as many neighborhood parents as possible. Rather than each parent (usually the mother) staying in relative isolation in their own home raising their own one or perhaps two preschoolers, daycare centers could be established so that most parents could take their children and do their "work" there. Perhaps they might even be paid by society for fulfilling this vitally important role. Further, this "collective" of parents could be trained in principles of bringing up children to get along well with other children and to behave with consideration for the wider community. From the age of five up society is willing to pay a great deal for this job to be done in primary, secondary, and higher education. We very seldom recognize that the expenses already incurred by these five-year-old children, if evaluated in economic terms at present-day wage rates, would amount to a huge chunk of the gross national product. If we as a society are left for any reason with a newborn babe on our hands—"in care"—the cost to us as a community, of caring for it, is alarmingly high. The job of child rearing before the age of five is not considered as important even in this sense as that of a typist. There are no lunch and coffee breaks, no conditions of employment, no unions, and no possibilities of strike action. The conditions under which parental care evolved were very different from those in which we live today. For example, parental behavior was a more communal activity and far more important to the community. If this could be brought back for those parents who wanted it, it might appear as a much more rewarding and creative activity than it is perceived to be by many today. It is also worth pointing out that there is certainly no reason why only women have to carry the burden of child-rearing in the society. The fathers should be participants in this cultural endeavor as well. In the future we may see more and more families in which the male is the homemaker and the female pursues the career, or where they split the same job, with each member sharing responsibility for running the home. Certainly the wider society could benefit from the ensuing, increased socialization.

THE MASS MEDIA

It has been amply documented by now that our attitudes and values can be demonstrably altered by what we observe on television. Chapter 7 reviewed much of the scientific evidence for this conclusion. There have been many experiments conducted by behavioral scientists assessing the impact of television film on viewers' behavior. Many industrial countries have held hearings and commissions of inquiry into the problem. All have confirmed the potential power that television has over our lives. It is for this very reason that we are so fearful of television falling into the "wrong hands." Totalitarian governments could (and do) control all news outlets and sources of information. This, we believe correctly, leads the recipients of such news items to have a very distorted view of the world. It is the acknowledged power of television in shaping our thoughts that leads political parties to guard so jealously their rights to equal air-time. Should the president of the United States, or the prime ministers of Canada or the United Kingdom be seen as needing to address the Nation too often, the rival party's leader will demand an opportunity to reply. It is the powerful influence of television that makes this fact a major point of contention. It is no secret that nowadays, by and large, the political party that spends the most money on television advertising will be the party that wins the election. Our behavior, yours and mine, is influenced by what we watch, even if we feel that it is not, as is recognized by both the advertisers and the television networks. Advertisers spend billions of dollars annually to show their products being used (modeled) on television by attractive and conspicuous others who then receive extremely positive consequences (reinforcement) for such use. Alternatively, they simply associate (classically condition) their products with some highly positively valenced set of stimuli (sexual glamour, friendly people, a fulfilling life style). Such applications of the laws of learning affect the products we buy and the expectancies we have of what the "good life" is. Market research by the advertising companies demonstrates this to be so; billions of dollars are spent annually on advertising. It is clear that television has a great deal of power to affect our behavior.

Television network chiefs present a quite unwarranted duplicity of attitude on this issue. On the one hand, they like to believe that they are wielders of extraordinary power and social influence (which they are). They make this quite explicit when they charge enormous sums of money to advertisers to sell their products (differential rates depending on when the products are shown to the viewers). On the other hand, when behavioral scientists point out how powerful the mass media are in influencing the attitudes of viewers, the media chiefs immediately start to deny their power. Bandura (1973) discussed these issues and commented that it is not a matter of changing the attitudes of the people in a position of power, for their behavior is not really governed by consideration of what behavioral scientists say. Television violence is shown for good reason—it spices up very dull scripts and is inexpensive to product. The alternative of offering a lot of money to good playwrights to produce compelling drama with depth of character and weeks of rehearsal appears to be unacceptable to the media industry. Television programming is geared to one overriding purpose—to sell products (thus reinforcing the media chiefs for showing the programs they do).

The networks themselves purport an alternative view as to why they show so much violence. They claim that "violence sells," that this is what the viewers want, and that therefore they are only filling a need. Blaming the viewers for the amount of violence in programming is untenable. In a recent study by Diener and DeFour (1978), the amount of violent content in television programs was correlated with the national Nielsen viewer index. No significant relationship emerged ($r = +.05$). In a second study by these authors, an experiment was performed in which the adventure program *Police Woman* was presented to subjects either uncut or with the violence deleted. Although the uncut version was perceived as significantly more violent, it was not liked significantly more. There is presently little evidence indicating that violence enhances program popularity. Indeed, a large percentage of the population objects to the amount of television violence and believes that it should be restricted (Opinion Research Center 1973).

There are, in addition, much broader attitudes pervasively portrayed on television that some might think of as problematic for an altruistic society. Advertising per se is an example. By showing successful people on television as also materially successful and as consumers of advertised products, the norms being internalized of what constitutes the good life are materialistic. Millions of people who are not rich enough to afford all the portrayed life styles must feel continuous personal frustration and thwarted desire as a result of the social comparisons they inevitably must make. It is little wonder that unemployed ghetto youths, who are the most likely to contribute to the crime rate, behave as they do. To some extent, the frustrating social comparisons must occur to many professional people too, for even their life styles will not compare to many of the mass media fantasies continually being absorbed. Since we learn from salient models and these models are continuously being presented to us on the television screen, it is inevitable that we will internalize some of the standards they portray. These might include highly inappropriate expectations of life, thus relegating us to continuous self-absorbed dissatisfaction, including the concommitant misery, selfishness, and frustration-bred hostility produced by such disconfirmed expectations. It is worth noting, for example, that poverty per se or even poverty in the midst of plenty, are not sufficient to produce social upheaval. Such conditions occur throughout most of the world without producing the crime rates that occur in the United States. The problem appears to be, at least in part, the material expectations people have for their own lives, and that they have acquired norms of self-indulgence rather than norms of self-control.

The inescapable conclusion from all of the above is that that which is portrayed on our television screens must be drastically altered. It is perhaps worth repeating the conclusions of the Canadian Royal Commission about the problem of television:

> If the amount of depicted violence that exists in the North American intellectual environment could be expressed in terms of a potentially dangerous food or drink additive . . . there is little doubt that society long since would have demanded a stop to it. . . . (*Ontario*, vol. 1, 1977, p. 51)

A number of different steps could be taken to control the mass media. Bandura (1973) listed four different strategies for reducing the level of televised violence.

One approach mentioned, and as quickly dismissed, is to rely on the industry's system of self-regulation. Unfortunately, no matter how well-intentioned media practitioners might be, it can be expected that when left to internal regulation, profits will dictate content. A second approach is to publicly evaluate the performance of the broadcasting industry. For example, a respected, privately funded violence-monitoring service might be established independent of both government and industry control, that would compute and publicize separate violence rates for the different networks, sponsors, and programs. Gerbner (e.g., Gerbner & Gross 1976) developed a sensitive method of measuring the amount of violence shown on television through content analysis of its output. The standard coding system records the number and kinds of violent actions, and provides an index of the rate of violent episodes per hour of broadcasting. Bandura (1973) suggested that the dissemination and attendant publicization of these ratings, for example, through TV guides and parent-teacher organizations, might well lead the worst offenders to improve their image relative to their more positive competitors. Certainly other consumer advocates have found disclosures of objectionable practices to result in some amelioration of the practices. In the present case, presumably, the main effect would be made by the exertion of pressure on the advertising sponsors of the program.

A third approach advocated by Bandura is to rely on "the power of positive example" (1973, p. 281) by encouraging a viable public broadcasting system, free of commercial pressures, which would compete with the commercial television stations. If it can be shown that nonviolent programming can attract significant audiences, as it did with *Sesame Street,* then the commercial networks will be inclined to follow.

A final approach to the problem of television violence is to appeal to governmental agencies to regulate the commercial marketing of violence. Although Bandura himself does not recommend this particular view, it must be noted that many other countries have done this to the extent of actually banning the importation of particularly violent U.S.-made programs. In the United States, federal guidelines or even controls could be enacted with which the broadcasting industry would have to comply or face heavy fines or even loss of license through the power of the Federal Communications Commission. Although to some this might seem to be a drastic solution and the networks themselves would certainly shout censorship, it might be noted that all other large industries are regulated by a variety of governmental legislation. It is no more acceptable to pollute the intellectual environment for profit than it is the industrial one.

At the moment, the advertising and television industry exercise virtually unlimited control in the service of their corporate interests, and the public has no direct access to the use of public airways. There is clearly a need for some mechanism which would enable the public to voice an opinion. The present restricted access to television time raises the issue of *corporate* censorship of televised offerings. By restricting access to television time and excluding that which would conflict with sponsor interests, network officials exercise selective control over what people are shown. Stronger regulatory guidelines appear to be part of the answer. If industrial self-regulation does not work, and consumer advocacy and the example from more prosocial competitors fail to exert an influence, perhaps the recourse will have to be to public legislation in order to give the public a greater voice.

THE EDUCATIONAL SYSTEM

It is in the educational system that society perhaps can most readily make a significant and active contribution to increasing prosocial competencies and altruistic motivation. We can educate our children and ourselves to engage in altruistic cooperation to satisfy mutual goals, rather than to strive selfishly to satisfy personal desires. If the educational systems are examined closely, we can see that they are far from ideal. In most cases, school is a place where individual competition is fostered. Students compete with one another for top marks. There are winners and there are losers. The losers soon realize this and opt out of the academic competition to compete on other levels. Often such students are the most difficult to control and disrupt the class. In ghetto (and some suburban) schools, where most students see little point in the academic reinforcement system, the peer reinforcement-approval system is such that teachers can do little even to control the class. Assaults on teachers, including rape, is not uncommon in some inner city schools. Such happenings are probably unique to the United States. What is to be done?

One possibility is to turn to a far more intensive and disciplined program of prosocial education, in the widest sense of the term, than is currently being undertaken. As discussed in chapter 8, there are a number of viewpoints of how best to pursue prosocial education. In North America and Western Europe, prosocial "moral" education is in its infancy. Here we are likely to see massive extensions in the future. There is also no reason why this cannot begin at a very early age, particularly if more daycare centers and nursery schools were established. At the primary and secondary school level many of the implications mentioned in chapter 8 could be implemented. Large classes could be broken down into small groups (e.g., a row of five to eight students), and these groups could work more interdependently. There could be emphasis on getting along well with others, fulfilling responsibilities, belonging to the collective, and showing initiative and leadership. Groups could work on moral dilemmas connected with "self versus other" issues with some emphasis on the importance of rules and principles to guide the interaction between self and others. Such procedures may counteract the negative effects of excessive individualism. Naturally it would be quite inappropriate to go to the other extreme of excessive collectivism with a concommitant stifling of individual initiative. Rather, what is required is the encouragement of individual self-reliance within the framework of shared responsibility and concern for others.

There are other aspects of the education system that, with only slight modification, could result in substantial changes in outlook, not only for our own culture but for world culture as a whole. The first of these modifications is the massive extension of science and the scientific method. The world is filled with a million wonders, and young children are filled with curiosity about them. There is no reason why science, as a procedure for discovering how and why, cannot be introduced on the nursery school level. Science, in its broadest sense (a systematic, objective [replicable] observation of facts) can be generalized to all subjects, particularly to such areas of social science as history and geography. In early high school there is no reason why psychology and sociology (and evolutionary theory and animal behavior) could not be taught. The unity of knowledge could be stressed and perhaps made more relevant to the observation and living of daily life. With emphasis on the scientific method, there might be an increased desire to analyze prejudices and to see more clearly the continuity of community across national, racial, and religious borders.

For teaching history and social science, specific aspects of science also could be implemented. For example, the history of *Homo sapiens* as a species could be stressed, rather than, say, that of "Western Civilization." Mixed in with this history, when possible, could be lessons about the nature of humans, for example, the tendency of *Homo sapiens* to divide into competing factions (of class, race, religion, and nationality). It can be stressed how basically "tribal" humans are. By attempting to foster a more global view of our species, specific subgroups such as "American," and "Canadian," "Israeli," and "Arab" can be seen in broader perspective. By stressing the scientific approach, universal rather than parochial knowledge is emphasized. Historical events can be interpreted as conflict between differentially interested groups of *Homo sapiens* with different degrees of economic and military power, rather than, currently, on the glorious "will"of national peoples. Democracy, capitalism, fascism, and socialism can be seen as different ways of organizing power and resources determined partly by economic forces, rather than caused by the "good sense" of those like us or the "political backwardness" of those not like us. In these ways we can perhaps produce a new way of thinking in our children, one that is more deeply critical about social issues and that would increase awareness of a world identity and, indeed, a feeling of global altruism sufficient to ensure the survival of the human race.

SOCIO-POLITICAL CONSIDERATIONS

This book primarily has analysed altruistic behavior as a product of the social learning experiences people have had. This approach has the distinct advantage of being specific and operationalizable. Factors such as those discussed throughout this book: for example, modeling and reinforcement, and family, educational, and television systems, can be altered in ways that promote altruism within a society. The conceptual approach of social learning theory has therefore rested on firm empirical foundations. Data have been marshalled to support the view that the processes described and the systems that implement the processes do in fact exert influence. Challenging issues for further study remain. For example, *how* important are the processes and systems just described? How much of the real life altruism found within and among societies is due to the variables outlined here? Are more important variables found on quite different levels of explanation? If so, what might these other levels be?

One argument that might be mounted against the analysis outlined in this book is that the individual person has been falsely singled out as the primary source of influence; i.e., it is implied that humans internalize a set of emotional dispositions and standards which then serve to guide their behavior in a variety of environmental settings. The consequences that occur in these settings in turn feed back into and modify these same guiding standards and emotional dispositions. This is indeed the basis of the approach outlined here. A concern that might be raised about this analysis, however, is that since humans are confined in their actions by a variety of social and role constraints (which operate regardless of who fills those particular roles), a more appropriate level of explanation would include the group and/or sociological determinants of these roles. Certainly it is true that studies cited earlier such as that by Strayer, Wareing, and Rushton 1979 demonstrate social constraints even on the behavior of preschoolers. Thus the peer group and relations within it are of critical importance. This does not mean, however, that a social learning analysis is inappropriate. Far from it. Social and role restraints are created and maintained by humans who have learned those restraints and also learned to impose them on others. As discussed in chapter 3, social learning theory views causal processes in terms of triadic reciprocal influences between personal factors, behavior, and environmental influences (Bandura 1978b). Changing an individual's attitudes and behavior through social learning will lead him or her to respond quite differently to the nature of social constraints. Socially disadvantaged groups have made this abundantly clear in recent years by altering the inequitable social conditions that had persisted for decades, and even centuries. Determinism is thus reciprocal in nature. Social constraints determine attitudes and behavior; but changes in attitudes and ideas can lead to alterations in behavior and in the social constraints.

Some macro approaches prefer an even more sociological level of explanation. For example, Marxists believe that the ultimate determinants are economic and that educational systems, television industries, and family structures are, relatively speaking, "superstructures" built upon and determined by the basic underlying economic system. Certainly the means of producing goods is of critical importance. Hunter-gatherers have very different forms of social organization and altruism than do agricultural people. Large, powerful, agricultural civilizations usually had some form of feudal aristocratic social organization with a very different set of social obligations and altruistic expectations. Early mercantile and liberal capitalistic societies again, produced an entirely different set of social organizations. In this latter type of society, for example, very great emphasis is placed on the individual and his or her own drive, effort and responsibility. Altruism can seem detrimental to ideologies produced by the necessities of such economies. Ayn Rand (1964), for example, argued that altruism is harmful for the survival of capitalism. Utopian socialist societies, on the other hand, whether conceived of by behaviorist psychologists, as in Skinner's (1948) *Walden Two,* or by the leaders of Communist societies in the real world, believe that altruism is a virtue and that individuals should consider the wider interests of their community. For these ideologies there are sometimes economic implications. For example, individual farm holding is seen as an evil leading to selfish behavior. Farms, they argue, should be owned and worked collectively.

According to this particular macro approach, the ultimate determinant of social relationships within a society is the organizational procedure used in generating its wealth; that is, the society is based on the type of economic system it has—hunter-gatherer (primitive communism), feudal, capitalist, or socialist. Should this be the case, Marxists would argue, there would be little value in attempting to tinker with peripheral elements of the society such as the television industry and educational system. Instead, it would be necessary to alter the basic economic system. It would be argued, for example, that one could not hope to change the competitive nature of the American educational system, with its emphasis upon the individual, until the competitive nature of the American economic system was changed. According to Marxist theory, the competitive nature of the free-enterprise American economic system *requires* a competitive free-enterprise philosophy within the schools. Strong exponents of this view would probably argue also that even if one could alter people's attitudes within the school system through various programs of prosocial education, these would not generalize to the nonacademic situation where economic competition between individuals was the norm. The proposition that the existence of large pools of unemployed individuals serves to decrease solidarity among workers (who are faced with competing with each other for available jobs and to stop themselves from falling back into the unemployed pool) cannot be totally erroneous. Thus, Marxists would argue, the more appropriate level of analysis is that of society and the social roles it generates.

Although the social learning idea of reciprocal determinism would reject an extreme, undirectional view of the economic determinism of human behavior, nonetheless, analyses of altruism from such economic and sociological perspectives as the one just presented (regardless of its veridicality) can be integrated usefully into the social learning model. Reciprocal determinism is a general analytic principle for analyzing psychosocial phenomena at the level of organizational and societal systems, as well as the interpersonal level. It incorporates all sources of influence at many different levels and only rejects extreme undirectional determinism (whether economic, biologic, or whatever). According to the analysis being presented here, all sources of influence interact at the person-behavior-environment interface. On the one hand, the economic and political environment determines the individual's behavior and his or her philosophical idea-systems, emotional responses, and biological dispositions. By the same analysis, these dispositions, responses, and idea-systems within the individual help to determine the economic environment. This is not to deny that, at any point in time, one source of influence may be stronger than another. When there are unjust social conditions (for example, leading to a lack of altruism), the point of interest might become the ascertaining of mechanisms that would allow for the exercise of more reciprocal influence.

WILL OUR SOCIETY SURVIVE?

For the last six thousand years of human history, great empires and civilizations have risen and then fallen. Egyptian, Sumerian, Greek, Carthaginian, Roman, and Chinese empires have pushed outwards incorporating diverse peoples and parochial customs and outlooks into metropolitan civilizations. It was these large supranational organizations that produced some of the finest accomplishments in literature, the arts, and human thought. Occasionally, as among the Greeks, the Empire was only loosely knit together, as in trading cities. In others, as in the Roman, there was clear political unification that went along with the economic basis. No matter how great the civilization became, however, it eventually fell.

The factors that cause civilizations to decay (or grow for that matter) are certainly not known. Decline might be caused by competition from an even bigger and more viable economic and political empire, although this does not seem to have been the case with a number of such civilizations. Rather, it has often been felt by historians, the decline was due to internal factors. Thus Gibbon's (1932) history of the fall of the Roman Empire indicated moral decline from within as the basic cause.

Today the ascendant empire of the world is an American one. The great advances in science, economics, and human thought today occur primarily in the United States of America and among its allies in the West. Many predict, however, that the Western world also is in decline and will be superceded by the Communist world. Such predictions are often based on notions of a collapse of "will" from within. Sometimes the criticism comes from the political right and this will is couched in terms of "moral decay." At other times the prediction comes from the political left and the internal dissolution is attributed to the "contradictions of capitalism." In either case, it is possible to define a solution. Whether that solution will be acted on, of course, is a different matter.

States today, in the "post-capitalist" (Dahrendorf 1959), or technological world, have a great capacity to control many of the external factors that determine their future evolution. By deliberately controlling these external factors we can in effect control our own destiny. We can control our own future evolution, both on the level of society and of the individual. This will, of course, require the implementation of the planned society. We can no longer leave the contingencies that determine our behavior to be controlled by chance. We must control them ourselves in order to survive.

At no other time in human history have we, as a species, had as much wealth and power as we do today. The overwhelming majority of this power and wealth is concentrated in less than one quarter of the world. Nonetheless its benefits and potential benefits are worldwide. Diseases such as smallpox, diptheria, scarlet fever, and bubonic plague are controlled by the determined efforts of medical science and philanthropic international organizations. Hundreds of millions of *Homo sapiens* now take for granted electric stoves, refrigerators, air-conditioning, television, and computerization. Air travel across thousands of miles is common. Television watchers have even seen our species walking on the earth's moon. In biological terms *Homo sapiens* completely dominate the world's surface. We have filled most valuable ecological niches and are poised ready to expand into space. We have achieved this remarkable position for two primary reasons: our social organization and our intelligence.

Our incredible abilties of social organization and altruism have allowed us to create societies and even cities of several millions of people. The only species that rival our own in terms of possible long-term survival are the social insects, for they match our own abilities for social organization and altruism. They owe their entire behavioral repertoire to wired-in, fully determined, genetic makeups. The altruism that our own species, on the other hand, does exhibit is due mainly to learning. Our intelligence is much more flexible. We are genetically programmed to learn from our environment and from our life experiences. As has been discussed throughout the book, one of the most important of our particular species-specific ways of learning social behavior is through observation of what significant others in our environment do as well as the consequences we observe occurring in our own and others' behavior. (We learn also, of course, through direct tuition.) The flexibility of our intelligence is a distinguishing feature of our species. It has even enabled us to discover how the process of social learning affects the amount of altruism and cooperation exhibited! Perhaps now we can use that knowledge to help increase such behaviors.

Even if all the suggestions made in this chapter were to be implemented, and even if they all succeeded in increasing the amount of social solidarity and altruism that exists in our society, it still would not ensure survival. This is because our society cannot be limited to just one country, or even a block of countries. Current society must be viewed as world society. Extension of the arguments presented makes it clear that ultimately we must create a world society in which consideration for others is the message received and acquired by all citizens. The brotherhood and sisterhood of man and woman, which has been dreamed of, thought about, and written of by so many, will become a reality only through the application of positivistic behavioral science. Many of the techniques are now at our disposal. We must find a way to implement them.

SUMMARY

The last three chapters have documented a bleak situation: The family is an increasingly ineffective socializer of children; the television system is socializing them in an increasingly antisocial direction; and the educational system is not socializing them at all. Furthermore there is, unfortunately, an accumulation of evidence that this gloomy scenario is actually producing the predicted "undersocialized personality." How can we effect changes in our society that would increase the amount of consideration for others that is shown?

One solution to the problem of undersocialization is to increase the frequency of adult-child interactions, thus providing more opportunities for limit-setting and prosocial socialization. One way of doing this would be to help parents to be home when their children return from school. Perhaps factories and businesses employing large numbers of workers could be encouraged to produce flexible work schedules that would enable parents to be home when their children return from school. Another solution is to try to keep families intact and to decrease the number of illegitimate births. The social welfare system might be examined in this regard to see whether it is inadvertently reinforcing undesirable behavior. Social policy can also be used more positively. Perhaps communal raising of children in well-staffed daycare centers could be useful. Indeed there is no reason why parents who want to spend time raising their children might not be paid to do this at the daycare centers, where they could also take turns helping to care for other children. Certainly the wider society could benefit from the ensuing increased socialization.

In regard to the mass media, it has been amply documented by now that our attitudes and values can be demonstrably altered by what we observe on television. Not only is violence and anti-social behavior being portrayed, but much broader attitudes that may be incompatible with an altruistic society are also depicted. By showing successful people on television as materially successful and as consumers of advertised products, the norms being internalized of what constitutes the good life are materialistic. Millions of people will feel frustration at the inevitable social comparisons that are being made. We must alter our conception of what television is: It has become one of the most powerful socializers that our society currently possesses. When this is realized, issues of power and control become important. At the moment, the advertising and television industry exercise virtually unlimited control in the service of their corporate interests, and the public has no direct access to the use of the public airways. Dissemination and attendant publicization of the violence rates for the different networks, sponsors, and programs might play a part in exerting influence. Certainly other consumer advocates have found that disclosure of objectionable practices can result in some amelioration of the practices. If this does not work then stronger regulatory guidelines and/or public legislation will be necesary to stop the pervasiveness of so much antisocial behavior.

It is in the educational system that society can most readily make a significant and active contribution to increasing prosocial competencies and motivations. It is time we turned to a far more intensive and disciplined program of prosocial education, in the widest sense of the term. As discussed in chapter 8, there are a number of viewpoints of how best to pursue prosocial education. These should all be implemented: The way a child behaves and reasons, and the way he or she clarifies and acts on his or her values, are all important and should be attended to more completely in schools than they are today. Cooperative school work could be encouraged, as could leadership and initiative in helping the less able students. Stress might also be placed, in social studies courses, on the scientific understanding of human society. In early high school there is no reason why psychology and sociology (and evolutionary theory and animal behavior) could not be taught. With emphasis on the scientific method, there might be an increased desire to analyze prejudices and to see more clearly the continuity of community across national, racial, and religious borders.

Finally we must consider whether our society can survive the incredible problems it will face in the next half century. Many civilizations and great empires have risen and then fallen. *It is the thesis of this book that altruism is the central problem facing society today.*

REFERENCES

Adams, J. S., & Jacobsen, P. R. Effects of wage inequities on work quality. *Journal of Abnormal and Social Psychology,* 1964, *69,* 19-25.

Aderman, D., & Berkowitz, L. Observational set, empathy, and helping. *Journal of Personality and Social Psychology,* 1970, *14,* 141-148.

Aderman, D., Brehm, S. S., & Katz, L. B. Empathic observation of an innocent victim: The just world revisited. *Journal of Personality and Social Psychology,* 1974, *29,* 342-347.

Ahlgren, A., & Johnson, D. W. Sex differences in cooperative and competitive attitudes from the 2nd through the 12th grades. *Developmental Psychology,* 1979, *15,* 45-49.

Allen, E. K., Hart, B. M., Buell, J. S., Harris, F. R., & Wolf, M. M. Effects of social reinforcement on isolate behavior of a nursery school child. *Child Development*, 1964, *35*, 511-518.

Allport, G. W., Vernon, P. E., & Lindzey, G. A. *A study of values.* Boston: Houghton Mifflin, 1960.

Anchor, K. N., & Cross, H. J. Maladaptive aggression, moral perspective, and the socialization process. *Journal of Personality and Social Psychology*, 1974, *30*, 163-168.

Ardrey, R. *African genesis.* New York: Bantam Books, 1961.

Aronfreed, J. The socialization of altruistic and sympathetic behavior: Some theoretical and experimental analyses. In J. Macaulay & L. Berkowitz (Eds.), *Altruism and helping behavior.* New York: Academic Press, 1970.

Aronfreed, J., & Paskal, V. Altruism, empathy, and the conditioning of positive affect. *Unpublished manuscript, University of Pennsylvania,* 1965. Citied by J. Aronfreed in "The Socialization of altruistic and sympathetic behavior: Some theoretical and experimental analyses." In J. Macaulay & L. Berkowitz (Eds.), *Altruism and helping behavior.* New York: Academic Press, 1970.

Aronfreed, J., & Paskal, V. The development of sympathetic behavior in children: An experimental test of a two-phase hypothesis. *Unpublished manuscript, University of Pennsylvania,* 1966. Cited by J. Aronfreed in "The Socialization of altruistic and sympathetic behavior: Some theoretical and experimental analyses." In J. Macaulay & L. Berkowitz (Eds.), *Altruism and helping behavior.* New York: Academic Press, 1970.

Bandura, A. Vicarious processes: A case of no-trial learning. In L. Berkowitz (Ed.), *Advances in experimental social psychology* (Vol. 2). New York: Academic Press, 1965.

Bandura, A. *Principles of behavior modification.* New York: Holt, Rinehart & Winston, 1969.

Bandura, A. Vicarious and self-reinforcement processes. In R. Glaser (Ed.), *The nature of reinforcement.* New York: Academic Press, 1971.

Bandura, A. *Aggression: A social learning analysis.* Englewood Cliffs, N.J.: Prentice-Hall, 1973.

Bandura, A. Self-efficacy: Toward a unifying theory of behavioral change. *Psychological Review*, 1977, *84*, 191-215. (a)

Bandura, A. *Social learning theory.* Englewood Cliffs, N. J.: Prentice-Hall, 1977. (b)

Bandura, A. On paradigms and recycled ideologies. *Cognitive Therapy and Research*, 1978, *2*, 79-103. (a)

Bandura, A. The self-system in reciprocal determinism. *American Psychologist,* 1978, *33,* 344-358. (b)

Bandura, A., & Barab, P. G. Processes governing disinhibitory effects through symbolic modeling. *Journal of Abnormal Psychology,* 1973, *82,* 1-9.

Bandura, A., Blanchard, E. B., & Ritter, B. Relative efficacy of desensitization and modeling approaches for inducing behavioral, affective and attitudinal changes. *Journal of Personality and Social Psychology,* 1969, *13,* 173-199.

Bandura, A., Grusec, J. E., & Menlove, F. L. Some social determinants of self-monitoring reinforcement systems. *Journal of Personality and Social Psychology,* 1967, *5,* 449-455. (a)

Bandura, A., Grusec, J. E., & Menlove, F. L. Vicarious extinction of avoidance behavior. *Journal of Personality and Social Psychology,* 1967, *5,* 16-23. (b)

Bandura, A., & Harris, M. B. Modification of syntactic style. *Journal of Experimental Child Psychology,* 1966, *4,* 341-352.

Bandura, A., & Kupers, C. J. Transmission of patterns of self-reinforcement through modeling. *Journal of Abnormal and Social Psychology,* 1964, *69,* 1-9.

Bandura, A., & McDonald, F. J. Influences of social reinforcement and the behavior of models in shaping children's moral judgments. *Journal of Abnormal and Social Psychology,* 1963, *67,* 274-281.

Bandura, A., & Menlove, F. L. Factors determining vicarious extinction of avoidance behavior through symbolic modeling. *Journal of Personality and Social Psychology,* 1968, *8,* 99-108.

Bandura, A., & Mischel, W. Modification of self-imposed delay of reward through exposure to live and symbolic models. *Journal of Personality and Social Psychology,* 1965, *2,* 698-705.

Bandura, A., & Rosenthal, T. L. Vicarious classical conditioning as a function of arousal level. *Journal of Personality and Social Psychology,* 1966, *3,* 54-62.

Bandura, A., Ross, D., & Ross, S. Imitation of film-mediated aggressive models. *Journal of Abnormal and Social Psychology,* 1963, *66,* 3-11.

Bandura, A., & Whalen, C. K. The influence of antecedent reinforcement and divergent modeling cues on patterns of self-reward. *Journal of Personality and Social Psychology,* 1966, *3,* 373-382.

Barash, D. P. *Sociobiology and behavior.* New York: Elsevier, North Holland, 1977.

Barber, P. J., & Rushton, J. P. Experimenter bias and subliminal perception. *British Journal of Psychology,* 1975, *66,* 357-372.

Barber, T. X., & Silver, M. J. Fact, fiction, and the experimenter bias effect. *Psychological Bulletin,* 1968, *70,* 1-29.

Barnett, M. A., & Bryan, J. H. Effects of competition with outcome feedback on children's helping behavior. *Developmental Psychology*, 1974, *10*, 838-842.

Barnett, M. A., Matthews, K. A., & Howard, J. A. Relationship between competitiveness and empathy in 6- and 7-year-olds. *Developmental Psychology*, 1979, *15*, 221-222.

Baron, R. A. *Human aggression.* New York: Plenum Press, 1977.

Barrett, D. E., & Yarrow, M. R. Prosocial behavior, social inferential ability, and assertiveness in children. *Child Development*, 1977, *48*, 475-481.

Bar-Tal, D. *Prosocial behavior: Theory and research.* Washington, D.C.: Hemisphere, 1976.

Baumrind, D. *Early socialization and the discipline controversy.* Morristown, N. J.: General Learning Press, 1975.

Beattie, E. Magazines and violence. In *Ontario. Royal commission on violence in the communications industry. Report* (Vol. 4), *Violence in print and music.* (Research reports.) Toronto: Queen's Printer for Ontario, 1977.

Belson, W. A. *Television violence and the adolescent boy.* Lexington, Mass.: Heath, 1978.

Berger, S. M. Conditioning through vicarious instigation. *Psychological Review*, 1962, *69*, 450-466.

Berkowitz, L. Resistance to improper dependency relationships. *Journal of Experimental Social Psychology*, 1969, *5*, 282-294.

Berkowitz, L. The self, selfishness, and altruism. In J. Macaulay & L. Berkowitz (Eds.), *Altruism and helping behavior.* New York: Academic Press, 1970.

Berkowitz, L. Social norms, feelings, and other factors affecting helping and altruism. In L. Berkowitz (Ed.), *Advances in experimental social psychology* (Vol. 6). New York: Academic Press, 1972.

Berkowitz, L., & Connor, W. H. Success, failure, and social responsibility. *Journal of Personality and Social Psychology*, 1966, *4*, 664-669.

Berkowitz, L., & Daniels, L. R. Responsibility and dependency. *Journal of Abnormal and Social Psychology*, 1963, *66*, 429-436.

Berkowitz, L., & Daniels, L. R. Affecting the salience of the social responsibility norm: Effects of past help on the response to dependency relationships. *Journal of Abnormal and Social Psychology*, 1964, *68*, 275-281.

Berkowitz, L., & Friedman, P. Some social class differences in helping behavior. *Journal of Personality and Social Psychology*, 1967, *5*, 217-225.

Berkowitz, L., & Lutterman, K. G. The traditionally socially responsible personality. *Public Opinion Quarterly*, 1968, *32*, 169-187.

Berkowitz, L., & Rawlings, E. Effects of film violence on inhibitions against subsequent aggression. *Journal of Abnormal and Social Psychology,* 1963, *66,* 405-412.

Berkowitz, L., & Walster, E. (Eds.) Equity theory: Toward a general theory of social interaction. In L. Berkowitz (Ed.), *Advances in experimental social psychology* (Vol. 9). New York: Academic Press, 1976.

Berton, P. *Hollywood's Canada.* Toronto: McClelland and Stewart, 1975.

Borke, H. Interpersonal perception of young children: Egocentrism or empathy? *Developmental Psychology,* 1971, *5,* 263-269.

Borke, H. Piaget's mountains revisited: Changes in the egocentric landscape. *Developmental Psychology,* 1975, *11,* 240-243.

Brehm, S. S. *The application of social psychology to clinical practice.* New York: John Wiley, 1976.

Bronfenbrenner, U. *Two worlds of childhood: U. S. and U. S. S. R.* New York: Russell Sage Foundation, 1970.

Bronfenbrenner, U. Reality and research in the ecology of human development. *Proceedings of the American Philosophical Society,* 1975, *119,* 439-469.

Brown, J. Unwed teen mothers a big problem. *Detroit News,* May 14, 1978.

Brown v. Board of Education of Topeka, 98F. Supp. 797 (1951), 347 U. S. 438 (1954), 349 U. S. 294 (1955).

Bryan, J. H. Model affect and children's imitative altruism. *Child Development,* 1971, *42,* 2061-2065.

Bryan, J. H. Children's cooperation and helping behaviors. In E. M. Hetherington (Ed.), *Review of child development research* (Vol. 5). Chicago: University of Chicago Press, 1975.

Bryan, J. H. & London, P. Altruistic behavior by children. *Psychological Bulletin,* 1970, *73,* 200-211.

Bryan, J. H., & Schwartz, T. Effects of film material upon children's behavior. *Psychological Bulletin,* 1971, *75,* 50-59.

Bryan, J. H., & Test, M. A. Models and helping: Naturalistic studies in aiding behavior. *Journal of Personality and Social Psychology,* 1967, *6,* 400-407.

Bryan, J. H., & Walbek, N. H. The impact of words and deeds concerning altruism upon children. *Child Development,* 1970, *41,* 747-757. (a)

Bryan, J. H., & Walbek, N. H. Preaching and practicing generosity. Children's actions and reactions. *Child Development,* 1970, *41,* 329-353. (b)

Buckley, N., Siegel, L. S., & Ness, S. Egocentrism, empathy, and altruistic behavior in young children. *Developmental Psychology,* 1979, *15,* 329-330.

Burns, S. M., & Brainerd, C. J. Effects of constructive and dramatic play on perspective taking in very young children. *Developmental Psychology,* 1979, *15,* 512-521.

Burton, R. V. Generality of honesty reconsidered. *Psychological Review,* 1963, *70,* 481-499.

Burton, R. V. Honesty and dishonesty. In T. Lickona (Ed.), *Moral development and behavior: Theory, research and social issues.* New York: Holt, Rinehart & Winston, 1976.

Byrne, D. *The attraction paradigm.* New York: Academic Press, 1971.

Byrne, D., & Byrne, L. A. *Exploring human sexuality.* New York: Harper & Row, 1977.

Campbell, D. T. Ethnocentric and other altruistic motives. In D. Levine (Ed.), *Nebraska symposium on motivation.* Lincoln: University of Nebraska Press, 1965.

Campbell, D. T. On the genetics of altruism and the counter hedonic components in human culture. *Journal of Social Issues,* 1972, *28(3),* 21-37.

Campbell, D. T. On the conflicts between biological and social evolution and between psychology and moral tradition. *American Psychologist,* 1975, *30,* 1103-1126.

Carlsmith, J. M., & Gross, A. E. Some effects of guilt on compliance. *Journal of Personality and Social Psychology,* 1969, *11,* 232-240.

Carnegie Hero Fund Commission. Annual report, 1977. Address: 1932 Oliver Building, Pittsburgh, Pennsylvania 15222, U. S. A.

Chaffee, S. H. Television and adolescent aggressiveness (overview). In G. A. Comstock & E. A. Rubinstein (Eds.), *Television and social behavior* (Vol. 3). *Television and adolescent aggressiveness.* Washington, D. C.: U. S. Government Printing Office, 1972.

Chandler, M. J. Egocentrism and anti-social behavior: The assessment and training of social perspective-taking skills. *Developmental Psychology,* 1973, *9,* 326-332.

Christie, R., & Geis, G. (Eds.). *Studies in Machiavellianism.* New York: Academic Press, 1968.

Church, R. M. Emotional reactions of rats to the pain of others. *Journal of Comparative and Physiological Psychology,* 1959, *52,* 132-134.

Cialdini, R. B., Darby, B. L., & Vincent, J. E. Transgression and altruism: A case for hedonism. *Journal of Experimental Social Psychology,* 1973, *9,* 502-516.

Coates, B., & Pusser, H. E. Positive reinforcement and punishment in *Sesame Street* and *Mister Rogers' Neighborhood. Journal of Broadcasting,* 1975, *19,* 143-151.

Coates, B., Pusser, H. E., & Goodman, I. The influence of *Sesame Street* and *Mister Rogers' Neighborhood* on children's social behavior in the preschool. *Child Development,* 1976, *47,* 138-144.

Coke, J. S., Batson, C. D., & McDavis, K. Empathic mediation of helping: A two stage model. *Journal of Personality and Social Psychology,* 1978, *36,* 752-766.

Collins, W. A., & Getz, S. K. Children's social responses following modeled reactions to provocation: Prosocial effects of a television drama. *Journal of Personality,* 1976, *44,* 488-500.

Comstock, G., Chaffee, S., Katzman, N., McCombs, M., Roberts, D. *Television and human behavior.* New York: Columbia University Press, 1978.

Comte, A. *System of positive polity.* New York: B. Franklin (1966). (Original in French in 1851-1854.)

Cowan, P. A., Langer, J., Heavenrich, J., & Nathanson, M. Social learning and Piaget's cognitive theory of moral development. *Journal of Personality and Social Psychology,* 1969, *11,* 261-274.

Craig, K. D., & Lowery, H. J. Heart-rate components of conditioned vicarious autonomic responses. *Journal of Personality and Social Psychology,* 1969, *11,* 381-387.

Crowley, P. M. Effect of training upon objectivity of moral judgment in grade school children. *Journal of Personality and Social Psychology,* 1968, *8,* 228-232.

Dahlstrom, W. G., Welsh, G. S., & Dahlstrom, P. E. *An MMPI handbook.* (Rev. ed.). Minneapolis: University of Minnesota Press, 1972.

Dahrendorf, R. *Class and class conflict in industrial society.* Stanford, Calif.: Stanford University Press, 1959.

Darley, J. M., & Batson, C. D. From Jerusalem to Jericho: A study of situational and dispositional variables in helping behavior. *Journal of Personality and Social Psychology,* 1973, *27,* 100-108.

Dart, R. A. The predatory implemental technique of Australopithecus. *American Journal of Physical Anthropology,* 1949, *7,* 1-38.

Darwin, C. *On the origin of species by means of natural selection.* London: Murray, 1859.

Darwin, C. *The descent of man.* London, Murray, 1871.

Dawkins, R. *The selfish gene.* Oxford: Oxford University Press, 1976.

DeFleur, M. L. Occupational roles as portrayed on television. *Public Opinion Quarterly,* 1964, *28,* 57-74.

Diener, E., & DeFour, D. Does television violence enhance program popularity? *Journal of Personality and Social Psychology,* 1978, *36,* 333-341.

Dienstbier, R. A., Hillman, D., Lehnhoff, J., Hillman, J., & Valkenaar, M. C. An emotion-attribution approach to moral behavior: Interfacing cognitive and avoidance theories of moral development. *Psychological Review,* 1975, *82,* 299-315.

Dlugokinski, E. L., & Firestone, I. J. Congruence among four methods of measuring other-centeredness. *Child Development,* 1973, *44,* 304-308.

Dlugokinski, E. L., & Firestone, I. J. Other centeredness and susceptibility to charitable appeals: Effects of perceived discipline. *Developmental Psychology,* 1974, *10,* 21-28.

Donagher, P. C., Poulos, R. W., Liebert, R. M., & Davidson, E. S. Race, sex and social example: An analysis of character portrayals on interracial television entertainment. *Psychological Reports,* 1975, *37,* 1023-1034.

Drabman, R. S., & Thomas, M. H. Does media violence increase children's toleration of real-life aggression? *Developmental Psychology,* 1974, *10,* 418-421.

Dreman, S. B. Sharing behavior in Israeli school children: Cognitive and social learning factors. *Child Development,* 1976, *47,* 186-194.

Easterbrook, J. A. The effect of emotion on cue utilization and the organization of behavior. *Psychological Review,* 1959, *66,* 183-201.

Eisenberg-Berg, N. Relationship of prosocial moral reasoning to altruism, political liberalism, and intelligence. *Developmental Psychology,* 1979, *15,* 87-89.

Eisenberg-Berg, N., & Geisheker, E. Content of preachings and power of the model/preacher: The effect on children's generosity. *Developmental Psychology,* 1979, *15,* 168-175.

Eisenberg-Berg, N. & Hand, M. The relationship of preschoolers' reasoning about prosocial moral conflicts to prosocial behavior. *Child Development,* 1979, *50,* 356-363.

Eisenberg-Berg, N., & Mussen, P. Empathy and moral development in adolescence. *Developmental Psychology,* 1978, *14,* 185-186.

Ekman, P., & Friesen, W. V. Constants across cultures in face and emotions. *Journal of Personality and Social Psychology,* 1971, *17,* 124-129.

Elliot, R., & Vasta, R. The modeling of sharing: Effects associated with vicarious reinforcement, symbolization, age, and generalization. *Journal of Experimental Child Psychology,* 1970, *10,* 8-15.

Emler, N. P., & Rushton, J. P. Cognitive-developmental factors in children's generosity. *British Journal of Social and Clinical Psychology,* 1974, *13,* 277-281.

Endler, N. S., & Magnusson, D. Toward an interactional psychology of personality. *Psychological Bulletin,* 1976, *83,* 956-976.

England, C. Violence in literature for children and young adults. In *Ontario. Royal commission on violence in the communication industry. Report* (Vol. 4), *Violence in print and music.* (Research Reports). Toronto: Queen's Printer for Ontario, 1977.

Eron, L. D. Relationship of TV viewing habits and aggressive behavior in children. *Journal of Abnormal and Social Psychology,* 1963, *67,* 193-196.

Estes, R. D., & Goddard, J. Prey selection and hunting behavior of the African wild dog. *Journal of Wildlife Management,* 1967, *31,* 52-70.

Etaugh, C. Effects of maternal employment on children: A review of recent research. *Merrill-Palmer Quarterly of Behavior and Development,* 1974, *20,* 71-98.

Eysenck, H. J. *Crime and personality* (3rd edition). St. Albans, Hertfordshire, England: Granada Publishing Ltd., 1977.

Fellner, C. H., & Marshall, J. R. Twelve kidney donors. *Journal of the American Medical Association,* 1968, *206,* 2703-2707.

Feshbach, N. D. Studies of empathic behavior in children. In: B. A. Maher (Ed.), *Progress in experimental personality research* (Vol. 8). New York: Academic Press, 1978.

Feshbach, N. D., & Roe, K. Empathy in six- and seven-year-olds. *Child Development,* 1968, *39,* 133-145.

Feshbach, S., & Singer, R. D. *Television and aggression: An experimental field study.* San Francisco: Jossey-Bass, 1971.

Festinger, L. A theory of social comparison processes. *Human Relations,* 1954, *7,* 117-140.

Fincham, F., & Barling, J. Locus of control and generosity in learning disabled, normal achieving, and gifted children. *Child Development,* 1978, *49,* 530-533.

Fischer, W. F. Sharing in pre-school children as a function of amount and type of reinforcement. *Genetic Psychology Monographs,* 1963, *68,* 215-245.

Fisher, J. D., Harrison, C. L., & Nadler, A. Exploring the generalizability of donor-recipient similarity effects. *Personality and Social Psychology Bulletin,* 1978, *4,* 627-630.

Fisher, J. D., & Nadler, A. The effect of similarity between donor and recipient on recipient's reactions to aid. *Journal of Applied Social Psychology,* 1974, *4,* 230-243.

Flacks, R. The liberated generation: An exploration of the roots of student protest. *Journal of Social Issues,* 1967, *23(3),* 52-75.

Flavell, J. H. *The developmental psychology of Jean Piaget.* Princeton, N. J.: Van Nostrand, 1963.

Flavell, J. H., Botkin, P. T., Fry, C. L., Wright, J. W., & Jarvis, P. E. *The development of role-taking and communication skills in children.* New York: John Wiley, 1968.

Freedman, J. L. Transgression, compliance and guilt. In J. Macaulay & L. Berkowitz (Eds.), *Altruism and helping behavior.* New York: Academic Press, 1970.

Freedman, J. L., Wallington, S. A., & Bless, E. Compliance without pressure: The effects of guilt. *Journal of Personality and Social Psychology*, 1967, *7*, 117-124.

Friedrich, L. K., & Stein, A. H. Aggressive and pro-social television programs and the natural behavior of preschool children. *Monographs of the Society for Research in Child Development*, 1973, *38* (4, Serial No. 151).

Friedrich, L. K., & Stein, A. H. Pro-social television and young children: The effects of verbal labeling and role playing on learning and behavior. *Child Development*, 1975, *46*, 27-38.

Frisch, K. von. [*The dance language and orientation of bees*] (L. E. Chadwick, trans.) Cambridge: Harvard University Press, 1967.

Fryrear, J. L., & Thelen, M. H. Effect of sex of model and sex of observer on the imitation of affectionate behavior. *Developmental Psychology*, 1969, *1*, 298.

Fulford, R. Speaking the unspeakable: Violence in the literature of our time. In *Ontario. Royal commission on violence in the communications industry. Report* (Vol. 4), *Violence in print and music.* (Research reports). Toronto: Queen's Printer for Ontario, 1977.

Gabarino, J., & Bronfenbrenner, U. The socialization of moral judgment and behavior in cross-cultural perspective. In T. Lickona (Ed.), *Moral development and behavior: Theory, research, and social issues.* New York: Holt, Rinehart & Winston, 1976.

Gale, E. N., & Jacobson, M. B. The relationship between social comments as unconditioned stimuli and fear responding. *Behaviour Research and Therapy*, 1970, *8*, 301-307.

Gelfand, D. M., Hartmann, D. P., Cromer, C. C., Smith, C. L., & Page, B. C. The effects of instructional prompts and praise on children's donation rates. *Child Development*, 1975, *46*, 980-983.

Gerbner, G., & Gross, L. Living with television: The violence profile. *Journal of Communication*, 1976, *26*, 173-199.

Gergen, K. J., Ellsworth, P., Maslach, C., & Seipel, M. Obligation, donor resources, and reactions to aid in three cultures. *Journal of Personality and Social Psychology*, 1975, *31*, 390-400.

Gergen, K. J., Gergen, J. M., & Meter, K. Individual orientations to prosocial behavior. *Journal of Social Issues*, 1972, *28(3)*, 105-130.

Gibbon, E. *The decline and fall of the Roman empire.* New York: Modern Library, 1932.

Goddard, P. Violence and popular music. In *Ontario. Royal commission on violence in the communications industry. Report* (Vol. 4), *Violence in print and music.* (Research reports). Toronto: Queen's Printer for Ontario, 1977.

Goodall, J. The behavior of free-living chimpanzees in the Gombe Stream Reserve. *Animal Behavior Monographs,* 1968, *1,* 161-311.

Goodall, J. *In the shadow of man.* Boston: Houghton Mifflin, 1971.

Goranson, R. E. Media violence and aggressive behavior: A review of experimental research. In L. Berkowitz (Ed.), *Advances in experimental social psychology* (Vol. 5). New York: Academic Press, 1970.

Goranson, R. E. The impact of TV violence. *Contemporary Psychology,* 1975, *20,* 291-292.

Goranson, R. E. Television violence effects: Issues and evidence. In *Ontario. Royal commission on violence in the communications industry. Report* (Vol. 5), *Learning from the media.* (Research reports). Toronto: Queen's Printer for Ontario, 1977.

Goranson, R. E., & Berkowitz, L. Reciprocity and responsibility reactions to prior help. *Journal of Personality and Social Psychology,* 1966, *3,* 227-232.

Gorn, G. J., Goldberg, M. E., & Kanungo, R. N. The role of educational television in changing the intergroup attitudes of children. *Child Development,* 1976, *47,* 277-280.

Gough, H. G. *California Psychological Inventory,* Palo Alto, Calif.: Consulting Psychologists Press, 1956.

Gouldner, A. W. The norm of reciprocity: A preliminary statement. *American Sociological Review,* 1960, *25,* 161-178.

Grant, J. E., Weiner, A., & Rushton, J. P. Moral judgment and generosity in children. *Psychological Reports,* 1976, *39,* 451-454.

Green, F. P., & Schneider, F. W. Age differences in the behavior of boys on three measures of altruism. *Child Development,* 1974, *45,* 248-251.

Gregory, M. S., Silvers, A., & Sutch, D. *Sociobiology and human nature: An interdisciplinary critique and defense.* San Francisco: Jossey-Bass, 1978.

Gross, A. E., & Latané, J. G. Receiving help, reciprocation, and interpersonal attraction. *Journal of Applied Social Psychology,* 1974, *4,* 210-223.

Grusec, J. E. Power and the internalization of self-denial. *Child Development,* 1971, *42,* 93-105.

Grusec, J. E. Demand characteristics of the modeling experiment: Altruism as a function of age and aggression. *Journal of Personality and Social Psychology,* 1972, *22,* 139-148.

Grusec, J. E. The effects of co-observer evaluation on imitations: A developmental study. *Developmental Psychology,* 1973, *8,* 141.

Grusec, J. E., Kuczynski, L., Rushton, J. P., & Simutis, Z. M. Learning resistance to temptation through observation. *Developmental Psychology,* 1979, *15,* 233-240.

Grusec, J. E., Kuczynski, L., Rushton, J. P., & Simutis, Z. M. Modeling, direct instruction, and attributions: Effects on altruism. *Developmental Psychology*, 1978, *14*, 51-57.

Grusec, J. E., Saas-Kortsaak, P., & Simutis, Z. M. The role of example and moral exhortation in the training of altruism. *Child Development*, 1978, *49*, 920-923.

Grusec, J. E., & Skubiski, S. L. Model nurturance, demand characteristics of the modeling experiment, and altruism. *Journal of Personality and Social Psychology*, 1970, *14*, 352-359.

Haan, N., Smith, M. B., & Block, J. Moral reasoning of young adults: Political-social behavior, family background, and personality correlates. *Journal of Personality and Social Psychology*, 1968, *10*, 183-201.

Haldane, J. B. S. *The causes of evolution.* London, Longmans, 1932.

Halloran, J. D. Studying violence and the media: A sociological approach. In: C. Winick (Ed.), *Sage Annual Reviews of Studies in Deviance*, Volume 2, *Deviance and Mass Media.* Beverly Hills, Calif.: Sage Publications, 1978.

Hamilton, W. D. The genetical evolution of social behavior (I and II). *Journal of Theoretical Biology*, 1964, *7*, 1-16; 17-52.

Hamilton, W. D. Altruism and related phenomena, mainly in social insects. *Annual Review of Ecology and Systematics*, 1972, *3*, 193-232.

Handlon, B. J., & Gross, P. The development of sharing behavior. *Journal of Abnormal and Social Psychology*, 1959, *59*, 425-428.

Haney, C., Banks, W., & Zimbardo, P. Interpersonal dynamics in a simulated prison. *International Journal of Criminology and Penology*, 1973, *7*, 69-97.

Harmon, W.W. The coming transformation. *Futurist*, 1977, *11*, pp. 5-12; 106-112.

Harris, D. B. A scale for measuring attitudes of social responsibility in children. *Journal of Abnormal and Social Psychology*, 1957, *55*, 322-326.

Harris, M. B. Reciprocity and generosity: Some determinants of sharing in children. *Child Development*, 1970, *41*, 313-328.

Harris, M. B. Models, norms and sharing. *Psychological Reports*, 1971, *29*, 147-153.

Harris, S., Mussen, P., & Rutherford, E. Some cognitive, behavioral and personality correlates of maturity of moral judgment. *Journal of Genetic Psychology*, 1976, *128*, 123-135.

Hartshorne, H., & May, M. A. *Studies in the nature of character.* Vol. 1: *Studies in deceit.* New York: Macmillan, 1928.

Hartshorne, H., May, M. A., & Maller, J. B. *Studies in the nature of character.* Vol. II: *Studies in self-control.* New York: Macmillan, 1929.

Hartshorne, H., May, M. A., & Shuttleworth, F. K. *Studies in the nature of character.* Vol. III: *Studies in the organization of character.* New York: Macmillan, 1930.

Hartup, W. W., & Coates, B. Imitation of a peer as a function of reinforcement from the peer group and rewardingness of the model. *Child Development,* 1967, *38,* 1003-1016.

Hicks, D. J. Imitation and retention of film-mediated aggressive peer and adult models. *Journal of Personality and Social Psychology,* 1965, *2,* 97-100.

Hicks, D. J. Effects of co-observer's sanctions and adult presence on imitative aggression. *Child Development,* 1968, *39,* 303-309. (a)

Hicks, D. J. Short and long-term retention of affectively varied modeled behavior. *Psychonomic Science,* 1968, *11,* 369-370. (b)

Hill, J. H., Liebert, R. M., & Mott, D. E. W. Vicarious extinction of avoidance behavior through films: An initial test. *Psychological Reports,* 1968, *22,* 192.

Himmelweit, H. T., Oppenheim, A. N., & Vince, P. *Television and the child: An empirical study of the effects of television on the young.* London: Oxford University Press, 1958.

Himmelweit, H. T., & Swift, B. A model for the understanding of school as a socializing agent. In P. H. Mussen, J. Langer, & M. Covington (Eds.), *Trends and issues in developmental psychology.* New York: Holt, Rinehart & Winston, 1969.

Hoffman, M. L. Power assertion by the parent and its impact on the child. *Child Development,* 1960, *31,* 129-143.

Hoffman, M. L. Parent discipline and the child's consideration for others. *Child Development,* 1963, *34,* 573-588.

Hoffman, M. L. Altruistic behavior and the parent-child relationship. *Journal of Personality and Social Psychology,* 1975, *31,* 937-943. (a)

Hoffman, M. L. Moral internalization, parental power, and the nature of parent-child interaction. *Developmental Psychology,* 1975, *11,* 228-239. (b)

Hoffman, M. L. The development of altruistic motivation. In D. J. DePalma & J. M. Foley (Eds.), *Moral development: Current theory and research.* Hillsdale, N. J.: Lawrence Erlbaum Associates, 1975.

Hoffman, M. L. Personality and social development. In M. R. Rosenzweig & L. W. Porter (Eds.), *Annual Review of Psychology,* Vol. 28. Palo Alto, Calif.: Annual Reviews, 1977. (a)

Hoffman, M. L. Sex differences in empathy and related behaviors. *Psychological Bulletin,* 1977, *84,* 712-722. (b)

Hoffman, M. L., & Salzstein, H. D. Parent discipline and the child's moral development. *Journal of Personality and Social Psychology,* 1967, *5,* 45-57.

Hogan, R. Theoretical egocentrism and the problem of compliance. *American Psychologist*, 1975, *30*, 533-540.

Hornstein, H. A. *Cruelty and kindness: A new look at aggression and altruism.* Englewood Cliffs, N. J.: Prentice-Hall, 1976.

Hornstein, H. A., Fisch, E., & Holmes, M. Influence of a model's feelings about his behavior and his relevance as a comparison on other observers' helping behavior. *Journal of Personality and Social Psychology*, 1968, *10*, 222-226.

Horton, R. W., & Santogrossi, D. A. The effect of adult commentary on reducing the influence of televised violence. *Personality and Social Psychology Bulletin*, 1978, *4*, 337-340.

House, T. H., & Milligan, W. L. Autonomic responses to modeled distress in prison psychopaths. *Journal of Personality and Social Psychology*, 1976, *34*, 556-560.

Huesmann, L. R., Eron, L. D., Lefkowitz, M. M., & Walder, L. O. Television violence and aggression: The causal effect remains. *American Psychologist*, 1973, *28*, 617-620.

Hull, D., & Reuter, J. The development of charitable behavior in elementary school children. *Journal of Genetic Psychology*, 1977, *131*, 147-153.

Iannotti, R. J. Effect of role-taking experiences on role taking, empathy, altruism, and aggression. *Developmental Psychology*, 1978, *14*, 119-124.

Isen, A. M. Success, failure, attention and reaction to others: The warm glow of success. *Journal of Personality and Social Psychology*, 1970, *15*, 294-301.

Isen, A. M., Clark, M., & Schwartz, M. Duration of the effect of good mood on helping: "Footprints in the sands of time." *Journal of Personality and Social Psychology*, 1976, *34*, 385-393.

Isen, A. M., Horn, N., & Rosenhan, D. L. Effects of success and failure on children's generosity. *Journal of Personality and Social Psychology*, 1973, *27*, 239-247.

Isen, A. M., & Levin, P. F. Effect of feeling good on helping: Cookies and kindness. *Journal of Personality and Social Psychology*, 1972, *21*, 384-388.

Isen, A. M., Shalker, T. E., Clark, M., & Karp, L. Affect, accessibility of material in memory and behavior: A cognitive loop? *Journal of Personality and Social Psychology*, 1978, *36*, 1-13.

Jaffe, P. G., & Carlson, P. M. Modeling therapy for test anxiety: The role of model affect and consequences. *Behavior Research and Therapy*, 1972, *10*, 329-339.

Jenness, D. *Indians of Canada* (7th ed.). Toronto: University of Toronto Press, 1977.

Johanson, D. C., & White, T. D. A systematic assessment of early African hominids. *Science*, 1979, *203*, 321-330.

Johnson, D. W. Cooperativeness and social perspective taking. *Journal of Personality and Social Psychology*, 1975, *31*, 241-244.

Jones, M. C. The elimination of children's fears. *Journal of Experimental Psychology*, 1924, 7, 382-390.

Jowett, G. S., Reath, P., & Schouten, M. The control of mass media in Canada, the United States and Great Britain: Historical surveys. In *Ontario. Royal commission on violence in the communications industry. Report* (Vol. 4). *Violence in print and music.* (Research reports). Toronto: Queen's Printer for Ontario, 1977.

Kagan, S., & Madsen, M. C. Cooperation and competition of Mexican, Mexican-American, and Anglo-American children of two ages under four instructional sets. *Developmental Psychology*, 1971, *5*, 32-39.

Kanfer, F. H. Personal control, social control, and altruism: Can society survive the age of individualism? *American Psychologist*, 1979, *34*, 231-239.

Kaplan, R. M., & Singer, R. D. Television violence and viewer aggression: A re-examination of the evidence. *Journal of Social Issues*, 1976, *32*(4), 35-70.

Katzev, R., Edelsack, L., Steinmetz, G., Walker, T., & Wright, R. The effect of reprimanding transgressions on subsequent helping behavior: Two field experiments. *Personality and Social Psychology Bulletin*, 1978, *4*, 326-329.

Keasey, C. B. Experimentally induced changes in moral opinions and reasoning. *Journal of Personality and Social Psychology*, 1973, *26*, 30-38.

Keller, M. F., & Carlson, P. M. Social skills in preschool children with low levels of social responsiveness. *Child Development*, 1974, *45*, 912-919.

Kettlewell, H. B. D. Further selection experiments on industrial melanism in the Lepidoptera. *Heredity*, 1956, *10*, 287-301.

Kohlberg, L. Development of moral character and moral ideology. In M. Hoffman & L. Hoffman (Eds.), *Review of child development research.* New York: Russell Sage Foundation, 1964.

Kohlberg, L. Stage and sequence: The cognitive-developmental approach to socialization. In D. Goslin (Ed.), *Handbook of socialization theory and research.* Chicago: Rand McNally, 1969.

Kohlberg, L. Moral stages and moralization: The cognitive-developmental approach. In T. Lickona (Ed.), *Moral development and behavior: Theory, research, and social issues.* New York: Holt, Rinehart & Winston, 1976.

Kohlberg, L., & Kramer, R. Continuities and discontinuities in childhood and adult moral development. *Human Development*, 1969, *12*, 93-120.

Konečni, V. J. Some effects of guilt on compliance: A field replication. *Journal of Personality and Social Psychology*, 1972, *23*, 30-32.

Korte, C., & Kerr, N. Response to altruistic opportunities in urban and non-urban settings. *Journal of Social Psychology*, 1975, *95*, 183-184.

Krebs, D. L. Altruism—An examination of the concept and a review of the literature. *Psychological Bulletin,* 1970, *73,* 258-302.

Krebs, D. L. Empathy and altruism. *Journal of Personality and Social Psychology,* 1975, *32,* 1134-1146.

Krebs, D. L. A cognitive-developmental approach to altruism. In L. Wispé (Ed.), *Altruism, sympathy, and helping: Psychological and sociological principles.* New York: Academic Press, 1978.

Krebs, D. L., & Rosenwald, A. Moral reasoning and moral behavior in conventional adults. *Merrill-Palmer Quarterly of Behavior and Development,* 1977, *23,* 77-87.

Krebs, D. L., & Sturrup, B. Role-taking ability and altruistic behavior in elementary school children. *Personality and Social Psychology Bulletin,* 1974, *1,* 407-409.

Kühme, W. Communal food distribution and division of labor in African hunting dogs. *Nature,* 1965, *205,* 443-444.

Kurdek, L. Perspective taking as the cognitive basis of children's moral development: A review of the literature. *Merrill-Palmer Quarterly of Behavior and Development,* 1978, *24,* 3-28.

Kurtines, W., & Greif, E. B. The development of moral thought: Review and evaluation of Kohlberg's approach. *Psychological Bulletin,* 1974, *81,* 453-470.

Latané, B., & Darley, J. M. *The unresponsive bystander: Why doesn't he help?* New York: Appleton-Century-Crofts, 1970.

Leakey, R. E., & Lewin, R. *Origins.* New York: Dutton, 1977.

Lee, L. C. The concomitant development of cognitive and moral modes of thought: A test of selected deductions from Piaget's theory. *Genetic Psychology Monographs,* 1971, *83,* 93-146.

Lefkowitz, M., Blake, R. R., & Mouton, J. S. Status factors in pedestrian violation of traffic signals. *Journal of Abnormal and Social Psychology,* 1955, *51,* 704-706.

LeFurgy, W. G., & Woloshin, G. W. Immediate and long-term effects of experimentally induced social influences in the modification of adolescents' moral judgments. *Journal of Personality and Social Psychology,* 1969, *12,* 104-110.

Leifer, A. D., Gordon, N. J., & Graves, S. B. Children's television: More than mere entertainment. *Harvard Educational Review,* 1974, *44,* 213-245.

Lenrow, P. B. Studies in sympathy. In S. S. Tomkins & C. E. Izard (Eds.), *Affect, cognition, and personality. Empirical studies.* New York: Springer, 1965.

Lepper, M. R., Sagotsky, G., & Mailer, J. Generalization and persistence of effects of exposure to self-reinforcement models. *Child Development,* 1975, *46,* 618-630.

Lerner, M. J. The desire for justice and reactions to victims. In J. Macaulay & L. Berkowitz (Eds.), *Altruism and helping behavior.* New York: Academic Press, 1970.

Lerner, M. J. Social psychology of justice and interpersonal attraction. In T. Huston (Ed.), *Foundations of interpersonal attraction.* New York: Academic Press, 1974.

Lerner, M. J., & Simmons, C. H. Observer's reaction to the "innocent victim": Compassion or rejection? *Journal of Personality and Social Psychology,* 1966, *4,* 203-210.

Levin, P. F., & Isen, A. M. Further studies on the effect of feeling good on helping. *Sociometry,* 1975, *38,* 141-147.

Lewontin, R. C. and others. Against "Sociobiology." *New York Review of Books,* November 13, 1975, *22,* 43-44.

Liebert, R. M., & Baron, R. A. Some immediate effects of televised violence on children's behavior. *Developmental Psychology,* 1972, *6,* 469-475.

Liebert, R. M., Neale, J., & Davidson, E. S. *The early window: Effects of television on children and youth.* New York: Pergamon Press, 1973.

Liebert, R. M., & Schwartzberg, N. S. Effects of mass media. *Annual Review of Psychology,* 1977, *28,* 141-173.

Liebhart, E. H. Empathy and emergency helping: The effects of personality, self-concern, and acquaintance. *Journal of Experimental Social Psychology,* 1972, *8,* 404-411.

Lindzey, G., Loehlin, J., Manosevitz, M., & Thiessen, D. Behavioral genetics. *Annual Review of Psychology,* 1971, *22,* 39-94.

London, P. The rescuers: Motivational hypotheses about Christians who saved Jews from the Nazis. In J. Macaulay & L. Berkowitz (Eds.), *Altruism and helping behavior.* New York: Academic Press, 1970.

Long, G. T., & Lerner, M. J. Deserving, the "personal contract," and altruistic behavior by children. *Journal of Personality and Social Psychology,* 1974, *29,* 551-556.

Lorenz, K. *On aggression.* New York: Harcourt Brace Jovanovich, Inc., 1966.

Macaulay, J., & Berkowitz, L. (Eds.), *Altruism and helping behavior.* New York: Academic Press, 1970.

Machiavelli, N. [*The prince*] (L. Ricci, Trans.). New York: Oxford University Press, 1906. (Originally published, 1532.)

Madsen, M. C. Developmental and cross-cultural differences in the cooperative and competitive behavior of young children. *Journal of Cross-Cultural Psychology*, 1971, *2*, 365-371.

Madsen, M. C., & Connor, C. Cooperative and competitive behavior of retarded and nonretarded children at two ages. *Child Development*, 1973, *44*, 175-178.

Mailer, N. *An American Dream.* New York: Dial Press, 1965.

Mann, J. Vicarious desensitization of test anxiety through observation of video-taped treatment. *Journal of Counseling Psychology*, 1972, *19*, 1-7.

Manning, A. Drosophila and the evolution of behavior. In J. Carthy & C. Duddington (Eds.), *Viewpoints in biology.* London: Butterworth, 1965.

Marcus, R. F., Telleen, S., & Roke, E. J. Relation between cooperation and empathy in young children. *Developmental Psychology*, 1979, *15*, 346-347.

Marshall, J. R., & Fellner, C. H. Kidney donors revisited. *American Journal of Psychiatry*, 1977, *134*, 575-576.

Masserman, J. H., Wechkin, S., & Terris, W. "Altruistic" behavior in rhesus monkeys. *American Journal of Psychiatry*, 1964, *121*, 584-585.

Mauss, M. *The gift: Forms and functions of exchange in archaic societies.* Glencoe, Ill.: Free Press, 1954.

Mehrabian, A., & Epstein, N. A measure of emotional empathy. *Journal of Personality*, 1972, *40*, 525-543.

Melamed, B. G., Hawes, R. R., Heiby, E., & Glick, J. The use of filmed modeling to reduce uncooperative behavior of children during dental treatment. *Journal of Dental Research*, 1975, *54*, 797-801.

Melamed, B. G., & Siegel, L. J. Reduction of anxiety in children facing hospitalization and surgery by use of filmed modeling. *Journal of Consulting and Clinical Psychology*, 1975, *43*, 511-521.

Melamed, B. G., Weinstein, D., Hawes, R., & Katin-Borland, M. Reduction of fear-related dental management problems using filmed modeling. *Journal of the American Dental Association*, 1975, *90*, 822-826.

Merrens, M. R. Nonemergency helping behavior in various sized communities. *Journal of Social Psychology*, 1973, *90*, 327-328.

Midlarsky, E. Aiding under stress: The effects of competence, dependency, visibility, and fatalism. *Journal of Personality*, 1971, *39*, 132-149.

Midlarsky, E., & Bryan, J. H. Training charity in children. *Journal of Personality and Social Psychology*, 1967, *5*, 408-415.

Midlarsky, E., & Bryan, J. H. Affect expressions and children's imitative altruism. *Journal of Experimental Research in Personality*, 1972, *6*, 195-203.

Midlarsky, E., Bryan, J. H., & Brickman, P. Aversive approval: Interactive effects of modeling and reinforcement on altruistic behavior. *Child Development*, 1973, *44*, 321-328.

Midlarsky, E., & Midlarsky, M. Some determinants of aiding under experimentally induced stress. *Journal of Personality,* 1973, *41,* 305-327.

Midlarsky, M. & Midlarsky, E. Status inconsistency, aggressive attitude, and helping behavior. *Journal of Personality,* 1976, *44,* 371-391.

Milgram, S. Behavioral study of obedience. *Journal of Abnormal and Social Psychology,* 1963, *67,* 371-378.

Milgram, S. Some conditions of obedience and disobedience to authority. *Human Relations,* 1965, *18,* 57-75.

Milgram, S. The experience of living in cities. *Science,* 1970, *167,* 1461-1468.

Milgram, S., & Shotland, R. L. *Television and antisocial behavior: Field experiments.* New York: Academic Press, 1973.

Miller, D. T., & Smith, J. The effect of own deservingness and deservingness of others on children's helping behavior. *Child Development,* 1977, *48,* 617-620.

Miller, R. E., Caul, W. F., & Mirsky, I. F. Communication of affects between feral and socially isolated monkeys. *Journal of Personality and Social Psychology,* 1967, *7,* 231-239.

Mischel, W. *Personality and assessment.* New York: John Wiley, 1968.

Mischel, W. *Introduction to personality* (2nd Edition). New York: Holt, Rinehart & Winston, 1976.

Mischel, W., & Liebert, R. M. Effects of discrepancies between observed and imposed reward criteria on their acquisition and transmission. *Journal of Personality and Social Psychology,* 1966, *3,* 45-53.

Mittler, P. *The study of twins.* Harmondsworth, Middlesex, England: Penguin, 1971.

Montagu, M. F. A. (Ed.). *Man and aggression.* New York: Oxford University Press, 1968.

Moore, B. S., Underwood, B., & Rosenhan, D. L. Affect and altruism. *Developmental Psychology,* 1973, *8,* 99-104.

Moral dilemmas of American presidents: The agony of decision. New Rochelle, N. Y.: Pathescope Educational Films, 1974.

Moriarty, D., & McCabe, A. E. Studies of television and youth sport. In *Ontario. Royal commission on violence in the communications industry. Report* (Vol. 5); *Learning from the media.* (Research reports). Toronto: Queen's Printer for Ontario, 1977.

Morris, D. *The naked ape: A zoologist's study of the human animal.* New York: McGraw-Hill, 1967.

Moss, M. K., & Page, R. A. Reinforcement and helping behavior. *Journal of Applied Social Psychology,* 1972, *2,* 360-371.

Murray, J. P. Television and violence: Implications of the surgeon-general's research program. *American Psychologist,* 1973, *28,* 471-478.

Murray, J. P., & Kippax, S. From the early window to the late night show: International trends in the study of television's impact on children and adults. In L. Berkowitz (Ed.), *Advances in experimental social psychology* (Vol. 12). New York: Academic Press, 1979.

Mussen, P., & Eisenberg-Berg, N. *Roots of caring, sharing, and helping: The development of prosocial behavior in children.* San Francisco: W. H. Freeman & Company, Publishers, 1977.

Mussen, P., Rutherford, E., Harris, S., & Keasey, C. B. Honesty and altruism among preadolescents. *Developmental Psychology,* 1970, *3,* 169-194.

Nadler, A., Fisher, J. D., & Streufert, S. When helping hurts: The effects of donor-recipient similarity and the recipient's self-esteem on the reactions to aid. *Journal of Personality,* 1976, *44,* 392-409.

Nelsen, E. A., Grinder, R. E., & Mutterer, M. L. Sources of variance in behavioral measures of honesty in temptation situations: Methodological analyses. *Developmental Psychology,* 1969, *1,* 265-279.

Nisbett, R. E., & Wilson, T. D. Telling more than we can know: Verbal reports on mental processes. *Psychological Review,* 1977, *84,* 231-259.

Nissen, H. W., & Crawford, M. P. A preliminary study of food sharing behavior in young chimpanzees. *Journal of Comparative Psychology,* 1936, *22,* 383-419.

O'Bryant, S. L., & Brophy, J. E. Sex differences in altruistic behavior. *Developmental Psychology,* 1976, *12,* 554.

O'Connor, R. D. Modification of social withdrawal through symbolic modeling. *Journal of Applied Behavior Analysis,* 1969, *2,* 15-22.

O'Connor, R. D. Relative efficacy of modeling, shaping, and the combined procedures for modification of social withdrawal. *Journal of Abnormal Psychology,* 1972, *79,* 327-334.

Olver, R. R., & Hornsby, J. R. On equivalence. In J. S. Bruner, R. R. Olver, & P. M. Greenfield (Eds.), *Studies in cognitive growth.* New York: John Wiley, 1966.

Ontario. Royal commission on violence in the communications industry. Report.
    (Vol. 1), *Approaches, conclusions and recommendations.*
    (Vol. 2), *Violence and the media: A bibliography.*
    (Vol. 3), *Violence in television, films and news.*
    (Vol. 4), *Violence in print and music.*
    (Vol. 5), *Learning from the media.*
    (Vol. 6), *Vulnerability to media effects.*

(Vol. 7), *The media industries: From here to where?*. Toronto, Ontario: Queen's Printer for Ontario, 1977.

Opinion Research Center. *The Sunday Times* (London), 1973, *25*(2). In D. Howitt & G. Cumberbatch, *Mass media violence and society*. New York: John Wiley, 1975.

Parke, R. D., Berkowitz, L., Leyens, J. P., West, S., & Sebastian, R. J. Some effects of violent and nonviolent movies on the behavior of juvenile delinquents. In L. Berkowitz (Ed.), *Advances in experimental social psychology* (Vol. 10). New York: Academic Press, 1977.

Pavlov, I. P. *Conditioned reflexes.* London: Oxford University Press, 1927.

Piaget, J. *The moral judgment of the child.* London: Routledge & Kegan Paul, 1932.

Piliavin, I. M., Rodin, J., & Piliavin, J. A. Good samaritanism: An underground phenomenon? *Journal of Personality and Social Psychology,* 1969, *13,* 289-299.

Prentice, N. M. The influence of live and symbolic modeling on promoting moral judgments of adolescent delinquents. *Journal of Abnormal Psychology,* 1972, *80,* 157-161.

Presbie, R. J., & Coiteux, P. F. Learning to be generous or stingy: Imitation of sharing behavior as a function of model generosity and vicarious reinforcement. *Child Development,* 1971, *42,* 1033-1038.

Rand, A. *The virtue of selfishness.* New York: NAL, 1964.

Regan, D., Williams, M., & Sparling, S. Voluntary expiation of guilt: A field experiment. *Journal of Personality and Social Psychology,* 1972, *23,*30-32.

Rest, J. R. The hierarchical nature of moral judgment: A study of patterns of comprehension and preference of moral stages. *Journal of Personality,* 1973, *41,* 86-109.

Rest, J. R., Turiel, E., & Kohlberg, L. Level of moral development as a determinant of preference and comprehension of moral judgment made by others. *Journal of Personality,* 1969, *37,* 225-252.

Reykowski, J. Introduction. In J. Reykowski (Ed.), *Studies in the mechanisms of prosocial behavior.* Warsaw: Wydaevnictiva Universytetu, 1975.

Rheingold, H. L., Hay, D. F., & West, M. J. Sharing in the second year of life. *Child Development,* 1976, *47,* 1148-1158.

Rice, M. E., & Grusec, J. E. Saying and doing: Effects on observer performance. *Journal of Personality and Social Psychology,* 1975, *32,* 584-593.

Ringer, R. J. *Looking out for number one.* New York: Fawcett Books Group— CBS Publications, 1977.

Robinson, H., & Robinson, N. Longitudinal development of very young children in a comprehensive day care program. *Child Development,* 1971, *42,* 1673-1683.

Rokeach, M. *The nature of human values.* New York: Free Press, 1973.

Rosenbaum, M. The effect of stimulus and background factors on the volunteering response. *Journal of Abnormal and Social Psychology,* 1956, *53,* 118-121.

Rosenbaum, M., & Blake, R. R. Volunteering as a function of field structure. *Journal of Abnormal and Social Psychology,* 1955, *50,* 193-196.

Rosenhan, D. L. Some origins of concern for others. In P. Mussen, J. Langer, & M. Covington (Eds.), *Trends and issues in developmental psychology.* New York: Holt, Rinehart, & Winston, 1969.

Rosenhan, D. L. The natural socialization of altruistic autonomy. In J. Macaulay & L. Berkowitz (Eds.), *Altruism and helping behavior.* New York: Academic Press, 1970.

Rosenhan, D. L., Moore, B. S., & Underwood, B. The social psychology of moral behavior. In T. Lickona (Ed.), *Moral development and behavior: Theory, research, and social issues.* New York: Holt, Rinehart, & Winston, 1976.

Rosenhan, D. L., Underwood, B., & Moore, B. Affect moderates self-gratification and altruism. *Journal of Personality and Social Psychology,* 1974, *30,* 546-552.

Rosenhan, D. L., & White, G. M. Observation and rehearsal as determinants of prosocial behavior. *Journal of Personality and Social Psychology,* 1967, *5,* 424-431.

Rosenthal, T. L., & Bandura, A. Psychological modeling: Theory and practice. In S. L. Garfield & A. E. Bergin (Eds.), *Handbook of psychotherapy and behavior change.* New York: John Wiley, 1978.

Rosenthal, T. L., & Zimmerman, B. J. *Social learning and cognition.* New York: Academic Press, 1978.

Rotter, J. B. Some problems and misconceptions related to the construct of internal versus external control of reinforcement. *Journal of Consulting and Clinical Psychology,* 1975, *43,* 56-67.

Rubenstein, J. L., & Howes, C. Caregiving and infant behavior in day care and in homes. *Developmental Psychology,* 1979, *15,* 1-24.

Rubin, K. H., & Schneider, F. W. The relationship between moral judgment, egocentrism, and altruistic behavior. *Child Development,* 1973, *44,* 661-665.

Rushton, J. P. Generosity in children: Immediate and long term effects of modeling, preaching, and moral judgment. *Journal of Personality and Social Psychology,* 1975, *31,* 459-466.

Rushton, J. P. Socialization and the altruistic behavior of children. *Psychological Bulletin,* 1976, *83,* 898-913.

Rushton, J. P. Television and prosocial behavior. In *Ontario. Royal commission on violence in the communications industry. Report* (Vol. 5); *Learning from the media.* (Research reports). Toronto: Queen's Printer for Ontario, 1977.

Rushton, J. P. Urban density and altruism: Helping strangers in a Canadian city, suburb, and small town. *Psychological Reports,* 1978, *43,* 987-990.

Rushton, J. P. The effects of prosocial television and film material on the behavior of viewers. In L. Berkowitz (Ed.), *Advances in Experimental Social Psychology* (Vol. 12). New York: Academic Press, 1979.

Rushton, J. P., & Campbell, A. C. Modeling, vicarious reinforcement and extraversion on blood donating in adults. Immediate and long-term effects. *European Journal of Social Psychology,* 1977, *7,* 297-306.

Rushton, J. P., & Endler, N. S. Person by situation interactions in academic achievement. *Journal of Personality,* 1977, *45,* 297-309.

Rushton, J. P., & Littlefield, C. The effects of age, amount of modeling, and a success experience on seven- to eleven-year-old children's generosity. *Journal of Moral Education,* 1979, *9,* 55-56.

Rushton, J. P. & Owen, D. Immediate and delayed effects of TV modeling and preaching on children's generosity. *British Journal of Social and Clinical Psychology,* 1975, *14,* 309-310.

Rushton, J. P., & Teachman, G. The effects of positive reinforcement, attributions, and punishment on model induced altruism in children. *Personality and Social Psychology Bulletin,* 1978, *4,* 322-325.

Rushton, J. P., & Wheelwright, M. *A validation study of a laboratory measure of children's generosity.* Unpublished manuscript, University of Western Ontario, London, Ontario, Canada, 1979.

Rushton, J. P., & Wiener, J. Altruism and cognitive development in children. *British Journal of Social and Clinical Psychology,* 1975, *14,* 341-349.

Rutherford, E., & Mussen, P. Generosity in nursery school boys. *Child Development,* 1968, *39,* 755-765.

Sagi, A., & Hoffman, M. L. Empathic distress in the newborn. *Developmental Psychology,* 1976, *12,* 175-176.

Sarason, I. C., & Sarason, B. R. *Constructive classroom behavior.* New York: Behavioral Publications, 1974.

Schachter, S., & Hall, R. Group-derived restraints and audience persuasion. *Human Relations,* 1952, *5,* 397-406.

Schleifer, M., & Douglas, V. I. Effects of training on the moral judgment of young children. *Journal of Personality and Social Psychology,* 1973, *28,* 62-68.

Schubert, D. S. P., & Wagner, M. E. A subcultural change of MMPI norms in the 1960s due to adolescent role confusion and glamorization of alienation. *Journal of Abnormal Psychology,* 1975, *84,* 406-411.

Schwartz, S. H. Awareness of consequences and the influence of moral norms on interpersonal behavior. *Sociometry*, 1968, *31*, 355-369. (a)

Schwartz, S. H. Words, deeds, and the perceptions of consequences and responsibility in action situations. *Journal of Personality and Social Psychology*, 1968, *10*, 232-242. (b)

Schwartz, S. H. Normative influences on altruism. In L. Berkowitz (Ed.), *Advances in experimental social psychology* (Vol. 10). New York: Academic Press, 1977.

Schwartz, S. H. & Clausen, G. T. Responsibility, norms, and helping in an emergency. *Journal of Personality and Social Psychology*, 1970, *16*, 229-310.

Schwartz, S. H., Feldman, K. A., Brown, M. E., & Heingartner, A. Some personality correlates of conduct in two situations of moral conflict. *Journal of Personality*, 1969, *37*, 41-57.

Selman, R. L., & Byrne, D. F. A structural-developmental analysis of role taking in middle childhood. *Child Development*, 1974, *45*, 803-806.

Shantz, C. U. The development of social cognition. In E. M. Hetherington (Ed.), *Review of child development research* (Vol. 5). Chicago: University of Chicago Press, 1975.

Shaw, D. W., & Thoresen, C. E. Effects of modeling and desensitization in reducing dentist phobia. *Journal of Counseling Psychology*, 1974, *21*, 415-420.

Sherrod, D. R., & Downs, R. Environmental determinants of altruism: The effects of stimulus overload and perceived control on helping. *Journal of Experimental Social Psychology*, 1974, *10*, 468-479.

Siebenaler, J. B., & Caldwell, D. K. Cooperation among adult dolphins. *Journal of Mammology*, 1956, *37*, 126-128.

Siegel, P. Genetic analysis of male mating behavior in chickens, I. Artificial selection. *Animal Behaviour*, 1972, *20*, 564-570.

Silverman, I. *The human subject in the psychological laboratory.* Elmsford, N. Y.: Pergamon Press, 1977.

Simon, S. B., Howe, L. V., & Kirschenbaum, H. *Values clarification: A handbook of practical strategies for teachers and students.* New York: Hart, 1972.

Skinner, B. F. *Science and human behavior.* New York, Macmillan, 1953.

Skinner, B. F. *Walden Two.* New York: Macmillan, 1948.

Smythe, D. W. Reality as presented by television. *Public Opinion Quarterly*, 1954, *18*, 143-156.

Sorrentino, R. M., & Boutilier, R. G. Evaluation of a victim as a function of fate similarity/dissimilarity. *Journal of Experimental Social Psychology*, 1974, *10*, 84-93.

Southern, M. L., & Plant, W. T. Decade differences in personality of junior college and university freshmen. *Psychological Reports*, 1974, *34*, 383-388.

Sprafkin, J. M., Liebert, R. M., & Poulos, R. W. Effects of a pro-social example on children's helping. *Journal of Experimental Child Psychology,* 1975, *20,* 119-126.

Staats, A. W. Outline of an integrated learning theory of attitude formation and function. In M. Fishbein (Ed.), *Readings in attitude theory and measurement.* New York: John Wiley, 1967.

Staats, A. W., & Staats, C. K. Attitudes established by classical conditioning. *Journal of Abnormal and Social Psychology,* 1958, *57,* 37-40.

Staats, A. W., & Staats, C. K. *Complex human behavior: A systematic extension of learning principles.* New York: Holt, Rinehart & Winston, 1963.

Staats, C. K., & Staats, A. W. Meaning established by classical conditioning. *Journal of Experimental Psychology,* 1957, *54,* 74-80.

Stanley, P. R. A., & Riera, B. Replications of media violence. In *Ontario. Royal commission on violence in the communications industry. Report* (Vol. 5); *Learning from the media.* (Research reports.) Toronto: Queen's Printer for Ontario, 1977.

Staub, E. A child in distress: The influence of age and number of witnesses on children's attempts to help. *Journal of Personality and Social Psychology,* 1970, *14,* 130-140.

Staub, E. A child in distress: The influence of nurturance and modeling on children's attempts to help. *Developmental Psychology,* 1971, *5,* 124-133.

Staub, E. Helping a distressed person: Social, personality, and stimulus determinants. In L. Berkowitz (Ed.), *Advances in experimental social psychology* (Vol. 7). New York: Academic Press, 1974.

Staub, E. *Positive social behavior and morality* (Vol. 1). *Social and personal influences.* New York, Academic Press, 1978.

Staub, E. *Positive social behavior and morality* (Vol. 2). *Socialization and development.* New York, Academic Press, 1979.

Staub, E., & Baer, R. S., Jr. Stimulus characteristics of a sufferer and difficulty of escape as determinants of helping. *Journal of Personality and Social Psychology,* 1974, *30,* 279-285.

Staub, E., & Sherk, L. Need for approval, children's sharing behavior, and reciprocity in sharing. *Child Development,* 1970, *41,* 243-252.

Stein, A. H., & Friedrich, L. K. Television content and young children's behavior. In J. P. Murray, E. A. Rubinstein, & G. A. Comstock (Eds.), *Television and social behavior* (Vol. 2). *Television and social learning.* Washington, D. C.: U. S. Government Printing Office, 1972.

Stein, A. H., & Friedrich, L. K. Impact of television on children and youth. In E. M. Hetherington (Ed.), *Review of child development research* (Vol. 5). Chicago: University of Chicago Press, 1975.

Stein, G. M. Children's reactions to innocent victims. *Child Development,* 1973, *44,* 805-810.

Stein, G. M., & Bryan, J. H. The effect of a televised model upon rule adoption behavior of children. *Child Development*, 1972, *43*, 268-273.

Stephan, W. G. School desegregation: An evaluation of predictions made in *Brown* v. *Board of Education*. *Psychological Bulletin*, 1978, *85*, 217-237.

Sternglanz, S. H., & Serbin, L. A. Sex role stereotyping in children's television programs. *Developmental Psychology*, 1974, *10*, 710-715.

Steuer, F. B., Applefield, J. M., & Smith, R. Televised aggression and the interpersonal aggression of preschool children. *Journal of Experimental Child Psychology*, 1971, *11*, 442-447.

Stewart, C. G. Consistency, generality, magnitude, and significance of experimenter expectancy effects in human research. *Psychological Record*, 1971, *21*, 449-458.

Stokols, D., & Schopler, J. Reactions to victims under conditions of situational detachment: The effect of responsibility, severity, and unexpected future interaction. *Journal of Personality and Social Psychology*, 1973, *25*, 199-209.

Stotland, E. Exploratory investigations of empathy. In L. Berkowitz (Ed.), *Advances in experimental social psychology* (Vol. 4). New York: Academic Press, 1969.

Strayer, F. F., Wareing, S., & Rushton, J. P. Social constraints on naturally occurring preschool altruism. *Ethology and Sociobiology*, 1979, *1*, 3-11.

Stumphauzer, J. S. Increased delay of gratification in young prison inmates through imitation of high delay peer models. *Journal of Personality and Social Psychology*, 1972, *21*, 10-17.

Superka, D. P., Ahrens, C., Hedstrom, J. E., Ford, L. J., & Johnson, P. L. *Values education sourcebook: Conceptual approaches, materials, analyses, and an annotated bibliography*. Boulder, Colo.: Social Sciences Education Consortium, 1976.

Takooshian, H., Haber, S., & Lucido, D. J. Who wouldn't help a lost child? You maybe. *Psychology Today*, February 1977, p. 67.

Teleki, G. The omnivorous chimpanzee. *Scientific American*, January 1973, pp. 33-39.

Titmuss, R. M. *The gift relationship*. London: George Allen & Unwin, 1970.

Trivers, R. L. The evolution of reciprocal altruism. *Quarterly Review of Biology*, 1971, *46*, 35-57.

Turiel, E. An experimental test of the sequentiality of development stages in a child's moral judgments. *Journal of Personality and Social Psychology*, 1966, *3*, 611-618.

Turner, W. D. Altruism and its measurement in children. *Journal of Abnormal and Social Psychology*, 1948, *43*, 502-516.

Ugurel-Semin, R. Moral behavior and moral judgment of children. *Journal of Abnormal and Social Psychology*, 1952, *47*, 463-474.

Underwood, B., Berenson, J. F., Berenson, R. J., Cheng, K. K., Wilson, D., Kulik, J., Moore, B. S., & Wenzel, G. Attention, negative affect, and altruism: An ecological validation. *Personality and Social Psychology Bulletin,* 1977, *3,* 54-58.

Underwood, B., Froming, W. J., & Moore, B. S. Mood, attention, and altruism: A search for mediating variables. *Developmental Psychology,* 1977, *13,* 541-542.

United States Surgeon General's Scientific Advisory Committee on Television and Social Behavior. *Television and social behavior: Technical reports to the committee.*
(Vol. 1), Media content and control.
(Vol. 2), Television and social learning.
(Vol. 3), Television and adolescent aggressiveness.
(Vol. 4), Television in day-to-day life.
(Vol. 5), Television's effects: Further explorations.
Washington, D. C.: U. S. Government Printing Office, 1972.

Wallington, S. A. Consequences of transgression: Self-punishment and depression. *Journal of Personality and Social Psychology,* 1973, *28,* 1-7.

Walster, E., Walster, G. W., & Berscheid, E. *Equity theory and research.* Boston: Allyn & Bacon, 1978.

Walters, G. C., & Grusec, J. E. *Punishment.* San Francisco: W. H. Freeman & Company, Publishers, 1977.

Walters, R. H., Leat, M., & Mezei, L. Inhibition and disinhibition of responses through empathetic learning. *Canadian Journal of Psychology,* 1963, *17,* 235-243.

Watson, J. B., & Raynor, R. Conditioned emotional reactions. *Journal of Experimental Psychology,* 1920, *3,* 1-14.

Waxler, C. Z., Yarrow, M. R., & King, R. A. Child rearing and children's prosocial initiations toward victims of distress. *Child Development,* 1979, *50,* 319-330.

Waxler, C. Z., Yarrow, M. R., & Smith, J. B. Perspective taking and prosocial behavior. *Developmental Psychology,* 1977, *13,* 87-88.

Weiner, A. The smug generation. *The Canadian.* April 22, 1978.

Weissbrod, C. S. Noncontingent warmth induction, cognitive style, and children's imitative donation and rescue effort behaviors. *Journal of Personality and Social Psychology,* 1976, *34,* 274-281.

Weissbrod, C. S., & Bryan, J. H. Filmed treatment as an effective fear-reduction technique. *Journal of Abnormal Child Psychology,* 1973, *1,* 196-201.

White, E. E., & Smith, H. I. *A guide to behavior modification: A classroom teacher's handbook.* Palo Alto, Calif.: Peak Publications, 1972.

White, G. M. Immediate and deferred effects of model observation and guided and unguided rehearsal on donating and stealing. *Journal of Personality and Social Psychology*, 1972, *21*, 139-148.

Wiesel, E. [*Night*] (S. Rodway, Trans.). New York: Hill & Wang, 1960.

Williams, G. C. *Adaptation and natural selection*. Princeton, N. J.: Princeton University Press, 1966.

Williams, T. B., Zabrack, M. L., & Joy, L. A. A content analysis of entertainment television programming. In *Ontario. Royal commission on violence in the communications industry. Report* (Vol. 3); *Violence in television films and news.* Toronto: Queen's Printer for Ontario, 1977.

Willis, J. A., & Goethals, G. R. Social responsibility and threat to behavioral freedom as determinants of altruistic behavior. *Journal of Personality*, 1973, *41*, 376-384.

Wilson, E. O. *The insect societies.* Cambridge: Harvard University Press, 1971.

Wilson, E. O. *On human nature.* Cambridge: Harvard University Press, 1978.

Wilson, E. O. *Sociobiology: The new synthesis.* Cambridge: Harvard University Press, 1975.

Wilson, G. T., & O'Leary, K. D. *Principles of Behavior Theory.* Englewood Cliffs, N.J.: Prentice-Hall, 1980.

Wincze, J. P., & Caird, W. K. The effects of systematic desensitization and video desensitization in the treatment of essential sexual dysfunction in women. *Behavior Therapy*, 1976, *7*, 335-342.

Wispé, L. G. (Ed.). *Altruism, sympathy, and helping: Psychological and socio-logical principles.* New York: Academic Press, 1978.

Wispé, L. G. (Ed.). Positive forms of social behavior. *Journal of Social Issues*, 1972, *28* 3.

Wispé, L. G., & Thompson, J. N., Jr. (Eds.). The war between the words. Biological versus social evolution and some related issues. *American Psychologist*, 1976, *31*, 341-384.

Wolf, T. M. Effects of televised modeled verbalizations and behavior on resistance to deviation. *Developmental Psychology*, 1973, *8*, 51-56.

Wolf, T. M., & Cheyne, J. A. Persistence of effects of live behavioral, televised behavioral, and live verbal models on resistance to deviation. *Child Development*, 1972, *43*, 1429-1436.

Wolfe, T. The me decade and the third great awakening. In T. Wolfe *Mauve gloves and madmen, clutter and vine, and other stories, sketches, and essays.* New York: Farrar, Straus & Giroux, 1976.

Woolfenden, G. E. Nesting and survival in a population of Florida scrub jays. *Living Bird*, 1973, *12*, 25-49.

Wright, B. Altruism in children and the perceived conduct of others. *Journal of Abnormal and Social Psychology*, 1942, *37*, 218-233.

Wylie, R. C. *The self-concept: A review of methodological considerations and measuring instruments* (Rev. ed.). Lincoln: University of Nebraska Press, 1974.

Wynne-Edwards, V. C. *Animal dispersion in relation to social behaviour.* Edinburgh: Oliver and Boyd, 1962.

Yamaguchi, S., Harano, K., & Egawa, B. Effects of differentially modeled stimuli on vicarious autonomic arousal. *Perceptual and Motor Skills,* 1978, *46,* 643-680.

Yarrow, M. R., & Scott, P. M. Imitation of nurturant and nonnurturant models. *Journal of Personality and Social Psychology,* 1972, *23,* 259-270.

Yarrow, M. R., Scott, P. M., & Waxler, C. Z. Learning concern for others. *Developmental Psychology,* 1973, *8,* 240-260.

Yarrow, M. R., & Waxler, C. Z. Dimensions and correlates of prosocial behavior in young children. *Child Development,* 1976, *47,* 118-125.

Yates, G. C. R. Influence of televised modeling and verbalization on children's delay of gratification. *Journal of Experimental Child Psychology,* 1974, *18,* 333-339.

Zigler, E., & Seitz, V. Changing trends in socialization theory and research. *American Behavioral Scientist,* 1978, *21,* 731-756.

AUTHOR INDEX

SUBJECT INDEX